The
FOUNDERS'
FORTUNES

ALSO BY WILLARD STERNE RANDALL

Unshackling America: How the War of 1812 Truly Ended the American Revolution

Ethan Allen: His Life and Times

Alexander Hamilton: A Life

George Washington: A Life

Thomas Jefferson: A Life

Benedict Arnold: Patriot and Traitor

A Little Revenge: Benjamin Franklin and His Son

Building Six: The Tragedy at Bridesburg (with Stephen D. Solomon)

The Founding City (with David R. Boldt)

Thomas Chittenden's Town (with Nancy Nahra)

American Lives (with Nancy Nahra)

Forgotten Americans (with Nancy Nahra)

The FOUNDERS' FORTUNES

HOW MONEY SHAPED
THE BIRTH OF AMERICA

WILLARD STERNE RANDALL

DUTTON

DUTTON

An imprint of Penguin Random House LLC
1745 Broadway, New York, NY 10019
penguinrandomhouse.com

Copyright © 2022 by Willard Sterne Randall
Penguin Random House values and supports copyright. Copyright fuels creativity, encourages diverse voices, promotes free speech and creates a vibrant culture. Thank you for buying an authorized edition of this book and for complying with copyright laws by not reproducing, scanning, or distributing any part of it in any form without permission. You are supporting writers and allowing Penguin Random House to continue to publish books for every reader. Please note that no part of this book may be used or reproduced in any manner for the purpose of training artificial intelligence technologies or systems.

DUTTON and the D colophon are registered trademarks of Penguin Random House LLC.

LIBRARY OF CONGRESS CATALOGING-IN-PUBLICATION DATA
has been applied for.

ISBN 9781524745929 (hardcover)
ISBN 9781524745943 (ebook)
ISBN 9781524745936 (paperback)

While the author has made every effort to provide accurate telephone numbers, internet addresses, and other contact information at the time of publication, neither the publisher nor the author assumes any responsibility for errors or for changes that occur after publication. Further, the publisher does not have any control over and does not assume any responsibility for author or third- party websites or their content.

The authorized representative in the EU for product safety and compliance is
Penguin Random House Ireland, Morrison Chambers, 32 Nassau Street, Dublin D02 YH68, Ireland,
https://eu-contact.penguin.ie

149927040

To Nancy and Lucy

CONTENTS

PART THREE. "The Crisis Is Arrived"

PROLOGUE

As he prepared to leave Mount Vernon in April 1789 to journey to his inauguration in New York City, George Washington dashed off letters to his closest friends and relatives. Washington had not sought the presidency. After thirty-five years of intermittent warfare, he preferred "to live and die on [his] own plantation."[1] To Henry Knox, his Revolutionary War comrade in arms, he wrote, "My movements to the chair of government will be accompanied with feelings not unlike those of a culprit who is going to the place of execution. I greatly apprehend that my countrymen will expect too much from me."[2]

Like many Americans half a dozen years after the war, Washington was scraping by financially. For his eight years as commander in chief of the Continental Army, he had received neither salary nor pension, only reimbursement for well-documented expenses. He had been forced to neglect his farms, the principal source of his income. In all, the war had diminished Washington's net worth by half, and he had met with little success in recouping his fortune. Britain's high-handed postwar restrictions on American trade had eliminated the primary Caribbean markets for Washington's crops, while prewar Mediterranean markets for his wheat were falling prey to North African privateers. A postwar depression had dried up cash and credit nationwide. Some tenants on

Washington's frontier farms could no longer pay their rent, forcing him to take them to court and evict them.

To George Augustine Washington, his favorite nephew, Washington confided, "Necessity, if this [election] had not happened, would have forced me into [frugality], as my means are not adequate to the expense at which I have lived since my retirement to what is called private life."[3] Once inaugurated, he would receive a yearly salary of $25,000 (approximately $750,000 today), the highest in the United States at the time. Clearly, George Washington needed the job.

In that era of unparalleled change, Washington, like the other Founders of the new republic, made major decisions that were influenced by his personal financial circumstances.

In 1776, as they lined up in Philadelphia to sign the Declaration of Independence, the Founders attested quite literally to its final words: "We pledge our lives, our fortunes and our sacred honor."[4] If defeated, they would, as Benjamin Franklin put it, "most assuredly all hang separately,"[5] forfeiting their fortunes and their lives, probably in the gruesome execution ritual the English reserved for traitors: hanging, drawing, and quartering.

But what exactly were their fortunes? What impact would they have on critical political decisions and the formative policies of incipient institutions? What, if any, were the lingering consequences? By examining the financial affairs of the Founders and the unprecedented decisions they made to shape a new nation, this book attempts to answer these important, timely, and virtually unexplored questions, making the Founders' finances much more evident while explaining that, well aware of the high stakes, they did not necessarily expect commensurate rewards.

A little over a century ago, Columbia University professor Charles A. Beard rocked the foundations of normally staid and hagiographic American history by rejecting what he called the "juristic theory of the origin and nature of the Constitution."[6] He supplanted it with this hypothesis: that economic elements were the chief factors in the development of the nation's political institutions. In his 1913 book, *An Economic Interpretation of the Constitution of the United States*, Professor Beard argued that economic forces underlay the movement for the formation and adoption of the federal Constitution and determined its most important provisions. Launching the Progressive school of American history, Beard asserted that "substantially all of the merchants, money lenders, security holders, manufacturers, shippers, capitalists, and financiers and their professional associates" supported the Constitution, while any opposition came from unrepresented, non-slaveholding farmers and debtors. Beard concluded that the new Constitution was not the product of "the whole people" but of economic interests who expected to benefit from it.[7]

Able to draw on only the sparse records of individual states under the short-lived Confederation available to scholars in the early twentieth century, Beard published his study far before the availability of the voluminous personal papers and government documents that have since surfaced that have a bearing on the Founders and their influence on the foundation and policies of the new republic. In this book, I seek to update Professor Beard's famous hypothesis by providing a deeper understanding of the financial lives of the Founders, of their interests, and of what acted as the drivers of their decisions.

In our own time of intense public interest in the effects of personal wealth on the nation's governance, this book investigates and describes the extent and the impact of private finances on the founding generation of the nation's leaders, shedding new light on why and how the Revolution took place; how individual Founders, reacting to provocative British laws and policies, forged diffuse alliances of contending business interests based at least in part on their financial circumstances; and how and why the leaders of the newly united states opted for a federal Constitution more conservative than the Articles of Confederation.

This book shows how the Founders shifted allegiances as revolutionary ideology evolved in the tempestuous postwar decades and as they struggled to transform their theoretical debates into a practicable form of government.

During this critical period of breaking away from Britain, key moments of decision-making—over war and peace, trade and taxation—reveal how contesting individuals drew on their personal experiences, with their changing financial circumstances driving the formulation of new laws and institutions.

PART ONE

"THE WAY TO WEALTH"

CHAPTER ONE

"A Penny Saved"

Dirty, cold, and hungry, seventeen-year-old runaway apprentice Benjamin Franklin arrived in Philadelphia on a sunny Sunday morning in 1723 after sleeping all night in an open boat he had helped row across the Delaware River. From the foot of Market Street, he could see, beyond a waterfront crowded with ships and piles of cargo, solid rows of brick houses, a three-block-long covered market, and families dressed in clean clothes heading to the Friends Meeting House. Following them inside, he fell asleep; awakened by a smiling Quaker, he got directions to a nearby bakery, where he spent his last Dutch dollar.

Already a master printer, the tall, barrel-chested Ben Franklin came to the largest town in America, as George Washington would half a century later, with the promise of a job, something he felt he could never find in Boston, where he had antagonized Puritans and politicians with his satirical writings. Selling half his library, Franklin had found a berth on a Dutch ship that took him to even smaller New York City. There, he also failed to find work, but he had learned of an opening in a Philadelphia printshop, a ninety-mile trudge across New Jersey.

Born in Boston, the eighth of seventeen children of an immigrant candle and soap maker, Franklin was editing and publishing his own newspaper, the *Pennsylvania Gazette*, within five years of his arrival in Philadelphia, by age twenty-two.

In its premiere issue, in October 1729, Franklin advertised his first book publication, Isaac Watts's metrical Psalms of David, a perennial bestseller. Yet Franklin's greatest success as a publisher was to come from his own pen. In 1732, he launched *Poor Richard's Almanack*. Written in a witty, rural vernacular, it combined Puritan moralizing, weather forecasts, household hints, and memorable proverbs that counseled industry and thrift. It would go on to sell, on average, ten thousand copies a year—one copy a year for every one hundred colonists—making it, after the Bible, colonial America's most popular reading matter.

To sell such a large number of books, Franklin found that he had to operate on an ambitious, intercolonial scale. Setting type and printing pages in his own Philadelphia printshop, he then shipped the pages off to be bound and sold by printer partners, often his relatives and former apprentices, in Boston, Newport, New York, Williamsburg, and Charleston.

Franklin practiced what Poor Richard preached. "Keep thy shop and thy shop will keep thee," *Poor Richard* counseled in June 1735. In "Advice of a young Tradesman, written by an old one," Franklin admonished:

> Remember that TIME is money. . . . Remember that CREDIT is money. . . . The Way to Wealth is as plain as the Way to market. It depends chiefly on two words, INDUSTRY and FRUGALITY.

Posing as a "wise old man" delivering a "harangue" to "the People attending an Auction," Franklin filled "the little spaces" at the margins of his calendar with proverbs. "Clergy and the Gentry" purchased *Poor Richard*, he later explained in his autobiography, "to distribute gratis among their poor Parishioners and Tenants." Franklin's proverbs linked "the Means of procuring Wealth" with "securing Virtue, it being more difficult for a Man in Want to always act honestly. . . . It is hard for an empty Sack to stand upright."[1]

Opening a stationery shop in the front of his house on Market Street, he sold paper, tea, coffee, cheese, slates, pencils and lampblack, Crown soap that his siblings made in Boston, iron stoves of his own invention, lottery tickets, and even slaves, whom he advertised in the *Gazette*. He imported books from London; his 1744 catalog listed six hundred titles. To cater to "Friends here of Different Tastes," he ordered pamphlets about "everything good or bad that makes a Noise and has a Run."[2]

On November 8, 1739, the *Gazette* noted the arrival in Philadelphia of a young evangelist. The Reverend George Whitefield, a twenty-five-year-old Anglican priest, was preaching his way from Rhode Island to Georgia, everywhere drawing unprecedented crowds. His fire-and-brimstone sermons were igniting a religious revival movement that would shake the political and social foundations of the mainland British colonies while at the same time greatly enhancing Benjamin Franklin's fortune.

Eventually barred from most churches by envious clergy, Whitefield preached in the streets and in open fields in a voice so loud and so clear that he could be heard two blocks away by as many as twenty-five thousand auditors, at least according to Franklin's unverifiable estimate.

Whitefield had arrived in colonial America from Great Britain already so popular that few churches could safely accommodate his legion of listeners. At Old South Church in Boston, the *Gazette* reported, "vast numbers of people crowded in there before the time of the service." When "some persons [were] breaking a board to make a seat," some "imprudent person" shouted that the gallery was collapsing, setting off a panic:

> Some jumped out of the galleries into the seats below, others out of the windows, and those below pressing hastily to get out, several were thrown down and trod upon, whereby many were much bruised, and some had their bones broke.

According to the details provided the *Gazette*—probably by Franklin's sister Jane, a Whitefield devotee—five of the faithful perished.[3]

Sometimes warned by express riders of Whitefield's approach to a town, thousands would pour in from the countryside to see and hear the celebrated golden-haired evangelist. One report from the *Gazette*'s New-port correspondent (also a relative of Franklin's) noted that Whitefield had to preach twice in the same day in the Anglican church to overflow congregations.

The normally tightfisted Franklin attended one of Whitefield's Phila-delphia sermons. In his *Autobiography*, Franklin recalled that he was well aware beforehand of the evangelist's mission to raise funds to build an orphanage in Georgia:

> I perceived he intended to finish with a Collection, and I si-lently resolved he should get nothing from me. I had in my Pocket an Handful of Copper Money, three or four silver Dollars and five Pistoles in Gold. As he proceeded I began to soften, and concluded to give the Coppers. Another stroke of his Oratory made me ashamed of that, and determined me to give the Silver; and he finished so admirably, that I empty'd my Pockets wholly in to the Collector's Dish, Gold and all.[4]

Franklin recognized a business opportunity, and printer and preacher met before Whitefield concluded his first visit to Philadelphia. Together, the two men forged a mutually beneficial publishing partnership.

The itinerant evangelist went off preaching all the way to Georgia while Franklin rushed to publish his sermons. In addition, Franklin con-tracted to publish American editions of Whitefield's *Journals* and *Sermons*, as well as any other books he would write in America.

In November 1739, Franklin announced in the *Gazette* his first print-ing of the Whitefield sermons. Within days, orders for two hundred complete sets poured in. Whitefield's style, a blend of autobiography, Christian discourse, and travelogue written in plain English, proved an instant success. Soon Franklin was shipping boxes of the books up and down the Atlantic coast and deep into the hinterland to general stores, bookstores, and printshops. Between 1739 and 1741, Franklin printed 110 Whitefield titles. The profits from Franklin's association with the evangelist outstripped those from his own bestselling *Almanack*. In 1740 alone, the sales of Whitefield's writings and printed sermons accounted for 30 percent of all works published in America.[5]

Enjoying his most successful year ever, Franklin hurried to publish a popular versification of Ralph Erskine's *Gospel Sonnets* as well as a second edition of Watts's *Psalms*, and a first of his *Hymns and Spiritual Psalms*. He recruited two partners for the enterprise, his former apprentice James Parker in New York and Charles Harrison in Boston. Franklin printed the first and last sheets, Parker the rest, and Harrison bound them. It marked the first instance of dividing the production and distribution of books.

While he always made more money from the *Gazette* and the *Almanack*—together accounting for roughly half his income—Franklin grasped that book publishing was more prestigious and increased his reputation not only with other printer-publishers but with the reading public.

For the first time in America, Franklin published fellow printer Samuel Richardson's *Pamela: or, Virtue Rewarded*, arguably the first English novel. Selling at six shillings when a loaf of bread cost a penny (in other words, the equivalent of 120 loaves), the novel was considered a luxury. This time, Franklin shipped off unbound lots to Boston, New York, and Williamsburg, where one of his readers was young George Washington.

Selling subscriptions to his books through his *Gazette*, Franklin soon had more subscribers than copies, so he gave preference to anyone who paid in advance or came to his shop with cash in hand. His account ledgers show thousands of retail transactions.

When Franklin began to carry out scientific experiments, he publicized his innovations in newspapers from Massachusetts to Georgia, bringing him even more customers and readers. Investing the profits in real estate, he eventually acquired eighty-nine rental properties in Philadelphia.

Appointed by the province's assembly as Pennsylvania's official printer, Franklin found that each year's new laws guaranteed his newspaper's profitability. He soon also won appointment as clerk to the Pennsylvania Assembly. From his entrepreneurial springboard, Franklin won his first political office as a member of the town's common council.

And when the imperial postal lords in London criticized the tardy remittances of accounts by rival printer Andrew Bradford, Franklin lobbied through contacts in London for the lucrative post of Philadelphia's postmaster. His accurate record-keeping and ability to transform losses into profits paved the way for him to next win appointment as joint postmaster general for British North America.

Franklin soon proved to be as adept a postmaster general as he was a printer and publisher. He gave detailed instructions to postmasters and introduced a uniform system of accounting and standardized forms for all post offices, reforms that tripled the number of deliveries between Philadelphia and New York and doubled those to New England. Visiting all post offices as far south as Virginia, he tripled revenues, for the first time giving the British colonies an efficient postal service.

In a position carrying the prestige of a royal official, he shared an annual salary of £600 (roughly $110,000 today). For the first time, he received a rare government expense account that enabled him to travel the length of the continent at will and to ship his newspapers and *Poor Richard's Almanack* postage-free.

The Franklin-Whitefield publishing collaboration was so profitable that Franklin and his family were able to move to a larger house four doors down Market Street. Proof of their casting aside of Poor Richard's frugality appeared almost immediately in the *Gazette*: they were robbed. The list of stolen goods included a silk-lined coat and a beaver hat.

In the spring of 1742, news arrived that King George II had declared war on Spain. The *Gazette* spread the news that Spanish privateers were attacking British merchants who were trading illegally with Spanish colonies around the Caribbean. *Gazette* readers soon learned of the British invasion of Florida; of Frederick the Great's invasion of Silesia; and of the death of Emperor Charles VI.

As British coastal colonies braced for attacks, Scottish merchants in Philadelphia fitted out a privateer, the *George*, to carry the fight to the

Spanish, only to be rebuffed when they sought an appropriation from the pacifist, Quaker-dominated Pennsylvania Assembly. When France joined forces with Spain against Great Britain, the *Gazette*'s columns brimmed not only with accounts of distant fighting but with tales of Spanish and French privateers boldly sailing into Delaware Bay and capturing four ships bound for Philadelphia.

In New England, militias boarded a British fleet to besiege the French fortress at Louisbourg. In New York, French-led Indians from Canada attacked and burned Saratoga and attacked Albany. Pennsylvania German volunteers rode north with Franklin's only son, William, who wore the red uniform of a Grenadier Guards ensign. Leading dangerous patrols, young Franklin was promoted to the highest provincial rank: captain.

The war finally reached the peaceable domain of the Quakers. Portuguese and Spanish privateers raided up the Delaware River, sacking plantations within thirty miles of Philadelphia and capturing a ship only a few miles south of the undefended city. After sixty-five years of peaceful relations with the natives since its founding by William Penn, the province of Pennsylvania, owned outright by the Penn family, had never made any provision for defense.

As the raids drew closer to Philadelphia and the assembly still refused to appropriate funds for defense, Franklin, who had much to lose from an Indian raid, broke into print, arguing in his *Gazette* that Quaker doctrine was not "absolutely against defensive war."[6]

In *Plain Truth*, a pamphlet he wrote and distributed free in English and in German, Franklin argued that protection and obedience were reciprocal obligations. In exchange for the people's obedience, government was duty bound to protect them. Franklin summoned a mass meeting of citizens and called for five hundred signatures on a petition to the assembly. He got one thousand, but the assembly still refused.

Franklin then appealed for volunteers to form a militia: twenty thousand Scots Presbyterians and Pennsylvania Germans flocked to colors he designed. Franklin formed the Association for General Defense and created a lottery whose proceeds would be used to order cannon and small arms from Boston, then he rode off to New York City to borrow guns from that province's government. Franklin's militiamen drilled throughout Pennsylvania with "good Muskets, all fitted well with Bayonets," some of which Franklin had sold them.[7]

Franklin designed and, with hundreds of volunteers, built and armed two river forts. One, called the Association Fort, ran along some four hundred feet of shoreline and bristled with borrowed cannon. The other, an eleven-gun battery within walking distance of Franklin's home and businesses, protected Society Hill and his own considerable property. Franklin set an example for other merchants by contributing cash to the city's defense—and took his turn on guard duty at night.

Despite six years of constant imperial crisis, Franklin's business interests flourished, largely because of his association with George Whitefield. When European diplomats finally met in Paris and, to the disgust of Americans, halted the fighting, the rival empires returned all conquered territory to the status quo antebellum. After disbanding his militia, Franklin emerged as a leading intercolonial figure and spokesman for the new mercantile class. For the first time, he was elected to the Pennsylvania Assembly.

He made his former journeyman printer David Hall a full partner in his Philadelphia printing and book distribution business, and over the next eighteen years the profits from Franklin & Hall awarded Franklin with an average £467 per annum (about $76,000 today). Adding income from partnerships in New York and Charleston and receipts from his Philadelphia rental properties, Franklin's aggregate income amounted to £2,000 a year (approximately $300,000 today), making him among the wealthiest Americans.

Arriving in Philadelphia a threadbare fugitive at seventeen, Benjamin Franklin by age forty-two had become one of the most influential men in Pennsylvania, thanks largely to wealth he had accrued. Now he could afford to leave the daily routines of the printshop and devote himself to scientific experiments, to writing his bestselling almanac as well as economic and philosophical tracts, and to his growing political engagement.

CHAPTER TWO

"My Constant Gain Every Day"

Through his paternal grandmother, George Washington claimed descent from King Edward III. Whatever wealth such noble lineage might imply was hardly the reality for young George, growing up four centuries and an ocean away from Edward's reign. Orphaned at eleven, George had so little money by the time he was in his teens that he could not afford corn to feed his horse.

George's last English-born ancestor, Lawrence Washington, enjoyed better financial circumstances—at least for a while. As a youth, he left the family manor in Northamptonshire to study at Oxford, enrolling in Brasenose College. After graduation, he became its proctor—the university disciplinarian—whose duties during the English Civil War would include purging Puritans from its faculty. When the Puritans prevailed, Lawrence himself was purged, eventually dying in poverty. The great-great-grandfather of George Washington was ruined, thanks to his loyalty to the Crown.

The expulsion of royalists from Oxford cut off Lawrence's son, John, from a university education. Deciding to seek his fortune in the import-export business, John apprenticed himself to a London merchant in a countinghouse along the Thames waterfront, where cargoes from all over England's booming mercantile empire first arrived on English soil. It was there that he learned about commerce.

Harnessing his new experience, young John Washington decided to get into the tobacco re-export trade. Forty percent of all tobacco imported from the British American colonies was reshipped through London to European markets. John invested his small inheritance in a merchant ketch crammed with manufactured goods and, signing on as its first mate, sailed across the Atlantic to Virginia, which had declared itself a royalist sanctuary.

Dropping anchor in the Potomac River, he went ashore to barter. Just then, a squall blew up, shoving his ship aground. Washington managed to refloat the vessel, but most of its cargo had become waterlogged. His inheritance lost, he decided then and there not to return to England, and thus became the first American Washington.

Ashore, he met an elderly planter who deemed John Washington just the right bridegroom for his daughter. Nathaniel Pope, a member of the Maryland Assembly, advanced Washington £80 in gold (about $12,000 today) and dangled the bequest of seven hundred acres of riverfront land. Washington married Anne Pope and, overnight, assumed the same social status in Virginia that his family had once enjoyed in England.

John Washington's opportunism added two elements to the Washington family character. He relentlessly pursued money. By age thirty, he had succeeded as a merchant-planter; within ten years of his arrival in the New World, he had accumulated five thousand acres of undeveloped land. He also carved out a place in his new society as a public servant, albeit paid, prospering on emoluments from Virginia's royal governor as county coroner, trustee of estates, guardian of children, justice of the county court, and, most notably, lieutenant colonel of the county militia.

John's first son, Lawrence, was born in 1659, at about the same time John began to import indentured servants from England. The Virginia government, in order to promote settlements on its frontiers, offered "head rights" of fifty acres for each servant the colonists imported. In all, Washington "brought over" sixty-three white servants. His neighbors elected him to the Virginia House of Burgesses.

When Anne Pope Washington died, after giving birth to five children within nine years, John Washington promptly remarried. He chose

Anne Gerrard, already twice widowed. The second Mrs. Washington, a shrewd businesswoman, also imported servants. As her dowry, she brought John a mill and a tavern, plus a courthouse and a jail, all of which he leased to the colony's government. He also made a secret pact with the secretary of the colony whereby Washington would survey land just before it became public knowledge that the original land grant had expired and then quickly repatent it for themselves. It was through this inside trading that John Washington acquired the future site of Mount Vernon. His half share of this five-thousand-acre ruse placed the Washingtons squarely among the leading families of the Potomac region.

When John died, he left most of his land to his son Lawrence, who pocketed enough income from a string of public offices to live like a country gentleman. Elected to the House of Burgesses, Lawrence also became sheriff of Westmoreland County. He married Mildred Warner, the daughter of the late Speaker of the House of Burgesses, and together they had three children before Lawrence died at the age of thirty-seven.

Lawrence's second son, Augustine—George Washington's father— was three years old when his father passed away. His mother remarried and went with her new husband and her children to England. When she died soon after, her widower plunked Augustine into Appleby Grammar School in Westmoreland, where he spent four happy years while Mildred's Virginia relatives went to court to contest her will.

Brought back to Virginia, the boy was raised by an uncle, the sheriff of Stafford County. Augustine grew into an amiable blond giant whom everyone called Gus. Marrying at twenty-one, Gus became master of 1,740 acres. Using money judiciously, he developed iron-ore mining and built a blast furnace on his land.

When England went to war with Sweden, English iron imports disappeared, and an iron rush ensued in Virginia. Gus had unearthed rich ore deposits, and to barter the rights, he sailed to London to negotiate with British investors, who offered him a one-sixth interest in a new iron-mining and manufacturing works, the Principio Iron Works.

Returning to Virginia with a generous contract, he discovered that his wife and four-year-old daughter had died in his absence. Now alone with three surviving children, he promptly chose a new bride: Mary Ball was the daughter of a member of the House of Burgesses. Gus had initially met her back in London, where she had journeyed to be introduced into English society. They married in the spring of 1731, and months later, their first child together, George Washington, was born.

From Gus's 10,000 woodland acres, he harvested a modest living, reinvesting the produce of his fifty slaves' hard labor in better tobacco-growing land. As more children came, Gus put everyone on rafts and poled them forty miles upriver to a 2,500-acre farm called Epsewasson that he had assembled along the Potomac. It would be years before anyone renamed it Mount Vernon.

When George Washington was five, he met for the first time his half brothers Lawrence and Austin, both of whom were returning from schooling in England. George was especially fond of the elder, Lawrence, who was sensitive, intelligent, and elegant in manner, his speech littered with literary allusions. Gus turned over the house and farm at Epsewasson to Lawrence.

George was seven when the War of Jenkins's Ear broke out. The British Ministry ordered an attack by land and sea on Cartagena, Colombia, the strongest citadel in New Spain. For the first time, English settlers in America were ordered to serve in a British overseas expedition. Red-coated recruiting officers strutted from town to town with drummers and flags, raising the first American regiment. Lawrence Washington immediately applied and obtained a captain's commission.

Young George was dazzled by his brother's new scarlet breeches, navy blue jacket, and gold-laced hat. A shiny brass officer's gorget hung from Lawrence's neck, and he wore a crimson sash with a silver short sword dangling from it. Captain Washington sailed south to the Caribbean and into a howling fiasco, with 90 percent of his American regiment suffering casualties, most caused by an array of tropical diseases, including yellow fever and malaria.

For four years, little George rarely saw his father, who was often away on his restless quest for more land, more ore, more income. When Gus was home, George would follow him around their property, often riding with him over to the iron furnace to watch the blast. When Gus returned from one surveying trip to the West, George watched as he unstrapped his expensive surveying tools and locked them safely in a shed.

During his frequent absences, Gus arranged to have a convict teach George to read, write, and keep sums. George took a ferry each morning to a log schoolhouse in Fredericksburg, in preparation for Appleby Grammar School in England, the same school Gus had attended as a boy, and where Lawrence and Austin had been educated. But he would never make the crossing to England, and his formal education would soon be over.

George had just turned eleven when his father died, leaving behind 10,000 acres of Virginia soil, a one-sixth share in the Principio Iron Works, and a herd of cattle. The larger share of his property was passed to Lawrence. When George turned twenty-one, he was to receive the 260-acre Ferry Farm, 2,100 acres of undeveloped land, and ten slaves, an inheritance controlled by George's mother for the time being. Barely an adolescent, George Washington became a slaveholder.

Life at Ferry Farm grew progressively more austere. Mary Washington insisted on discipline. Her step-granddaughter (the wife of Robert E. Lee) passed down the tradition that she "required from those about her a prompt and literal obedience somewhat resembling that demanded by proper military subordination."[1] From his boyhood, George Washington knew what an order sounded like—and the pain of disobeying one. Mary was especially strict about who could ride her horses. No one was allowed to mount her prize bay mare. When George ignored this rule and leaped on the horse, it reared and fell, rupturing a blood vessel in its neck, which proved fatal. Mary may never have forgiven him for this headstrong act.

George, the oldest of Mary's six children, never wrote about his childhood and rarely spoke of his education. In all, he received about eight years of irregular schooling, including tutoring in grammar, logic, mathematics, history, geography, and surveying. His earliest surviving papers are three notebooks, some 218 pages of his longhand exercises in mathematics and surveying. A succession of tutors had him copy legal instruments and forms he would need to manage a plantation. He devoted fully twenty pages to copying 110 rules for good behavior from a sixteenth-century manual prepared by French Jesuits to train young noblemen. The book may have been printed by Benjamin Franklin, who regularly distributed *Rules of Civility* to the bookstore of the *Virginia Gazette* in Williamsburg.

Lawrence tutored George until he was fourteen, concealing it from his mother. Discreetly, Lawrence was preparing George for a military career, including fencing lessons from a Dutch tutor. What George learned under Captain Washington's watchful eye can be deciphered. In a lesson in his notebook dated and signed August 13, 1745, he began to master geometry at thirteen. He soon became an enthusiastic student of mathematics.

His notebooks contain fifty pages of exercises encapsulating the mathematical training needed by any planter, merchant, or merchant-mariner of his time, including a thorough grounding in currency and credit and Virginia's rates of exchange. One notebook contains nineteen pages of geometric theorems and definitions. Another includes decimals, simple interest, money conversion, geometry problems, rules of the square root, and plane trigonometry. And a final notebook is devoted to the "Art of Surveying and Measuring of Land." In its pages, Washington demonstrated that he was properly trained for a career as a "woodland" surveyor. At fifteen, George plotted his brother's turnip field, his first paid job.

Lawrence's influence on his young half brother did not stop at his education. In 1743, Lawrence married into one of the most powerful families in Virginia, exposing George to a rung of society he had scarcely known existed. Lord Thomas Fairfax, sixth Baron Fairfax, was the sole proprietor of the five-million-acre Northern Neck of Virginia. His cousin, Colonel William Fairfax, had recently built Belvoir, a magnificent manor house on the Potomac, four miles from Mount Vernon. Lawrence married Colonel Fairfax's daughter, Ann, who furnished Mount Vernon in the latest Georgian style.

Nothing at Ferry Farm had prepared George for a house where

everyone wore shoes, where there were separate parlors so one group could dance without disturbing another playing whist or loo, and where dinner table and drawing room repartee was peppered with references to Joseph Addison and Richard Steele's influential London daily, the *Spectator*. Discovering an abundance of old issues in Lord Fairfax's library, the young Washington devoured the *Spectator*, exposing himself to the wit and politics of Georgian England. He considered it more a primer than a satirical tabloid. The paper introduced him to a smattering of Greek and Latin, and he memorized the expressions he read until, years later, like any gentleman, he could sprinkle his correspondence and military orders with apt classical references.

It was at Belvoir that George first encountered an English nobleman: Baron Fairfax was the first peer to come live in America. Belvoir's drawing rooms, music room, dining room, and grand library were filled with guests garbed in the latest London fashions. Between rounds of cards and conversations by the fire, George Washington learned the rituals of deference that he would one day abhor and overthrow. Afternoons of listening to His Lordship rant about women often led to George streaking off with him after the fox. George's horsemanship impressed the baron.

As the years passed, Lord Fairfax became fond of the tall, elegantly mannered young Washington. When he decided to sell off some of his acres in the Shenandoah Valley, an area nearly the size of New Jersey, it came to His Lordship's attention that George had another useful skill. He was already an accomplished surveyor, and Fairfax was inclined to do the lad a favor. Lord Fairfax's best surveyor needed a strong young assistant to manhandle the supplies, care for the horses, clear the underbrush, haul the chains, carry the theodolite, and hold steady the rod for his sightings. By age sixteen, Washington had developed powerful arms and tough hands.

He also possessed what mattered most on a frontier expedition: endurance. On March 11, 1748, he set out on horseback from Belvoir for the expedition to the West. But first, George had to stop to get his mother's permission. After he pointed out that he would be paid, she gave her approval.

This first journey to the West was a pivotal moment in Washington's life, for it marked his independence. He may have needed to ask his mother for permission, but now he no longer needed to ask her for money. With hard-earned cash in his pocket, he began to keep a ledger. Whenever he was paid for a surveying job, he bought fashionable clothes. He purchased a sword and took fencing lessons. And he brought money home to help with his mother's expenses for his five younger siblings.

He also gained a new kind of stature. Men who ventured onto the frontier and returned safely earned respect they could receive no other way. Their retellings of their adventures made them the centerpieces of fireside society. George had left as a boy; he returned as a young man respected by other men. With his skill as an experienced surveyor, George Washington at age sixteen was ready to pursue a fortune.

Surveying was considered an important and respected skill in the largely undeveloped American colonies, and skilled surveyors were in demand. As a surveyor's assistant laying out building lots in the new town of Alexandria, George was able to pay the fees to obtain a surveyor's license less than six months after he turned seventeen. Two days later, he accepted his first full-fledged professional commission. Lord Fairfax again hired him, at more than the going rate, to lead his own team back into the Shenandoah Valley to measure for subdivision a four-thousand-acre tract near present-day Winchester.

Doubtless through Fairfax's influence, he also garnered, at seventeen, a three-year appointment as surveyor of newly created Culpeper County. Before he was eighteen, George Washington pocketed £125 ($18,250 today) a year from surveying, more cash than most Virginia planters saw in a year; between 1749 and 1752, he performed 190 surveys, earning roughly £400 ($60,000 today).[2]

As he earned higher fees, he bought land, sometimes taking land in lieu of cash. As a speculative fever swept Virginia, grandiose plans to carve up the vast western lands inspired Washington, at age eighteen, to make his first cash purchases of 549 acres in what is now West Virginia plus 1,312 acres on the Virginia–West Virginia line; a year later, he acquired 240 acres along the Potomac and two parcels in the new town of Winchester.

During his three years as Culpeper County's surveyor, he acquired 2,315 acres, roughly equal to Lawrence's estate at Mount Vernon. Before his twenty-first birthday, George Washington's ownership of 4,830 acres assured him a place in Virginia's gentry.[3]

CHAPTER THREE

"Join, or Die"

George Washington's first act of rebellion against British authority was due not to ideals of patriotism but to a levy on his own burgeoning personal income. Virginia's royal governor, Robert Dinwiddie, decided to enforce an old regulation requiring that all surveyors pay one-sixth of their income to support the College of William and Mary. Outraged that his hard work should be taxed to support the education of the sons of wealthy planters, Washington decided to pack away his surveying tools.

Tired of holding the reins for the Fairfaxes, he faced the fact that beyond his surveying work and a modest income from investments in land, he had little potential to earn enough money to live in the style to which he'd become accustomed. He would have to do something bold to catapult himself into the position in society to which he believed he was entitled by heritage.

He now set his sights on a career as a British Army officer. For four generations, Washingtons had distinguished themselves in the Virginia militia, Lawrence rising to its highest permanent (and salaried) post as adjutant general. George knew how far it had taken his brother into the ranks of Virginia's elite. George was presentable and an experienced frontiersman, but he lacked military experience. He would have to rely on family connections, the patronage of the powerful Fairfaxes, and sheer nerve.

In 1752, tragedy again struck young George's life. Lawrence's health deteriorated, and as he lay dying, George helped his half brother draw up his complex will. He discovered that he would eventually inherit a tangle of investments—and debts. In the short run, Lawrence made George his executor and left him in temporary control of their father's Principio Iron Works interests. If Lawrence's wife and daughter died without heirs, George would receive Mount Vernon. But Lawrence's most important legacy may have been his status as adjutant general of Virginia's militia.

George left Lawrence's bedside long enough to dash to Williamsburg to seek an audience with the royal governor. He had already made a strong impression on Dinwiddie, who had often signed patents for young Washington's land purchases and was well aware of George's backing by the Fairfaxes.

The House of Burgesses decided to divide Lawrence's former militia post into four districts. Dinwiddie appointed George adjutant of the southernmost (and least important) district, between the James River and the North Carolina border. With the rank of major, he was to oversee militia training. The £100-a-year salary (roughly $15,000 today) doubled his cash income. Washington borrowed all the military books he could find and, as Major Washington, continued to lobby the governor and his own patrons to help win over the northern district adjutancy, which he considered rightfully his. He succeeded.

His half brother's death also brought George something else of value: Lawrence's shares in a land-speculating firm, the Ohio Company, whose organizers included Lawrence and his brother Augustine. With the hope of establishing a settlement and a trading empire with the local Indians, the company had received a royal grant of two hundred thousand forested acres in the Ohio Valley. Stockholders envisioned constructing a highway linking the valley to the Chesapeake Bay, and thus the Atlantic Ocean.

Successfully appealing to British authorities, the company had received permission to offer free ship's passage from England to indentured servants who would work for the company for seven years, clearing forests and building roads and trading posts in return for the right to remain on the land as tenant farmers. The company's organizers had committed to settling one hundred families in three years around a small fort that they would build at stockholders' expense. They had to move quickly or lose their grant and their investment, but if they succeeded, they would receive an additional three-hundred-thousand-acre royal land grant. Blazing a highway eighty miles through the mountainous Virginia backcountry to the Cumberland Gap in present-day northwestern Maryland, they built a fortified trading post and began to sell land.

The value of the company's stock had soared after Robert Dinwiddie, a wealthy Scottish merchant and himself an investor in the Ohio Company, was appointed as Virginia's royal governor. He arrived in the colony with fresh capital and a ship loaded with cannon and goods to trade with the Indians, ready to wield his new position toward greater wealth. Dinwiddie attracted other highly placed British officials as investors in the Ohio Company, including the royal governors of Maryland and North Carolina, a majority of Virginia's House of Burgesses, and a duke, as well as London merchants. Whatever on-the-scene transactions Dinwiddie deemed necessary to assure the success of the Ohio Company now became British foreign policy. But the French government considered the activities of the company nothing more than a subterfuge for extending British imperial power.

With Lawrence Washington's death, Governor Dinwiddie had assumed the presidency of the Ohio Company, aware that neither the French nor their native allies recognized the company's claim to the region. To emphasize that they had not lost interest in the Ohio Valley, the French began to build a line of forts from Quebec southward around the Great Lakes.

It was at this moment, in February 1753, the same week Washington turned twenty-one and was sworn in as the adjutant general for northern Virginia, that the French launched their thrust into the Ohio Country.

Building Fort Machault at near present-day Franklin in northwestern Pennsylvania and at Presque Isle in Lake Erie off present-day Buffalo, New York, they destroyed the Ohio Company's trading post at Will's Creek, in northwestern Maryland, replacing it with their own stockade.

Governor Dinwiddie was instructed, in orders signed by King George II himself, to counter the French threat. He was to send an ultimatum to the French to leave the Ohio Country immediately. If they refused, "[we] do hereby strictly charge and command [you] to drive them off with force of arms."[1]

Learning from Colonel Fairfax that an emissary to the French would be chosen, Washington saw his opportunity. Through an emissary, Dinwiddie would be interposing the English—even if over a small private fort—between Virginia and New France. Whoever carried Dinwiddie's ultimatum would represent not only Virginia but also England. Washington rushed to Williamsburg to make his case directly to Dinwiddie. As an adjutant general, he was already an administrative deputy of the governor, and though he was the youngest of Virginia's three adjutants, Major Washington was the most experienced frontiersman.

An imposing giant for his time, young Washington stood a head taller than most men, his 209 pounds spread over a taut six-foot, four-and-a-half-inch frame. Dinwiddie could see there was nothing soft about this frontier-toughened, physically powerful young man who had already proved by his surveying missions that he had the endurance to carry off a thousand-mile trip in the wilderness. He could speak neither French nor any Indian language but, Washington argued, he could take along interpreters.

The young Washington got his appointment, becoming half diplomat, half intelligence officer. On April 16, 1753, Washington, clad in buckskin, set off with a translator, two hunters, and two fur traders. After slogging through heavy snows and rain for two weeks, Washington delivered Dinwiddie's ultimatum to the commandant at Fort Machault, who told him that "it was the absolute design [of the French] to take possession of the Ohio."

With a French escort, Washington's party rode north to Presque Isle to present the commandant there with Dinwiddie's letter. While the French officers huddled in a council of war, Washington learned that they planned to enlist the natives to hunt down "all our straggling traders." Indians had already taken eight scalps and sent other prisoners to Quebec. When Washington brought up the names of the missing traders, the French commandant suddenly answered the Virginia ultimatum. He would not withdraw his troops.

Washington rode into Williamsburg after a seventy-nine-day, thousand-mile journey by horseback, canoe, and snowshoe in terrible winter weather. His seven-thousand-word report created a sensation. Dinwiddie presented the report to an emergency session of his executive council, rushed it off to the colony's printer, and forwarded it, along with Washington's expert drawings and maps of the Ohio Valley, to the Board of Trade and Plantations in London. Washington's report was read throughout Virginia and reprinted in other colonies, including in Benjamin Franklin's *Gazette.*

To Governor Dinwiddie and his council, Major Washington proposed that Virginia build a fort at the confluence of the Allegheny and Monongahela Rivers, where the two formed the Ohio River. Dinwiddie succeeded in wringing enough money from the House of Burgesses to build the fort. The burgesses also authorized calling up two hundred militia to garrison it, with five hundred more promised. Washington was ordered to raise half the troops.

Dinwiddie found it difficult to commission a competent commanding officer for his new regiment. With no battle-seasoned officers, he finally settled on Joshua Fry, an aged professor of mathematics at William and Mary, to lead the expedition. A respected frontiersman, Fry had experience negotiating with the Indians, but he was too out of shape to lead such a mission—and soon died of injuries he sustained after falling off his horse.

After learning that hundreds of French were canoeing down the Ohio, Dinwiddie promoted Washington to lieutenant colonel. Ordered to leave at once with all the men he could muster, he was to race the French to the fork of the Ohio and build a substantial fort before the French could.

But the young colonel did not forget that he was a stockholder in the company through whose lands the troops would march. He persuaded his company commanders, all older and more experienced, that their first task was to clear a wide enough roadway for heavy wagons and artillery, a road for future civilian as much as for current military use, a road that would surely raise the value of his investment.

In the steamy heat of a dense forest, while Washington laid out the route with his surveyor's tools, his 159 raw troops began the backbreaking work of felling trees, hacking away underbrush, and grubbing out rocks and tree stumps. Incredibly, they managed to cut a passable road for forty miles over several Appalachian ridges. In a lush glen where two streams crisscrossed, known as the Great Meadows, Washington pitched his camp.

He soon learned that a sizable French detachment was camped only a few miles away. The French party, which consisted of around forty Frenchmen and Indians sleeping in makeshift huts, was commanded by Joseph Coulon de Villiers, Sieur de Jumonville. The group had been sent out from the half-completed Fort Duquesne, sited at the very spot where Washington proposed to build a British fort, to warn the Virginians to leave French territory.

Washington decided to strike. Creeping within a hundred yards of where the French contingent was camped, Washington bawled the order to attack. The Virginians kept up a withering fire for fully fifteen minutes. When the shooting stopped, ten French soldiers lay dead or wounded, including Jumonville. Washington was stunned when his new prisoners insisted they had been on a diplomatic mission.

British Americans who considered the land west of the Allegheny Mountains theirs for the taking would later hail Washington's gambit as a heroic blow against French depredations. But the attack gave the French justification for a major retaliation, and Washington found himself completely exposed deep in Indian country.

With the French army closing in, Washington decided he would have to make his stand in a hollow he now fatalistically named Fort Necessity. He had wasted more than a month building a road instead of a substantial fort on higher ground. Now, fully half his men, subsisting on only corn and uncured beef, were too sick from dysentery to fight. Making matters worse, Washington had no idea how to design a fort. He had his exhausted men cut down oak trees to fashion a crude stockade that protruded just eight feet aboveground. When he called the roll, he discovered that his Indian escort had vanished.

On rainy July 3, 1754, French soldiers, concealed behind trees, opened fire at the crowded, pitifully low stockade. Men were wounded or killed whenever they dared to raise their heads to fire. After nine hours, one-third of Washington's troops were killed or wounded, and the young officer finally faced the unescapable fact that no reinforcements were coming.

The French commander offered Washington written articles of capitulation. If the English returned to Virginia, they would not be taken prisoner. Washington would have to leave behind his cannon. With his former fencing master, the expedition's interpreter, critically wounded, Washington relied on the Dutchman's knowledge of French. In the guttering candlelight, he struggled to translate the word *assailir.* To the French, the word had only one possible meaning: assassination.

Washington's surrender was equivalent to a treaty recognizing French claims to the entire vast Ohio Country. The French were now in sole possession of the western slopes of the Alleghenies and all the tributaries of the Ohio River, in control of the interior of North America. Washington had to swear on his honor not to take up arms for a year before he could lead survivors forty miles on foot back to Wills Creek. Despite French assurances, the Indians looted Washington's baggage, including his costly surveying tools.

Governor Dinwiddie, learning of the debacle at Fort Necessity, demanded that Washington counterattack and protect the Ohio Company's investment. When Washington refused, Dinwiddie stripped him of his command, breaking his rank and pay back to an adjutant's. Nearly every trace of the expensive five-year-long Ohio Company investment in the Ohio Valley—and of Washington's quest to profit from his brother's share of it—was gone.

Yet when he rode into Williamsburg to report in person, he found to his utter amazement that he had become famous, his name bandied about in the press and in governors' reports to the king. Even newspapers in London reported on his exploits. Rather than Washington being disparaged for his failure, it was the governors of surrounding colonies who were being vilified for not providing him with reinforcements.

As war fever gripped England, young Colonel Washington—he had been promoted in his absence after Joshua Fry's death during the expedition—became the symbol of English resistance to French imperial expansion in the New World. A line he had written in a letter to his brother John was quoted in an article read by King George: "I have heard the bullets whistle and there is something charming in the sound."[2]

When Washington learned that his colonelcy had been eliminated, he did not even dignify Dinwiddie's offer of a new captain's commission. He wanted to turn his back on a military career and take up a planter's life. Suddenly, Mount Vernon became his. After Washington's widowed sister-in-law's baby daughter died, she remarried and moved away. Just after Christmas 1754, Washington inherited Mount Vernon and eighteen more slaves. He arrived at his new home in ill health and, once again, broke.

Even as George Washington capitulated, representatives of six colonies were arriving in Albany, New York, for the first American congress. Ordinarily, British colonies communicated only with authorities in London, not with one another, but in the May 9 edition of his *Pennsylvania Gazette*, Benjamin Franklin had published an account of the French advance into the Ohio Country and their building of Fort Duquesne, accompanying it with what probably was the first American political cartoon, a snake cut into eight sections over the caption "Join, or Die."

For three years, Franklin had been writing privately about the need for the colonies to join together and formulate a coordinated plan to meet the French threat. He proposed forming a colonial defense union under a military president general appointed and paid by the Crown. A grand council elected by the colonial assemblies—each colony to have two to seven delegates, depending on its contributions to a general treasury—would have legislative power subject to approval by the president general and the Crown. The president general and grand council would also have jurisdiction over Indian affairs, including new land purchases. One of Franklin's inspirations for the plan was the Great Law of Peace followed by the Iroquois Confederacy.

A federal council, meeting by turns in the various capitals, would be responsible for defense and be empowered to construct frontier forts and pay their garrisons, supported by a tax on liquor and an excise on what Franklin called "Superfluities [such] as Tea." The council would have more power than the colonial assemblies in their relations with the royal governors, but less than Parliament versus the king.

A total of twenty-five commissioners assembled in Albany, meeting inside the town's massive old three-story Dutch courthouse. In intervals between conferences with the Indians, a steering committee of one delegate from each colony for four days deliberated each clause of Franklin's plan. The committee rejected Franklin's proposal that the council's president general be a military man, and instead of raising revenue by singling out tea, it recommended that levies rather be aimed at "discouraging Luxury, than loading Industry with unnecessary burdens."

On July 10, 1754, the delegates to the Albany congress unanimously approved Franklin's Plan of Union. If adopted, it would have anticipated by three decades the Articles of Confederation. But as it stood, every colony's legislature rejected it. Without unanimous consent from the colonies, the British Board of Trade had no need to present the Albany Plan of Union to Parliament. "The Assemblies did not accept it as they all thought there was too much *Prerogative* in it; and in England it was judg'd to have too much of the *Democratic*."[3]

Benjamin Franklin was not totally surprised: most colonists, he was learning, were still narrowly provincial in outlook, mutually jealous and suspicious of any central taxing authority. In his *Autobiography*, he contended that if his plan had been adopted, "the subsequent separation of the colonies from the mother country might not so soon have happened:

> I am still of opinion it would have been happy for both sides of the water. . . . The colonies, so united, would have been sufficiently strong to have defended themselves; there would have been no need for troops from England; of course, the subsequent pretense for taxing America, and the bloody contest it occasioned, would have been avoided."[4]

CHAPTER FOUR

"Who Would Have Thought It?"

More than anything, George Washington aspired to be a British officer, not just a Virginia militiaman. He yearned for the respect he had seen accorded his half brother Lawrence and the accompanying ascent in social status that seemed to come with an officer's crimson uniform, sash, and short sword. Even though he could claim descent from royalty, and generations of Washingtons had served as militia officers in Virginia, he had seen that men would more readily follow a British officer's command than any provincial's—and that no British officer would defer to a colonist no matter his rank. He had seen his dashing scarlet-garbed brother welcomed in the courtly society of an English lord—and his marriage into an aristocratic family. A young man of modest means, one who wasn't in line to inherit great wealth, young Washington imagined military honors as the route to the offices, privileges, and place in Tidewater society that he considered his birthright.

In February 1755, the personification of his life's ambition arrived by sea. Sixteen British troop transports dropped anchor off Norfolk and disgorged the first British regulars ever to land on Virginia soil, and the largest force ever sent to America from England. The pageantry of the British regulars, clad in red coats trimmed with brightly burnished brass buttons and buff breeches, and marching behind forty pounding drums, three dozen shrill fifes, and fluttering flags with rose-and-thistle-wreathed

Roman numerals, stirred the young Washington. He later wrote that he had loved the spectacle. His defeat at Fort Necessity notwithstanding, he was now, more than ever, determined to pursue a military career.

When the British home government had learned of the French fortress at the head of the Ohio River, the king's Privy Council convened at Whitehall. King George II declared his utter aversion to sending British troops to North America to fight the French; England and France were still negotiating the final details of a treaty to end the last war.

The king's councillors disagreed. The Earl of Halifax, who was president of the Board of Trade and Plantations and technically responsible for colonial affairs, insisted that a joint Anglo-American offensive was absolutely necessary to drive the French back to Canada. He was supported by Prince William Augustus, Duke of Cumberland, head of the British Army and an inveterate enemy of the French, who blamed them for supporting the recent Scottish rising of 1745.

Widely known as the "Butcher of Culloden," Prince William insisted on confronting the French in the Ohio Valley. He chose as commander of the expedition Major General Edward Braddock. A former royal governor of Gibraltar, Braddock had seen little combat.

Rowed ashore from the flagship *Centurion*, General Braddock arrived in Norfolk with a £50,000 (roughly $5.25 million today) war chest of silver and gold coins appropriated by Parliament, along with assurance of carte blanche. In addition to the two thousand troops he brought with him, he was empowered to raise an equal number of colonial troops. His orders: Destroy Fort Duquesne, then lead his army north to help American regiments evict the French from Fort Niagara and the Lake Champlain forts. All this presupposed little French objection to English chastisement.

Several blind spots were to plague the expedition. Among them was the fact that the British Ministry evidently lacked anyone who had ever seen the distances and natural obstacles involved. A more direct route to Fort Duquesne would have run west from Philadelphia through Pennsylvania.

In Virginia, as soon as he learned of the British strategy, Governor

Dinwiddie renamed the Ohio Company's trading post at Wills Creek as Fort Cumberland and designated it as the advance base for Braddock's expedition. Any improvements Braddock made to the old post would greatly enhance the value of the company's properties. Then Dinwiddie issued lucrative contracts to his cronies to build up a mountain of supplies.

Learning the details of Braddock's plan, George Washington decided to offer his services, even if it meant violating his word that he would not set foot on French-claimed soil for one full year. When Lord Fairfax hosted a lavish reception for Braddock and his officers, he invited Washington, who spent a giddy evening surrounded by elegant British officers who made up the general's "family."

Washington saw an opportunity to win a regular army commission by distinguishing himself. He sent Braddock a salutary letter of welcome that mostly detailed his own past services. In the patronage system of the times, such a blatant bid for a new patron was normal, expected, and necessary, especially since Washington had fallen out of the royal governor's favor.

A few weeks later, a red-coated courier delivered to Mount Vernon a letter from Braddock's chief of staff. Washington's response was a bit surprising. He wanted nothing more than to attach himself to Braddock but, he explained, he was "unprepared."[1] Hemming and hawing, he could not bring himself to say that he could not afford to accept the general's invitation. Instead, he said he could not join Braddock until he hired a farm manager and planted his tobacco crop. After more weeks of awkward negotiations, Washington agreed to join Braddock's staff as an unpaid aide-de-camp with the temporary rank of captain.

Never able to leave his money troubles behind, Washington had to borrow his neighbor Sally Fairfax's saddle pony. It took him another week to find a horse of his own, and then only after he had dashed off an urgent plea for a loan of £50 (about $7,500) from Lord Fairfax.

When he finally overtook Braddock, according to his own account, he discovered that he often had Braddock all to himself, the tall, solemn young Virginian and the braggadocio armchair general hitting it off. As he groomed a future British officer, Braddock rewarded Washington's adulation by allowing him to offer commissions to his own colonial officers.

Immersing himself in the details of army life, Washington studied firsthand how to be a general. Each day, he borrowed the orders of the day and copied them into his journal, learning to emulate their form and language. He made friends with Braddock's aides and officers, who shared with him their military manuals and pamphlets.

Washington found that the general was stymied in his attempt to procure horses and wagons to haul supplies, food, ammunition, and personal baggage over the 110 miles from Fort Cumberland to the Ohio River. The governor of Maryland had promised 2,500 horses; at the moment there were only 25. For several days, Braddock seriously considered calling off the expedition.

Army quartermasters found that the local German farmers were reluctant to extend credit to the English Crown. Only a clever ruse by Benjamin Franklin, accompanying the expedition in his dual capacities of chairman of Pennsylvania's defense committee and deputy postmaster general, finally got the army rolling again.

Franklin, attending the governors' conference at Alexandria, had noticed that Sir John Sinclair, the British quartermaster general, wore a Hussar-like caped jacket over one shoulder. That detail, he suspected, might be the key to convincing Pennsylvania's farmers to turn over their covered wagons and teams for the war effort. With Braddock's blessing, Franklin wrote and ordered printed a handbill warning the German farmers, many of whom had seen such capes all too frequently during wars in Europe before they had emigrated, that "Sir John Sinclair, the Hussar," was preparing "with a body of soldiers" to seize their wagons and burn their farms unless they cooperated.

Franklin had to promise the farmers that, if their wagon or horses were lost, they would be compensated. After running out of the cash Braddock had given him, Franklin advanced £200 (about $30,000 today) of his own money. But the farmers, "alleging that they did not know General Braddock, or what Dependence might be had on his Promise, insisted on [Franklin's] Bond for the Performance." Franklin gave them promissory notes totaling £1,000 (about $150,000). Soon enough, some 150 Conestoga wagons, their teams and drivers, and 259 packhorses were on the march toward Braddock's camp.[2]

Dining with the officers, Franklin learned that many of Braddock's junior officers "were generally not in affluence" and could ill afford to supply themselves for a long march in "this dear country" where "nothing could be purchased." Franklin said he would use his influence in the Pennsylvania Assembly to provide "some relief."

Writing to the assembly, he recommended a "Present" of "Necessaries and Refreshments." He asked his son, William, "who had some experience of a Camp Life," to draw up a list and present it in Philadelphia. Two weeks later, William returned with a horse for each officer burdened with his "presents":

> 6 lb. loaf sugar; 6 lbs. good Muscovado [brown sugar] 1 lb. good Green Tea; 1 lb. good Bohea; 6 lb. good ground Coffee; 6 lb. Chocolate; ½ Hundredweight best white Biscuit; ½ lb. Pepper; 1 Quart best white Wine Vinegar; 1 Gloucester Cheese; 1 Keg containing 20 lb. good Butter; 2 Doz. Old Madeira Wine; 2 Gallons Jamaica Spirits; 1 Bottle Flour of Mustard; 2 well-cur'd Hams; ½ Doz. Dried Tongues; 6 lb. Rice; 6 lb. Raisins.[3]

It was Captain Washington's task, as General Braddock's paymaster, to count out the gold coins for Benjamin Franklin. Yet his most crucial role, as a member of the staff of the highest-ranking British officer in North America, was as chief logistician of the expedition. He argued against exposing a four-to-five-mile-long cavalcade of wagons to Indian attack. And from his recent experience, he knew how poor the road ahead was. In some places only twelve feet wide, the road was clogged with men, horse-drawn wagons, and herds of cattle. He urged Braddock to employ packtrains of horses instead of wagons, which would require widening the existing road.

Braddock thanked Washington for his advice, and then ignored it. He regarded his road as a "tremendous opportunity of transporting the heavy artillery over the mountains."[4] Never before had artillery been brought to bear in the American interior, and Braddock believed that it would be decisive, especially against the Indians, who had never faced it. Despite Washington's urging, the general continued laboriously building the road ahead of him.

The conditions were hardly in his favor. Many officers, including Washington, were suffering from dysentery, due to a diet limited to mostly Royal Navy rations of salt beef. No fresh meat, vegetables, or butter had reached the army for weeks.

Braddock kept his young acolyte busy. He ordered Washington to ride to Williamsburg to fetch £4,000 (about $215,000 today) in cash to pay the troops. Knowing the mission was fraught with peril, Washington requested a cavalry escort, but none materialized and he had no luck in raising a militia troop. He wrote to his brother John, "You may, with almost equal success, attempt to raise the dead to life again as [a] force in this country."[5]

In observing Braddock closely for three months, Washington was able to study the frustrations and failures the British experienced in trying to deal effectively with their colonies, even during an emergency. Throughout June 1755, Braddock's spit-and-polish parade-ground army, along a route so familiar to Washington, labored through dense oak forests until it squeezed through the Cumberland Gap and emerged on the western slope of the Alleghenies, the thin red line advancing only half a mile a day.

The brutal hard work of building a road in summer heat and transporting the army was meted out to colonial teamsters hired on the frontier and to "pioneer" labor brigades, paid in gold to cut down trees marked by royal engineers. Washington did not record his emotions as he rode past the burned remains of Fort Necessity, almost a year since the day of his humiliation there.

He watched as Braddock butted his head against chronic colonial problems. Many Indians had become convinced by Washington's fiasco at Fort Necessity that the French would win in a wilderness war and stayed safely in their longhouses. Unhelpfully, Braddock insulted a delegation of Delaware, Shawnee, and Mingo by declaring that "no savage would inherit the land" he liberated from the French. They went over immediately to the French. When fifty warriors did arrive but insisted their wives be allowed to join them, Braddock at first refused. After several wild nights involving rum, soldiers, and Indian women, Braddock ordered the women out of his camp; the men followed.

Weeks of Braddock's time went toward diplomacy as he tried unsuccessfully to get the colonial legislatures to honor Dinwiddie's pledge to match the British war chest. In what may have been his first political argument, Washington found himself upholding American honor against an onslaught by a raging British general who did not possess any humility or self-restraint.

As they headed west, real affection developed between Braddock and Washington, despite the hardships. Braddock bore his youthful aide with good-natured patience. At Fort Cumberland, after he watched Redcoats drill all day, Washington lectured Braddock that European tactics would not repel an Indian attack in the forest. Braddock, turning to the other officers, chuckled and said, "What think you of this from a beardless boy?"[6]

After repeated warnings that his army's plodding pace was giving the French ample time to bring reinforcements from Canada, Braddock summoned his advisers one at a time into his command tent and asked for suggestions on how to speed things up. Captain Washington was the first he sent for.

Washington was, Braddock knew, the only British officer who understood the terrain. This time, Braddock listened closely as Washington gave drastic advice: Divide the army. Split it in two. Send a fast-moving handpicked force ahead with some artillery to begin the attack on Fort Duquesne. The slower troops could come along behind, continuing to build the supply road. Braddock and his headquarters unit would follow while the sick and most of the wagons were sent to the rear. When

Braddock called in his senior officers, he did not attribute the idea to Washington. A majority of British officers concurred.

Washington was proud that the regimental commanders supported his proposal, but he let Braddock's subordinates believe it was the general's idea, and he was careful not to take credit for it.

Considering seriously the British show of force, the French had rushed thousands of troops to Canada. For the first time, two European armies of professional soldiers would face off, vying for control of North America. The Seven Years' War, the climactic struggle for trade routes and colonies around the world, commenced.

Just before two o'clock in the morning on July 9, 1755, Washington and the rest of Braddock's staff awakened and dressed in their best uniforms. Washington would ride at Braddock's side, ready to carry orders to unit commanders. Each unit marched briskly past in review, uniforms immaculate, muskets gleaming. Washington would later say it was the most thrilling sight of his life. He watched in awe as the advance column crossed the Monongahela and climbed the embankment, the crimson current disappearing into the dark, majestic forest.

Braddock sent Washington with orders for his men, who had gone hungry the day before, to eat now. They gnawed on dried biscuits and watched as batmen milked cows and made rum punch and served it, along with some of Benjamin Franklin's Gloucester cheese, to their officers.

The French inside Fort Duquesne were up early, too. Their commander, Captain Claude Pierre Pécaudy, Sieur de Contrecoeur, decided to risk everything before Braddock could get close enough to bombard the fort with heavy artillery.

By midafternoon, the British vanguard was within seven miles of the French fort. Passing a heavily wooded slope, Braddock's scouts suddenly saw, running toward them, a French officer wearing a gleaming gorget on his otherwise bare breast. The scouts fired immediately at the shirtless officer, who fell dead.

The French and Indians divided and surrounded the British, dashing from tree to tree, blending with the terrain until they became invisible. Some of them had even dyed their torsos the color of tree trunks in order to remain undetected. Picking off the mounted red-coated British officers first, they quickly reduced the ranks of regulars to an undifferentiated mass of terrified men. The buckskin-clad Virginians, fanning out, took cover in the trees. British officers mistook them for French Canadians and ordered volley after volley, shooting many of their allies in the back.

As the Redcoats turned and ran, Braddock and Washington galloped up and down the road, trying to rally them. Washington was now Braddock's only surviving aide. He never forgot Braddock's bravery as he reined his horse back and forth, flailing at men with the flat of his sword. Twice, Washington's mounts were killed, one horse rolling over and briefly pinning him. Each time, he managed to grab a riderless horse. As he dodged through smoke-filled woods, his tall form made him a conspicuous target. Then Braddock was shot, the ball crashing through his right arm and chest and into his lungs.

Washington and the Virginians screened the British retreat. One of the last to cross the water, Washington found a small covered wagon and got Braddock into it. Before losing consciousness, Braddock told Washington to bring up the reserves. He still thought victory possible.

Washington rode all night through "shocking scenes that are not to be described. . . . The dead, the dying, the groans and cries of the wounded for help were enough to pierce a heart of adamant," he remembered years later.[7] At the spot where he had attacked Jumonville, he found the reserves and ordered them forward. Sleeping eleven hours, Washington awoke to find that most of the British had fled.

In terrible pain as he jolted along in a cart, Braddock asked Washington, "Who would have thought it?" He gave his last order: Captain Washington was to bury him. After the general took his final breath, Washington ordered a deep trench dug, lowered Braddock in his best uniform into the ground, and recited the Anglican prayers for the dead. Then he ordered every wagon driven over the grave to pack down the earth so the Indians wouldn't find it. What was left of Braddock's defeated army passed over him. George Washington, who had learned so much from Braddock about how and how not to be an officer, never uttered a word against him. But two decades later, Benjamin Franklin, in his *Autobiography*, took a dim view of "this whole Transaction" that "gave us Americans the first Suspicion that our exalted Ideas of the Prowess of British Regulars had not been well founded."

> From their Landing till they got beyond the Settlements, they had plundered and stripped the Inhabitants, totally ruining some poor Families, besides insulting, abusing and confining the People if they remonstrated. This was enough to put us out of conceit of such Defenders if we had really wanted any.[8]

For Washington, his discovery of Britain's refusal to adapt to conditions in America was sobering. He had seen soldiers in bright red uniforms march in formation into a forest ambush, surrounded by men stripped to the waist, camouflaged in Indian style.

After the carnage, Washington heard a haunting murmur, a mixture of excitement and horror, echoing through the frontier settlements: "The British are beaten! The British are beaten!" For the first time, George Washington realized that the mighty British Army *could* be beaten.

Washington had every reason to be disenchanted when he rode home to Mount Vernon in the late summer of 1755. Two years of hardship on the frontier seemed to have yielded nothing but defeat. A combination of dysentery and malaria had brought him close to death, and his weight had dropped by thirty-five pounds. His time away, serving with no salary, meant he had been forced to neglect his farms, his main source of income. He believed he was a failure.

No sooner did he arrive home than he discovered, to his immense surprise, that his valor and steadfastness as Braddock's aide and his courage under fire had made him the only hero of the Fort Duquesne debacle. His poor advice to divide the army had made timely reinforcement impossible, but that secret had died with Braddock. And so had

Braddock's promise of a permanent commission for Washington as a British officer.

In Williamsburg, the House of Burgesses honored him by pressing on him a commission to form a new Virginia regiment. The burgesses awarded him £300 (about $45,000 today) for his losses—including his prized surveying tools—in the past three campaigns.

Washington had studied an officer's prerogatives in Braddock's camp; now he drove a hard bargain. His shrewd decision to serve Braddock without pay now paid a handsome dividend.

George Washington's transition to professional soldier was now complete. At age twenty-three, he would command a small Virginia army that he designed himself. With a complement of 1,200 soldiers, it was the largest permanent military establishment in the British American colonies.

He would have the rank of colonel and could appoint his own officers. He was to receive a salary of £500 a year (about $75,000) plus generous expenses that included £100 (about $15,000) for his table plus an allowance for batmen. And following the British custom of the day, he was to act as regimental commissary and paymaster, receiving a 2 percent commission on all the money he handled. Only adding to his prestige, he was to receive a military war chest to "use as [he saw] the nature and good of the service requires."[9]

It is hard to imagine how George Washington could have struck a more successful deal in his first bargaining session with politicians.

CHAPTER FIVE

"Tribune of the People"

On the Post Road just north of Philadelphia, Washington and his friend George Mercer were returning from a visit to British headquarters in Boston when they encountered Benjamin Franklin and his son, William. Franklin and Washington had not met since the Braddock debacle, and now they had much to discuss. Both had concluded that something better had to be done about defending the American colonies. Like Franklin, Washington had come to believe that one underlying problem was the method of settlement. Newly arrived immigrants bought cheap land as far as they could from existing settlements, assuring their isolation and vulnerability to Indian raids.

Washington endorsed Franklin's idea that closely spaced stockades with small, highly trained garrisons of fast-moving rangers to carry out constant patrols and periodic sweeps of the frontier could retard Indian attacks. They agreed that Braddock's defeat made reevaluation of British military tactics imperative.

Washington may not have been the only soldier in America who was trying to puzzle out how to build a new model army more suitable for frontier warfare, but after his bitter experience at Fort Necessity, he was sure that militia were not the solution.

Franklin, too, decried sole reliance on militia, writing that the tactics that could be taught to a militia "are known by experience to be of little or no use in the woods." But, he wrote, he had recent reason to stop short of Washington's blanket condemnation of a civilian force.

For seventy-five years of Quaker rule in Pennsylvania, there had been no need to defend the province from the Indians. Exemplary relations by founding proprietor William Penn with the natives had made Pennsylvania a safe haven for settlers. Penn had made the Walking Purchase from Delaware Indian leaders, who offered him all the land he could cover in a day and a half's walk. It had been a leisurely stroll, with breaks for smoking the calumet, eating lunch, and sleeping overnight, and it had given the Penn family a fifteen-mile arc extending from the Delaware River through Bucks County.

But Penn's sons by his third marriage were now absentee landlords, merchants living in London and keen to sell more land. They produced a bogus deed that asserted their right to a second walking purchase. This time, they ordered a wide path cleared and hired four fleet-footed runners who ran in tandem and didn't stop for sixty-seven miles, leaving the Indians far behind and extending Pennsylvania north to New York's southern border. Evicted from their traditional hunting and burial lands, the Delaware retreated to the Ohio Valley, where they now fought alongside the French.

In the autumn of 1755, when no British retaliation came for the defeat of Braddock, the French sent raiding parties from Fort Duquesne to attack isolated settlements. By October, bands of up to two hundred Delaware and Shawnee were raiding hundreds of miles farther east. One large war party struck a settlement on the Susquehanna River within one hundred miles of Philadelphia. A survivor warned Franklin by postrider: "We expect the enemy every hour. I have cut holes through my house . . . and am determined to hold out to the last extremity, hoping for protection from the province soon."[1]

Franklin, now the chairman of the Pennsylvania Assembly's committee on defense, fired off to London "the bad news" that "thirteen men and women were found scalped and dead and twelve children are missing."[2]

Quakers in their meetinghouses rose to warn against deviating from their pacifist doctrine even as emboldened Indians raided within a two-day ride of Philadelphia, razing the cabins of Scots Irish settlers and setting fire to scores of houses. The terror intensified when farmers recognized old Indian neighbors among the war parties. In all, forty settlements were burned and four hundred settlers slain. Frightened families packed what they could into their wagons and fled east. Indians once again held dominion over the forests of Pennsylvania.

Complicating Pennsylvania's inability to resist attacks was the struggle between the Penn family, owners of the ninety-million-acre proprietorship, and the Quaker-controlled assembly. The Penns wanted to defend their interests but without giving up their proprietary prerogatives or spending any of their own money. The assembly, largely Quaker, advocated taxing the Penns' estates to pay a share of the expenses of defense, but the Quaker party was no longer Quaker-led.

If Pennsylvania had any leader, it was Benjamin Franklin. A successful businessman—indeed, one of the colony's wealthiest citizens—he had become its acknowledged civic leader. Franklin's drive to tax proprietary estates to pay for frontier defenses had gradually made him acceptable to the assembly's majority. Franklin believed that "Quakerism" was being used by the Proprietary Party to impede its political enemies.

While orthodox Quakers opposed war out of principle, Quaker merchants did not want a fight with the Indians for another reason: war would disrupt business. To an increasingly profitable extent, the Quakers' customers were Indians. In exchange for furs, Quaker merchants sold them English-made iron kettles, English woolen blankets, and English-made hatchets, knives, and guns.

The result of the political standoff: no tax, no defense.

For nearly six months, the great new statehouse bell had summoned the assembly to agonize over the province's peril. Assemblymen were pulled one way by preachers who beseeched them to "not fear them that kill the body"; another by refugees' appeals for arms, food, and clothing; and a third by the Penns' latest attempt to make Quakers pay for the privilege of war. In his *Gazette*, Franklin launched an editorial attack on the Penns' prerogatives: Even the king did not claim exemption of taxes for his private estates.[3]

In November, Franklin introduced a militia bill. Once before he had raised a volunteer army. This time, he was not anonymously seeking volunteers. He was demanding a public vote to create an official provincial militia. Franklin's bill would limit enlistments to three weeks, excusing all conscientious objectors and boys and servants under twenty-one and forbidding more than a three days' march from a militiaman's home, rendering offensive warfare all but impossible. But orthodox Quakers still deferred a final vote by referring it into Franklin's defense committee.

Early on the evening of November 24, after another exasperating day's debate, Benjamin Franklin started for home. Ordinarily, the carriages of assemblymen would roll up the street in procession, each assemblyman peeling off when he reached his brick townhouse row. Tonight, the streets were unusually clogged. Franklin saw an unprecedented number of Conestoga wagons pouring into town. German farmers were obviously not only bringing their goods to market; they were marching angrily on Philadelphia to demand protection.

Their arrival was not a welcome sight to many Philadelphians. Germans in the province outnumbered Quakers two to one. As their numbers had grown, hostility toward them had risen commensurately. Franklin had shared in the antipathy at first. One of his comments would later cost him dearly. The Germans, he wrote in a pamphlet on demographics published in England, were "Palatine boors herding together."[4]

Once wooed to settle in Pennsylvania, the Germans were all too aware of the prejudice against them. Their resentment became conspicuous when they ignored Franklin's pleas in the assembly for an all-volunteer militia. When French-led Indians continued to burn their farms and murder their neighbors, they knew better than to rely on pacifist Quakers to protect them.

Gathering up their dead and their living, they marched on the capital. Four hundred brightly lacquered red-and-black Conestoga wagons pulled by black dray horses made a caravan extending eight miles to Germantown. Eighteen hundred angry refugees—their furniture, chests of clothing, sacks of food, and rolls of bedding piled high—rolled toward the residence of Governor Robert Hunter Morris. When one wagon stopped at the front entrance, a contingent gently removed its contents, reverently arranging the scalped, mutilated bodies of a dozen murdered relatives and friends.

Blaming everything on the Quakers, Governor Morris announced that the Penns had just authorized him to withhold £5,000 (about $750,000) from the settlers' annual rents "as a free gift" for defense. (He did not tell them that the money was to come from uncollectable rents on lands already in the hands of the Indians.) Cheering, the crowd shouted "Huzzah!" three times, collected the bodies, and rolled away toward the statehouse.

There, once again they delicately arranged their grizzly cargo on the sidewalk. After hearing vague words of reassurance from the speaker of the assembly, they withdrew. By nightfall, German refugees were bivouacking around cook fires on the commons across the street from Benjamin Franklin's house.

That afternoon, the assembly broke the long legislative logjam and approved Franklin's militia bill, appropriating £55,000 pounds (about $5.8 million) "for the King's use," their euphemism for "war." The assembly then created a defense commission to supervise the war effort, to build forts on the frontier, and to draft and arm the province's militia. Benjamin Franklin won the vote as chairman of the commission.

All parties to the spreading French and Indian War coveted the Lehigh Valley, sixty miles north of Philadelphia. To the Delaware, the valley, surrounded by graceful rings of hills, was holy, their birthplace and burial grounds. The Shawnee, promised the valley by French agents if they cleared it of English settlers, had warned the last unarmed Delaware that they must either daub on war paint and take up the hatchet or expect to be treated as Englishmen. To the French, the Lehigh Gap was the only break in the Kittatinny Mountains wide enough to permit the passage of artillery for an attack on Philadelphia.

The valley had become the heartland of the settlements of Moravians, the German pacifist forerunners of the Methodists. They had purchased most of the valley from William Penn and established un-armed towns with biblical names: Bethlehem, Nazareth, Emmaus. Building missions, they preached to the Indians a Christian salvation. They alone among the peaceful Pennsylvanians methodically studied Native American culture and dialects.

At the heart of their wilderness utopia stood Bethlehem, with its hospital, colleges for men and women, woolen mills, shops, grist mills that served surrounding valleys, running water from the first waterworks in America, apothecary gardens, and a cocoonery for producing silk.

The Moravians were housed in steep-roofed, fieldstone-and-timber dormitories according to age, sex, marital status, and occupation. For recreation, they loved to sing in a cappella choirs, the well-scrubbed women in long black dresses and white caps, the brethren in starched white linen roundabouts and linen trousers. On summer evenings, violin and French horn, oboe and trombone music floated out to the Delaware Indians who came to visit and pray.

On November 25, 1755, there was no music. In the chilly early dawn, Bethlehem awoke to the doleful tolling of the town bells. The Moravian bishop told his people of the terrible massacre at Gnadenhutten, the principal Moravian mission twenty miles up the Lehigh River.

Delaware Indians lived in substantial stone cottages across the river from a church, dormitories, stores, barns, a sawmill, and a school where Delaware and Mohican languages were taught to young missionaries. About one hundred Delaware, mostly women and children, had remained in the village while the older boys and men were away on the annual winter hunt.

On the same day that the German settlers displayed their neighbors' corpses in Philadelphia, a Shawnee war party attacked Gnadenhutten. Since the men had gone off with all the guns, the resident Delaware were helpless. The war party killed eleven missionaries, stripped the food from the stores, butchered sixty cattle, set the buildings on fire, and made off with their plunder. Of five missionaries who had escaped into the woods, one was found dead four months later, lying on his back, his hands folded in prayer.

Franklin still had not recuperated fully from the recurring pleurisy brought on by the rigors of Braddock's campaign, but now the prospect of once again defending his adoptive province reinvigorated him.

Franklin's son, William, was on good terms with all factions of Philadelphia society. He played cards with members of the Penns' social set and danced with their wives and daughters. From his circle of aristocratic young friends, he assembled the best-equipped and best-trained horsemen in Pennsylvania. He also recruited five hundred men from Philadelphia and surrounding counties, many of them veterans of King George's War.

On December 18, 1755, fifty uniformed horsemen of the First Troop Philadelphia City Cavalry dismounted outside the small redbrick house of Defense Commissioner Benjamin Franklin while he finished reading the galley proof of a plea in his *Gazette* for more recruits.

At a word from Commissioner Franklin, Captain Franklin, in his scarlet Grenadier Guards uniform, signaled a bugler to sound the call to assemble. Franklin wanted to make an ostentatious display of his reconstituted Philadelphia Association militia. Captain Franklin rode out ahead, leading the column as it marched thirty-five miles over twisting, narrow roads.

When the Franklins stared down at Bethlehem from South Mountain the next afternoon, they could see the dramatic change in the once-peaceful Moravians since the slaughter at Gnadenhutten: they had decided to defend themselves. They had requested from the province's governor authorization to build a fort to command the Lehigh Gap, but it had not come, and now Scots-Irish refugees were crowding in.

The Moravian elders had decided to build their own fortifications, a log stockade linking twelve major stone buildings, with paving stones cemented over the lower halves of all the buildings.

The next morning, the Franklins decided to move on to Easton, the Penns' latest settlement, also overrun by Scots-Irish refugees. Sending wagonloads of food ahead to the refugees, the Franklins began to execute Benjamin's plan to build a chain of outposts, setting up a strong defensive base in each town.

After issuing arms, the Franklins worked ten days and nights training new volunteers. Then they rode west seventy-five miles, leading a wagonload of guns and escorted by Franklin's militia to the stockaded town of Reading. Along the way, spaced at ten-mile intervals so that no settler would ever be more than five miles from the nearest stockade, they planned to build and garrison small forts of Franklin's own design.

Franklin had studied a thick tome of military engineering titled *A Short Treatise on Fortification and Geometry*. Indians rarely attacked a fortified place, he reasoned, and a log fort, however rickety, was safe against an enemy with no artillery. He sketched out a prototype frontier fort, fifty feet square. Armed with swivel guns taken from ships in Philadelphia harbor, it could be defended by sharpshooters firing through loopholes from platforms and from twin blockhouses.

At the junction of the Lehigh River and Mahoning Creek, the militiamen dug trenches three feet deep and, loading dirt into baskets and binding them together, made musket-proof breastworks within three hours. Franklin marked off a fort with a circumference of 455 feet made of pine timbers, each a foot in diameter. Unslinging the Conestoga wagons, he used their wheels to help horses drag timbers eighteen feet long, cut, trimmed, and pointed by seventy Moravian axmen.

For five months, Franklin had planned, schemed, and harangued to get other men to fortify the frontier; in just five days, his own volunteers built Fort Allen, the key fortress of Pennsylvania's first-ever line of defense. Thirty miles behind enemy lines, it spiked the French winter offensive.

When the Pennsylvania Assembly came to order on February 7, 1756, Benjamin Franklin rose to urge assemblymen to oppose any continuation of the folly that had brought their province to the brink of civil war. The Proprietary Party must be opposed, if necessary by force. Outside the statehouse, as if to underscore the urgency of his arguments, two regiments of troops, one loyal to him, the other recruited by the Penns' handpicked governor, Morris, maneuvered in the streets.

Day after day, Franklin had risen to oppose Morris's plan for an all-out attack on the French. Franklin had become convinced that political action was no longer sufficient to stop the governor. Backed by some Quakers, by the Scots-Irish, and by the Germans, Franklin raised more troops, this time forming the Philadelphia Association regiment of infantry and an artillery company.

Advancing £1,000 pounds (about $150,000) of his own money, Franklin ordered cannon from New York. Morris, supported by a small number of Anglicans, merchants, and proprietary officeholders, refused Franklin's officers' commissions, stalling as he made a final attempt to buy Franklin off. If Franklin would lead Morris's troops west to attack the French, the governor would make him a general.

What Franklin probably didn't know was that Governor Morris had just made the same offer to George Washington when he had made a courtesy call on his way back to Virginia. Morris's son, Braddock's secretary, had been kind to Washington. Washington's visit in uniform may have given Morris the idea that he had found a well-qualified candidate for commander in chief of the Pennsylvania militia.

Washington seems to have encouraged the idea. If he could not win the support he needed for the defense of Virginia, he might be willing to become Pennsylvania's commander in chief. Gossip quickly circulated that Washington had met with Morris to discuss plans for a joint Virginia-Pennsylvania assault on Fort Duquesne, which Washington would lead.

When Washington rode off, Morris commissioned Benjamin Franklin a colonel, an act of duplicity, since he was also issuing commissions to his own officers; no regiment could legally have two sets of officers. Accepting Morris's commission, Colonel Franklin decided to move fast.

In just four hours, Captain William Franklin gathered seven hundred armed men and led them to the statehouse yard. After parading them past the assembly, he quick-marched them east to the Academy of Philadelphia, where at that moment pro-Penn officers were forming their own regiment. Franklin's troops surrounded the academy and shouted for the Proprietary leaders to come out. Most of the Proprietary officers, who were college students, slipped out a side door and fled.

When the governor's backers derided the Franklin militia, Franklin decided on a show of force. Twelve hundred Franklin militiamen drilled in the snow for a week before the Franklins led them in a grand review. Preceded by boys playing oboes, fifes, and drums and by German axmen in buckskins, the Philadelphia Regiment in green-and-red uniforms marched past the governor's mansion. The governor stayed inside. As Franklin's troops reached specially built reviewing stands on Society Hill, thousands of spectators cheered. Each platoon fired a salute and retreated.

To ram the point home, Franklin saved the heaviest firing for last. One hundred artillerymen paraded thirteen heavy guns drawn by teams of Conestoga horses past the stands, then wheeled and arranged them facing the river. For two more hours, Franklin's troops marched through the streets; at the center of the column, in the post of honor, rode Colonel Benjamin Franklin. A few days later, Governor Morris sent his letter of resignation to Thomas Penn in London.

In a development Franklin had not foreseen, that summer, disgusted with the formal British declaration of war against their old friends the Indians and ashamed of their own involvement in the bloodshed of recent years, the Quakers of Philadelphia resigned en masse from the assembly. The "Holy Experiment" was over. Returning from a postal inspection in the South, Franklin could not restrain his jubilation. "All the Stiff-rumps except one," he wrote to a friend in London, "have voluntarily quitted the Assembly."[5]

The resulting power vacuum allowed Franklin to take complete control of the statehouse in the fall elections. To their astonishment, Penn partisans discovered that Franklin had already won the support of the leading Anglicans, men they had expected to fill Quaker seats. One disgusted Proprietary official wrote to Thomas Penn, "The Old Churchmen are infected, they are mere Franklinists."[6]

As long ago as July 1755, when Franklin had been rounding up supplies for the Braddock expedition, Chief Justice William Allen, the most powerful member of the pro-Penn Proprietary Party, had secretly circulated a petition asking the royal government to take action against the popular Franklin party. He had warned London officials that "if the malevolent party that is opposed to [the Penn] interest and government do [*sic*] not receive a check from England, both their [the Penns'] power and their estate will be rendered precarious. . . . There is a conspiracy among the leaders of the opposition to destroy both."[7]

On the day the Pennsylvania Militia Act was signed into law, Allen wrote to London to ask the king to intervene, revealing the real fear of many pro-Penn Englishmen in the province:

> One-half the inhabitants of this province are foreigners. . . . They have, in their own country, generally been soldiers. . . . They in the militia bill have the choice of their own officers. . . . They may join the enemy and drive out the English inhabitants.[8]

Allen implied that their organizer and leader, Benjamin Franklin, would be at the head of an anti-British army.

For many years, Thomas Penn had been alarmed by Franklin's ability to gather men about him in emergencies. Penn had once denounced him as capable of founding another "military commonwealth" like Oliver Cromwell's. Franklin's activities were "a little less than treason. . . . He is a dangerous man. . . . He is a sort of a tribune of the people."[9] When Allen told him that Franklin's militiamen had the effrontery to march with sabers bared through the streets, Penn decided he could make a strong case before the Board of Trade and Plantations that Franklin was a dangerous republican and had to be stopped.

Colonial laws could only be passed subject to the approval of the Crown. The king's Privy Council could recommend that the king veto any law at his pleasure. Penn had powerful connections, including Lord Halifax, president of the Board of Trade, and the Duke of Cumberland, who had little patience with popular movements. Until the question could be resolved by Parliament, no upstart colonial legislature would be allowed to pass its own militia law. At a stroke of King George II's pen, the Pennsylvania Militia Act was nullified.

Along the frontier and in Philadelphia's statehouse, there was consternation. All commissions from the assembly, all military and defensive plans, all treaties with the Indians, were in jeopardy. Specifically, Benjamin Franklin's commissions as commander of frontier militia, as well as the defense commission itself, were abolished. And to follow up on his stunning behind-the-scenes victory, Thomas Penn launched a campaign to punish Franklin for his opposition. He attempted to have him stripped of his lucrative source of income, the deputy postmastership, the highest civilian office in America.

Franklin had grown mortally tired of jousting with the Penn party and of Philadelphia politics. It was now abundantly clear to him that he must go to England to plead his cause personally before Parliament, to defend not only Pennsylvania's interests but his own. By now, the Quaker party had come to blame the Indian attacks on the avarice of the Penn family. With the support of the majority Quaker party, Franklin won appointment to journey to London and lobby Parliament on its behalf to strip the Penns of their proprietary charter and turn Pennsylvania into a royal province.

In his Albany Plan of Union, Benjamin had advocated for permanent frontier forts manned by an intercolonial peacekeeping force. He had also suggested a buffer zone of new provinces west of the Appalachians. The plan had been too visionary for most colonists then, but now the major justifications were once again evident. The Quakers would never consent to support a permanent militia, the Penns would never pay for one, the German pacifists would never serve in one, and, except under direct attack by invaders, Philadelphia's merchants would never contribute to the province's defense.

Stockades, Franklin knew, were only a frail expedient, an illusion of security to induce frontier settlers to return to their farms. But if endless warfare was to be averted, endless vigilance was necessary. Franklin believed that there were men who, if paid in land, would be willing to move west to set up new colonies in river valleys where the rich, unclaimed forests and lush grazing and hunting lands could accommodate thousands of new settlers.

In a letter to his old friend George Whitefield, Franklin intimated the scope of his ambition:

> You mention your frequent wish that you were a chaplain to an American army. I sometimes wish that you and I were jointly employed by the Crown to settle a colony on the Ohio. I imagine that we could do it effectually, without putting the nation to much expense. . . .
>
> What a glorious thing it would be to settle in that fine country a large and strong body of religious and industrious people! What a security to the other colonies and advantage to Britain by increasing her people, territory, strength and commerce.[10]

While securing temporarily the safety of his adoptive province—and his own considerable property—Benjamin Franklin had effectively become its military and political leader, wielding considerable influence over its legislature. But he knew his hold was evanescent. Since the colonies refused a mutual defense alliance, to keep the French and their Indian allies at bay he saw the need for a military buffer zone. So far from seeking independence from Britain, Franklin now set out for London to persuade the Crown to make Pennsylvania a royal colony.

CHAPTER SIX

"Between Two Fires"

After more than three years of frontier warfare, George Washington at twenty-six was an emaciated figure in a baggy blue uniform. Ever since he had eaten rotten meat during Braddock's march, he had suffered from a chronic intestinal ailment. Winter months in a stockade kept half-warm by smoky fireplaces had contributed to a severe case of pleurisy that he worried was tuberculosis. Heartily sick of war, he was frustrated and depressed by his fitful attempts at a military career.

Yet, in a short time after returning home to Mount Vernon, he recovered sufficiently to supervise spring planting. He began to realize the potential for a handsome country seat. With the proceeds of his first successful tobacco harvest, he set about renovating his estate. He placed an order with a distant cousin, John Washington, a London merchant, for a chimneypiece, 250 windowpanes, wallpaper, tables, chairs, and door locks.[1]

He had become intent on reshaping his life into that of a Tidewater planter—his way of life, but not his methods. As the head of a small frontier army responsible for four frontier forts, he had chosen to be a micromanager rather than to delegate authority. He had selected, whenever he could, his own officers, who reported everything to him, while he gave all orders and made all decisions, large and small. At Mount

Vernon, he merely shifted over the same system to agriculture. He chose his farm managers and told them in great detail exactly what he wanted and expected. He personally inspected their work to see that his instructions had been carried out. As a planter, he was becoming a good general and a good businessman. He took full responsibility for what he knew and could control, and what he did not understand he tended to blame on some higher authority.

After overseeing the spring planting, Washington rode to Williamsburg to consult a physician about his lingering maladies. He arrived just in time to learn of the latest British plans for the coming season of war. England would provide all the arms, ammunition, and equipment while the colonists would have to raise and pay their own soldiers. Colonial officers serving with the British would no longer be subservient to British officers of the same grade. Virginia's House of Burgesses would double its forces and call up its militia for a fresh assault on Fort Duquesne. In all, some four thousand Virginia troops were to join in the latest Ohio Valley expedition.

The news electrified Washington. He headed for home, stopping only to pay a call on one Martha Dandridge Custis. In the close-knit society of Tidewater Virginia, it is unlikely that Washington had escaped hearing that Martha's rich husband had died, leaving her as the wealthiest widow in Virginia.

She was small, under five feet, and, after giving birth four times, plump. Attractive, with dark hair, beautiful skin, and refined manners, she was known as kind, thoughtful, loyal to friends, and extremely humble. Descended from a line of scholars and churchmen, she had grown up on a modest plantation, her father the county clerk. She had early learned the rituals of maintaining a facade of elegance superimposed over a system short on cash.

During the customary yearlong period of mourning following her husband's death, Martha had been besieged by visitors whose grief was sometimes indistinguishable from courtship. From her late husband she had inherited 17,438 acres of tobacco-growing lands appraised at £23,632 (about $3.4 million today), as well as £9,000 in cash (about $465,000 to-day). Naturally, she was considered an extremely eligible candidate for a strategic remarriage.

When Washington stopped by Martha's home en route from Williamsburg, she was visiting her next-door neighbor—the line of suitors at her doorstep had been so long that she had fled. But in about a week, Washington and Martha were engaged to be married. In all, they had patched together less than twenty-four hours together, and as events turned out, he would get to see his fiancée only once more in the next nine months.

The British Ministry was now led by the brilliant William Pitt, who was preparing an all-out campaign that would make use of large numbers of American troops. General John Forbes, the commander assigned to the Fort Duquesne prong of the offensive, made it known that Virginia forces were to be built up to division strength under the command of George Washington, if he wanted it. Furthermore, Washington would command all American troops.

While he may have given up all hope of a military career, Washington could not desert his command until Virginia was safe from attack. His marriage would have to wait until the war was over. Yet, before departing, he hired a master builder and left behind plans to make Mount Vernon a suitable home for Martha, shelling out a whopping £325 (about $50,000 today), excluding slave labor—three times his full salary.

As preparation was underway for the expedition to Fort Duquesne, Washington made an important step forward in his pursuit of influence within Virginian society. For nearly four years, he had been lining up support to run for a seat in Virginia's House of Burgesses. As a burgess, he would be able to see how the government dealt with the province's defense, and have a voice in expediting it.

His first bid for office in 1757, lacking organization and money, had resulted in defeat, yielding him his first political lesson. This time, Washington tapped into his social and business connections to drum up support, leaning heavily on the Fairfax family. Furthermore, he laid out what was to him a considerable sum of money, £40 (about $6,000 today), to ply voters with beer, rum, and wine on election day. Soldiers and settlers streamed into the taverns and then staggered off to the polls. In a four-way race, Washington drubbed the incumbent by a 7–1 margin. He had proved himself a popular, confident leader who inspired other men. They would fight for him and endure hardships and harsh discipline—and then would vote for him.

In late June 1758, Washington rode at the head of his buckskin-clad Virginia regiment to the Cumberland Gap. Far from being satisfied with his new command, he grew incensed as the new offensive dragged along. What's more, he had grown irate at the British command's decision to build a new road over the Alleghenies to the Forks of the Ohio rather than improve the old Ohio Company road that stretched northwest from the Cumberland Gap.

If Forbes went ahead with the new route, Washington argued, more time would be lost. All Virginia troops and their supplies would have to be transported from Fort Cumberland eastward and then north before crossing the Alleghenies to join Forbes, another long and costly delay.

The line of supply from Virginia to the Cumberland Gap—and all postwar trade—would be shifted north to Pennsylvania. Not only were Virginia and Pennsylvania interests clashing, but also the Ohio Company stood to lose, and heavily. Settlers who would pour into the Ohio Valley as soon as the French were cleared out would come through Philadelphia, not Alexandria.

Was Washington oblivious to his obvious conflict of interest as he pressured the British commander to improve the road that passed close to his own lands in western Virginia? Or was he, as the new burgess from Westmoreland County, Virginia, justifiably plumping for British gold to improve his new legislative district's economy in the short and long term?

Arguing loudly that it was foolish to take the time to build a new road, Washington railed to an old friend from Braddock's staff now serving at Forbes headquarters that if Forbes did not follow the Virginia route, "all is lost! All is lost by heavens! Our enterprise ruined!"

But Forbes remained adamant. When Washington continued to criticize Forbes's decision, the general summoned him to his headquarters. He told Washington "plainly" that, whatever he thought, the British command had "proceeded from the best intelligence that could be got for the good and convenience of the army" that had not been actuated by any preference for "one province or another." He accused Washington of "weakness" in his "attachment" to Virginia, "having never heard from one Pennsylvania person one word."

Forbes calling him on the carpet for provincialism was the sternest rebuke Washington had ever received. But if Forbes knew of Washington's financial interest in the opening up of Ohio Company lands, he ignored it.[2]

Washington's humiliating dressing-down came with more bad news: his own troops' assault on Fort Duquesne had resulted in a fiasco. When several companies of Washington's Virginians marched up close to the silent fort, the big gates had swung open and French and Indians had poured out. With all British officers shot, the Virginians fought a dogged rearguard action as, once again, the Redcoats fled. It was the Braddock fiasco all over again in miniature. Washington was not consoled when Forbes complimented him on the bravery of his men. Washington was beginning to believe that American courage was as axiomatic as British bungling.

Finally, he saw some action—and wished he had not. As the British desperately attempted to reach Fort Duquesne before winter, Forbes sent Washington's second in command, Major George Mercer, ahead and ordered Washington to reinforce him. On a foggy night, mistaking Washington's force for the enemy, Mercer's troops "commenced a heavy fire . . . which drew fire in return." As Washington ran "between two fires, knocking up [their firearms] with his sword," fourteen of his men were killed, twenty-six wounded. Washington later wrote that he was never in more imminent danger.[3]

Forbes rewarded Washington for his bravery by promoting him to the brevet (temporary) rank of brigadier (brigadier general to Americans). Washington had achieved his dream, becoming a general in the British Army commanding an all-American force. But in the process, he had grown thoroughly disgusted. When the French abandoned Fort Duquesne and Forbes didn't permit him to pursue the enemy, Washington resigned his commission.

George Washington's first war formed him. He had learned to endure terrible hardships. He came close to dying from disease and was shot at on at least five occasions. He was the only British officer who survived Braddock's debacle without a wound. Except when he surprised a patrol of half-asleep Frenchmen, he never won more than a skirmish. He lost a fort. He surrendered a regiment. He failed in his mission to protect the Virginia frontier, and he went home before the war was over and missed out on the final defeat of the French. Yet even when his own men attacked one another and inflicted heavy casualties all around him, he received one promotion after another.

Washington was tremendously lucky. He not only survived five years of appalling hardship and many serious mistakes, but he escaped blame for most of the fiascos in which he found himself involved. Yet in his own mind he was a failure. Complicating matters, his time on the battlefield had forced him to neglect his farm, which caused him to lose money.

Resigning his commission of the last day of 1758, Washington decided to begin a new life as that most revered of figures in Virginia: a planter.

On Twelfth Night 1759, George Washington and Martha Dandridge Custis were married in her White House estate on the Pamunkey River before an audience of forty guests, including the royal governor, all of whom had braved bitter-cold winds to come from all over Tidewater Virginia. Martha's wedding gown of silk with shiny pink ribbons contrasted sharply with George's somber blue coat, breeches, and white stockings. (A more fashionable—and no doubt more expensive—Manchester velvet suit he had ordered from England nine months earlier did not arrive for another three months.) After a brief Anglican ceremony, the newlyweds began forty years together as George and Martha Washington.

A month later, on his twenty-seventh birthday, Washington took his seat in the House of Burgesses. The Speaker of the House read a resolution honoring him "for his brave and steady behavior from the first encroachments and hostilities of the French and their Indians." As he settled into his new life, Washington took care of business, and of pleasure. He bought a racehorse, escorted his wife to the governor's annual ball in Williamsburg, and gave a party for all the members of the assembly.

By April, the newlyweds were ready for their move to Mount Vernon. Washington intended to transplant from Martha's estate to his own the accoutrements of a great plantation. The list of goods they were taking with them included Martha's "chariot," fifteen horses, sixty gallons of rum, fifty bushels of oats, 141 yards of Irish linen, and 49 yards of flannel. Washington helped himself to tools, leather, and lead to flesh out the workshops of his bare-bones plantation. Martha directed her slaves in loading a mahogany dining room table and chairs along with ten beds with their bolsters, counterpanes, and bedsheets, as well as desks, bureaus, and mirrors. For informal meals, Martha selected 134 pewter plates; for fancier dinners, "8 dozen and 8 China plates & 15 [serving] dishes."

The journey to Mount Vernon would take four days: 160 miles over roads sodden with spring rains. Before the wagon train set out, Washington sent orders ahead for the house to be thoroughly cleaned, fires kindled in the ten fireplaces, and eggs and chickens prepared for dinner the day of their arrival.

For the first time in his life, Washington, newly rich by marriage, spent freely. Celebrating his advancement in Tidewater society, the once-penniless boy now enjoyed taking his place in the top echelon of Virginia's social and political hierarchy.

CHAPTER SEVEN

"THE CHILD INDEPENDENCE
IS BORN"

A century and a half of chronic struggle for North American domination ended, in 1759, in a series of stunning British victories. Peace with the French promised peace with the Indians, removing the constant threat of attack from the two-thousand-mile backcountry of the British American colonies. Settlers could now safely surge across the mountains from crowded coastal towns. Investors could subdivide the forested, fur-rich empire. Trade with the Indians would be unimaginably lucrative.

Money flowed to Britain from its American colonies, and convoys of ships crammed with luxury goods returned with cargoes that sold as fast as they could be unloaded. Shipyards employing a thousand artisans transformed hardwood forests into vessels to carry the imports south and west.

Amid the jubilation, in 1760, King George II died suddenly, leaving to his twenty-two-year-old grandson, George III, the world's largest empire. In the customary yearlong interregnum before a new king's coronation, courtiers of the old king and the new jockeyed for position.

As prime minister, William Pitt, known as the Great Commoner, had planned and bankrolled the worldwide struggle with British gold. Three weeks after the coronation of George III, Pitt resigned, forced out by Lord Bute, the new king's boyhood tutor and the Queen Mother's favorite. The unpopular Bute was fairly typical of the 125 nobles who composed Britain's oligarchy, 25 of whom revolved through meetings of committees of the king's Privy Council.

Finding itself with a far-flung empire and staggering bills from the war, Parliament, after nearly a century of winking at colonial trade laws, plunged into a thorough review of its taxes in America. A glimpse at the national debt must have horrified any new minister—a staggering £137 million (about $20 trillion today) carrying annual interest of £5 million ($750 million today), while the cost of administering the empire, including its newly conquered territories, had ballooned to £8 million (about $1.2 trillion).

The average Englishman believed that his American cousin was far wealthier than the overburdened taxpayer of the mother country. Officers returning from the war spun tales of opulence, of Boston merchants' wives wearing silks and laces and living in three-story mansions, of Southern plantation owners with liveried outriders riding in carriages pulled by six matched horses, with their black slaves pouring them imported Madeira wine on languid summer days.

Not all the stories were so far-fetched. In Portsmouth, New Hampshire, Governor Benning Wentworth, who had grown rich by selling timber from pine forests for masts to the Royal Navy, lived in a sprawling fifty-four-room waterfront mansion.

In Norwich, Connecticut, two London-trained physicians, the Lathrop brothers, had parlayed their apothecary—the only one between Boston and New York City—into a lucrative contract to provide medical supplies for all British forces in New England and Canada. At home, their apothecary deliveries arrived in a yellow carriage pulled by four matched horses.

Indeed, many American colonists measured their wealth in consumer goods they imported from Europe, especially from England, to festoon houses often more opulent than their cousins' in Britain. In Philadelphia's Society Hill neighborhood, a square mile of spacious brick mansions built with the profits of trade, homes boasted Chippendale-style mahogany and maple highboys and dining room sets, silk brocaded settees and tall case clocks, Oriental rugs and gilded mirrors. Eighty-nine of the city's 25,000 citizens were wealthy enough to drive around the city streets in their own carriages. Wearing silks and satins, members drawn from eighty wealthy families gathered every other Friday, from February through May, for America's first assembly balls. Sipping cider served by uniformed footmen, they drew lottery tickets for partners for contra dancing. When the Delaware River froze over, they donned furs and assembled for skating parties; during hot and muggy summers, they retreated to airy jonquil-colored houses on nearby hills.

In New York City, brick townhouses with marble floors, figured Dutch wallpaper, and cellars brimming with Madeira wines lined Broadway, their interiors wainscoted with Honduran mahogany and draped with yellow silk damask. In New Bern, the colonial capital of North Carolina, visitors strolled through the mazes of the royal governor's elaborate formal gardens. In Williamsburg, Virginia's elite plantation society gathered at the Governor's Palace for Christmas balls and, during court days, wagered on races of thoroughbred horses bred by prize Andalusian stallions. In a society based more on wealth they had earned than on bloodlines with coats of arms, they nonetheless mimicked the English aristocracy.

The Seven Years' War had divided the loyalties of American merchants. Some had profited from both sides, a practice the British considered treason. Others, enriched by government subsidies to supply British and colonial troops, had armed their merchant ships to act as privateers—a deputized form of piracy. They harried French supply lines, selling captured ships and cargoes at auction for handsome profits. Still others took advantage of wartime shortages on the mainland to trade with the French enemy in the Caribbean.

New York City, headquarters of the British Army, became the leading privateering port. Its financiers included provincial Supreme Court justices and high-ranking American officers. Sir Peter Warren, leader of colonial forces in the siege of Louisbourg, owned a three-hundred-acre farm covering much of today's Greenwich Village. His privateer, the *Launceton*, captured fifteen French ships. In the course of the war, New York's armada of 128 privateering ships harvested 80 French ships valued at £1 million (about $150 million today).

One wartime practice condemned by British officials was the sale of "flags of truce" by royal governors to ship captains. Blank or bearing fictitious names, these documents facilitated the sale of illicit cargoes to the enemy in the French West Indies.

Intended to allow prisoner-of-war exchanges, the fictitious flags became a lucrative source of income. Rhode Island's wealthiest merchants, the Brown brothers, purchased "flags" from Governor Stephen Hopkins, a future member of the Continental Congress and signer of the Declaration of Independence. The Royal Navy captured several of the Browns' vessels, the Admiralty court condemning the Browns for engaging in "wicked, illegal, unwarrantable, clandestine and prohibited trade."[1]

The key to Britain's commerce with its North American colonies was sugar. Sugar, in the form of molasses, was shipped from the West Indies to New England, where it was turned into rum that was then shipped across the Atlantic to Africa to buy cargoes of gold dust and slaves, which, in turn, were taken to the West Indies and exchanged for more sugar. The profits from this triangular trade—molasses, rum, slaves, molasses—enriched American colonists but cut out the British from its rewards.

For nearly a century New Englanders had evaded a series of British acts of navigation and trade that collided with the colonists' notion of their right to trade freely. The acts mandated that any colonist-owned cargo must touch a port of England before being sold, no matter its destination. The first act stated explicitly that no goods from Asia, Africa, or America could be brought into England, Ireland, or the British colonies except in English ships crewed by a majority of Englishmen: "English goods in English bottoms."

American colonists had to buy all manufactured goods from or through Britain and were not free to establish their own manufacturing plants. To protect English growers, the mother country would buy only a fraction of American harvests. To further protect the profits of British merchants, Americans could export to Britain, and only to Britain, certain "enumerated" commodities, and then only in British ships to British ports.

For nearly a century, the acts had remained little more than words on parchment, British enforcement haphazard and prohibitively costly. A status quo had existed ever since the settling of the first mainland colonies. Planters in the West Indies depended on North American colonists for horses, fish and flour, livestock and lumber, barrel staves and naval stores, as well as the ships that brought them.

In exchange, the islanders provided the mainland with unlimited sugar and molasses. Yet the West Indians could not produce enough of this basic commodity to keep pace with the mainland colonies' growth.

To offset the shortfall, British officials turned a blind eye as North Americans traded with the Caribbean island possessions of their imperial rivals, the Spanish, French, and Dutch. The British government remained content with the profits from the sale of manufactured goods—furniture, glass, fine clothing, wines, carriages—exported to America by British merchants.

While the balance of trade favored the British, Americans preferred British manufactured goods that were cheaper and better made than similar products from Europe. Colonial merchants' profits seldom resided in America for six months before they were remitted to Britain in exchange for luxury goods.

Under an unwritten British colonial policy of "salutary neglect," these laissez-faire practices went unchallenged until the Molasses Act of 1733. Then, West Indian plantation owners who sat in Parliament demanded a monopoly on the rich sugar trade and, asserting Parliament's right to regulate colonial trade, pushed through the Molasses Act.

The new duty, six pence to the gallon, was steep—too steep for many mainland merchants, who simply evaded the duty and devised systematic practices that circumvented it. What had been acceptable business practice now became illegal.

Overnight, in the eyes of the British, legitimate merchants who did not abandon their customary practices became smugglers. Mainland merchants quickly learned that sugar and molasses could either be brought from French or Spanish ports directly to the mainland or bought from cynical British West Indian merchants. Illicit cargoes were now unloaded surreptitiously along thousands of miles of Atlantic seacoast at a profit.

Thomas Hancock, uncle of the Declaration of Independence signer John Hancock, instructed his ships' captains with cargoes consigned to Boston to unload them on Cape Cod. Evading customs collectors, they shipped the goods overland to market in Boston. Great family fortunes—the Browns of Rhode Island, the Hancocks of Boston, the Trumbulls of Connecticut, and the Whartons of Philadelphia— flourished in this clandestine system.

According to Board of Trade records in London, every Connecticut and Rhode Island shipper who dealt with the French and Spanish in the Caribbean in the molasses trade between 1733 and 1765 was a smuggler. *Nothing* was credited for these two colonies to an "account of all the duties collected under the Molasses Act," even while, of all the northern provinces, their industries were most dependent on the French sugar islands.[2]

Defying the fundamental principle of British mercantile law, New England ship owners imported from Dutch Caribbean islands an ever-broader array of manufactured goods. To Massachusetts aboard Dutch ships came "reels of Yarn or spun Hemp, paper, Gunpowder, Iron, Goods of various sorts used for Men's and Women's Clothing."

Despite a growing list of British trade restrictions, the port of New York, surpassing Boston and Philadelphia in the West Indies trade, thrived, the number of ships owned by New Yorkers quadrupling between 1747 and 1762. Efforts to collect customs duties lagged: For every ship seized by customs officials, an estimated dozen eluded detection.

So widespread had smuggling become that, as the French and Indian War wound down, reports of merchants' and government officials' questionable patriotism began to reach the highest levels in Britain. James

Hamilton, lieutenant governor of Pennsylvania, reported to the Board of Trade that the "very great part of the principal merchants of this city [Philadelphia]" had traded illegally with French Caribbean islands. The Board of Trade reported to its parent Privy Council that every one of the American colonies had engaged in the contraband trade with the French enemy.[3]

In a circular letter to provincial governors, a frustrated Pitt had denounced the practice "by which the Enemy is, to the greatest Reproach & Detriment of Government, supplied with Provisions . . . whereby they are principally, if not alone, enabled to sustain, and protract, this long and expensive War."

Pitt ordered the captains of Royal Navy ships to raid the French and Dutch islands in the West Indies that were acting as way stations between mainland merchants and the French enemy. But the cost of the combined customs service and navy crackdown—an estimated £8,000 (roughly $1.2 million today) annually—had far exceeded revenues.

Use of the king's ships as customs collectors had added little to the royal revenues of the past thirty years. In all, the Navigation Acts had produced only £35,000 ($5 million) in thirty years; the Molasses Act, a mere £21,000 ($3 million).

From the salutary neglect of King George II, British policy toward America shifted immediately and radically under George III. The young king's kaleidoscope of cabinet ministers understood that they had a mandate to drastically overhaul the government's American affairs.

The members of the Board of Trade, still espousing the seventeenth-century doctrine of mercantilism, enjoyed the support of the majority of ordinary English subjects, who believed that the colonies existed to supply the mother country with raw materials to fashion into manufactured commodities and sell at a profit to the colonists, keeping them dependent on the mother country for everything from hats to shoes.

But after accepting imperial limitations for decades, many Americans who had fought alongside the English against the French now were no longer willing to accept tightening British controls.

While Britain's victory should have brought a massive expansion of trade by English colonists into the void left by the expulsion of the French, for many Americans peace only induced a long depression. During wartime, in exchange for feeding, housing, and transporting British troops and supplies and the colonial troops who had made up fully half of the fighting men, the colonies had received not only hard-money subsidies that paid their militias but also bounties for the hemp, oak, and pine needed for shipbuilding, as well as wheat, corn, cotton, barrel hoops, staves—anything that could help in the war effort. The evaporation of these subsidies brought on the collapse of the colonial economies. Further shocking the markets was this first serious attempt to regulate American trade and enforce customs duties.

As the depression deepened, the colonists' viewpoint increasingly diverged from British sensibilities. Britain's war debt amounted to £18 ($2,700) per subject at home, while, on average, only eighteen shillings (about $135) in the American colonies. This disparity rendered new taxes or increased levies in the British Isles unthinkable. But the debt in some colonies was nearly as high.

New Jersey was burdened with the high costs of maintaining ports that harbored British ships, in addition to the main road and bridges that connected New York City and Philadelphia. Yet the rural colony produced only agricultural and forest products. Its assembly, like those in other colonies, had been allowed to issue vast amounts of paper money, much of which debt-ridden colonists sent to Britain to retire longstanding accounts incurred in pounds sterling. When the boom evaporated at war's end, New Jersey's artificial prosperity deflated. The second smallest populace in America woke up saddled with a £300,000 debt ($45 million today), the highest in America, amounting to £15 ($2,250) for every male between eighteen and sixty, rivaling the burden in Britain.

If ordinary Englishmen had grown restless paying for a bloated government and military, they were increasingly irate at reports that so many Americans had profited from trading with the enemy. British public opinion strongly supported a government crackdown on the perceived American evasion of a fair share of the tax burden. The old acts of navigation and trade should be enforced, the averaged Briton opined;

Britain was entitled to reap the rewards of the colonial trade it had engendered.

In London, the British Ministry was determined to halt such blatant evasion of the empire's trade laws. Smuggling must be stopped, the Navigation Acts and subsequent trade laws must be enforced, and revenues from colonial trade must be shared with the mother country.

As soon as British victory had been assured in 1759, British customs collectors in Massachusetts became determined to crack down on smugglers. In 1755, as the war had begun, customs officials requested that Governor William Shirley issue writs of assistance—general search warrants—authorizing customs agents to enter and search warehouses and ships to seize contraband. When merchants challenged the legality of these special warrants, Shirley ordered customs officers to apply for the warrants to the Massachusetts Superior Court, which complied, granting a number of writs in the next five years. When there were no large seizures, there were no protests.

At the death of George II in 1760, the writs of assistance had automatically expired; no more could be issued until the new king's coronation. With the war over, since Shirley's writs had been intended only to break up illegal wartime trafficking in French contraband, merchants were sure no more writs would be issued.

Yet, in the wake of the French surrender, customs officials in Boston, armed with the writs, swooped down on the waterfront and began to seize illicit cargoes. Every Boston merchant knew that the customs collectors profited handsomely from the sale of any goods they confiscated: a third of the proceeds went to the Crown, a third to the province's treasury, and the remainder to the customs collectors themselves. Paid informants who tipped off a collector were so hated that customs didn't even have to identify them to the Admiralty court, only the amount arranged, which came from the Crown's share. The potential from such unfair personal gain on the part of the customs collectors no doubt fed the merchants' resentment.

In the autumn of 1760, a Dutch ship arrived in Boston Harbor carrying an extraordinarily rich, not to mention illicit, cargo valued at an estimated £10,000 (about $1.5 million today). The ship's presence prompted Charles Paxton, surveyor of customs at Boston, apparently responding to instructions from London, to apply to the Massachusetts Superior Court for writs of assistance in the name of George III to conduct raids not just in Boston but in all Massachusetts ports.

Merchants in the colony yowled. Why, they demanded, was Massachusetts being singled out? Everybody knew that Rhode Island was where illicit cargoes were routinely smuggled in. Why were warrants being issued only for Massachusetts?

A delegation of merchants objected to the Dutch ship's seizure in a petition to provincial chief justice Jonathan Sewall. In England, they pointed out, search warrants could be issued only by the Court of the Exchequer. Did the Massachusetts Superior Court have the same authority, the same powers, as the Court of the Exchequer in England? If it did not, the seizure was illegal.

Sewall wavered, unsure that the Massachusetts court's authority had ever been tested. When Sewall said he couldn't be certain, sixty-three merchant shippers petitioned to the Superior Court to deny the writs. But shortly after scheduling a hearing for February 1761, Sewall died.

A newly arrived royal governor, Francis Bernard, promptly replaced Sewall as chief justice with Thomas Hutchinson, the Harvard-educated scion of a wealthy mercantile family. The appointment further outraged the merchants, who knew that Sewall had promised the judgeship to Colonel James Otis. They had hired his son, James, as their lawyer.

All that winter, Bostonians grew more indignant that they should be subjected to general search warrants. They considered them beyond illegal—the warrants were unconstitutional, contrary to the rights of Englishmen, a throwback to the reign of the despotic Stuarts!

What had become of the British constitution? It was not a written-down list of laws and rules, but it included all the ancient charters of the past ten centuries. It embodied the Magna Carta, the Bill of Rights won by the Glorious Revolution of 1688, John Locke's *Treatise on Government*, John Milton's *Areopagitica*, and the writings of John Wycliffe and Algernon Sydney. Writs of assistance were an outrage to New Englanders, contrary to the laws of nature and *right reason* as Sir Edward Coke enunciated them.

To these Boston merchants, "unconstitutional" meant the violation of principles higher than those of Parliament, of the king, of all the committees and boards of trade made up of men who were totally ignorant of America. None of these courtiers had ever visited the colonies. Their only goal was to make the colonies profitable to Britain, to keep the balance of trade favorable to England.

The day before the Paxton case—named for the customs official who had requested the writs—came to trial in February 1761, twenty-five-year-old John Adams and his cousin Samuel Quincy rode the ten miles over deep snow and ice from rural Braintree (now Quincy) into Boston, where they spent the night, ready to appear at the "Town House" early enough the next morning to be sure of a place.

The public was barred from the old council chamber; only the merchant petitioners and a stated number of barristers were allowed to enter. Adams still had not qualified to wear the long black robe and powdered wig of a barrister, but he persuaded a court official to allow him and his cousin to sit at the long council table.

For John Adams, the British crackdown on smuggling in Boston abruptly interrupted an uneventful life as a country lawyer. Son of a Braintree farmer, selectman, Congregational deacon, and sometime shoemaker, Adams first and last wanted to be a farmer. His devoutly Puritan father, however, insisted he attend Harvard College and, like his uncle Joseph, become a clergyman. It would cost his father nothing; Harvard extended free tuition to ministerial students.

During his years at Harvard, John cultivated a lifelong passion for studying, but he refused to become a clergyman, instead fixing his sights on a career as a lawyer as the pathway to a wider sphere of influence. After graduation, he read law with James Putnam in Worcester for three years. Teaching school to support himself, he worked so hard that he became gravely ill.

Sworn in as an attorney in 1758, he returned to Braintree to practice law. He got his first taste of office-holding during a two-year stint as a town selectman. He became thoroughly bored with the country lawyer's life of "fumbling and racking amidst the rubbish of writs, pleas and ejectments," of creating by his law practice "more quarrels than he composed." He had little appetite for enriching himself "at the expense of impoverishing others more honest and deserving."[4]

By nine o'clock, the great square courtroom, with its cavernous fireplace and central chandelier, filled quickly with merchants, sixty-three of them, sitting in long rows of chairs. Beneath full-length, gold-framed portraits, the hated Stuart kings, James II and Charles II, faced each other. After Governor Bernard and his executive councillors took their places with Chief Justice Hutchinson, all five judges of the Superior Court filed in, taking their seats near the fire.

At the special request of Bernard and Hutchinson, they had dressed as if for an important criminal trial: long crimson robes with wide white bands and outsize judicial wigs. Boston's august barrister Jeremiah Gridley would argue the case for the Crown; his two former students Oxenbridge Thacher and James Otis, for the merchants. Otis had resigned his Crown appointment as advocate general of the Admiralty court to take the case without fee.

Gridley opened by declaring that the Superior Court of Judicature was acting as both the Courts of King's Bench and Common Pleas and the Exchequer "within His Majesty's Kingdom of England." The necessity of the case, he contended, took away "the common privileges of Englishmen."

Even if the merchants were indignant when tax collectors entered their homes, arrested them, and seized their property, wasn't the collection of revenue to support fleets and armies more important than the liberty of any individual? There were many precedents for the exercise of writs of assistance in England, he argued. "If it is the law in England, it is the law here, extended to this country by act of Parliament."[5]

If was midafternoon before James Otis rose, bowed, and launched a fiery counterattack. "This writ is against the fundamental principles of English law," he contended. According to Locke's *Second Treatise on Government*, unrestricted general warrants were unconstitutional. It was an Englishman's right to keep his home secure against search and seizure.

> A man is as secure in his house as a prince in his castle. This is the Privilege of the House, and it obtains if a man be deeply in debt or if civil process be served against him. Only for felonies may an officer break and enter—and then by special, not general warrant. For general warrants there is only the precedent of the Star Chamber of the Stuarts. All legal precedents are under control of the fundamental principles of English law.

It was the right of English subjects not to be taxed without their consent. English colonists were full English subjects; they had the same rights as Englishmen on English soil. As such, they could not be taxed without representation in Parliament. "If an act of Parliament should be passed in the very words of this petition for writs of assistance, it would be void."[6]

Otis's argument against the writs became less important than the path he took to make his point: man's right to liberty is inherent, as inalienable as his right to life. Bondservants had these rights, the slave against his master. The merchants must have squirmed at this; Massachusetts held five thousand Africans enslaved and thirty thousand bondservants.

Merchants listening intently to Otis's arguments knew that British-American colonists had always believed that they held rights assured by "the laws of God and Nature," but no one had ever before objected to Parliament's authority to make laws regulating trade. While they objected to any excise tax—an internal tax raising revenue for the government's use—without a vote by the colonists' representatives, external taxes based on external legislation passed by Parliament had long been accepted.[7]

Indeed, British authority had long stifled American commerce. The Woolen Act of 1699 outlawed transporting woolens by water; even if someone transported wool across a stream, it became contraband. As a result, no colonial woolen trade had developed. The Hat Act of 1732 barred exportation of American-made hats, and hatmakers were restricted to two apprentices. The Iron Act of 1750 forbade slitting mills, plating forges, and steel furnaces. American colonists could not even make a nail to shoe their horses; instead, raw iron had to be shipped to England and manufactured for export to the colonies.

By asserting colonists' rights as British subjects, Otis was defying Parliament to abridge if not abrogate their natural rights as Englishmen. Otis went on lecturing the room until candles had to be lit—he had talked for nearly five hours. Finally, he bowed to the judges, and Chief Justice Hutchinson declared court adjourned until the next day.

Leaving the courtroom, a stunned John Adams understood that Otis was appealing to fundamental beliefs he had learned in childhood: His right to liberty was as inalienable as his right to life.

After three days of attorneys battering one another with citations of sources and legal precedents, Hutchinson stopped the hearing. He would make no decision but would continue the case until the next court term. Meanwhile, he would write to the Board of Trade in London for advice, allowing customs officials to continue exercising the writs, continuing their searches and seizures.

That November, the Paxton case once again came before the province's Supreme Court of Judicature. The judges, ignoring Hutchinson and deliberating for a single day, decided unanimously in favor of the writs. Fully six years later, in London, Britain's attorney general and solicitor general upheld Otis's pleading for the merchants, declaring that writs of assistance were invalid in America. Indeed, such writs could be issued only by the Court of the Exchequer in England. Meanwhile, the

illegal searches and seizures and fines had gone on, ruining more merchants.

More than half a century and a revolution later, John Adams wrote
that it had been on that winter day in the old town hall that many Bostonians became ready, for the first time, to defy the distant Parliament.
"Here, this day, in the old Council Chamber," Adams wrote, "the child
Independence was born."[8]

CHAPTER EIGHT

"An Ill-Judged Measure"

George Washington might have remained quietly at Mount Vernon, enjoying the leisurely life of an English country squire, had the British not begun to systematically hollow out everything he had worked to build and hoped to build, diminishing his rights, his privileges, and, significantly, his income.

The source of his discontent was land, the basis of the fortune he had, and the even bigger one he sought. Washington's appetite for land was unquenchable. He coveted properties near and far from Mount Vernon, yet his years in the field had left him with a passion to develop the American interior. He expected that one day he would own something like one hundred thousand acres of rich riverfront land in the Ohio Valley.

He was not alone in this dream. Ever since the French had abandoned Fort Duquesne, settlers had surged over the new military road from Philadelphia into the Ohio Valley. Their incursion ignored Pennsylvania's promises to the Indians assembled at the 1758 Treaty of Easton that there would be no further settlements west of the Alleghenies. No sooner had peace between England and France been declared than resentful Indians rose up; another two years would pass before the frontier became safe for new settlers.

Almost immediately after the signing of the Treaty of Paris in 1763,

officially ending the Seven Years' War, a royal proclamation dashed speculators' dreams of newfound fortunes in the western forests. On May 5,
1763, Lord Egremont, secretary of state for the Southern Department,
wrote to Lord Shelburne, president of the Board of Trade, that it had
become necessary to "fix upon some line for a western boundary to our
ancient provinces beyond which our people at present should not be
permitted to settle." A strict limit, if enforced, would destroy the prospects of land-hungry speculators.

Egremont wrote that he preferred emigrants to settle in Nova Scotia
or the more southerly provinces, "where they would be more useful to
their Mother Country instead of planting themselves in the Heart of
America, out of reach of Government where from the great difficulty of
procuring European commodities, they would be compelled to commerce and manufacturing to the infinite prejudice of Britain."[1]

Egremont decreed that all new land purchases from the Indians must
be made through imperial Indian agents or provincial proprietors. Lands
could no longer be purchased directly from the Indians. Since the Indians were nomads, as the British saw it, the British government did not
recognize the sovereignty of natives over any soil; Indians did not possess an absolute title, and they could not bestow one.

Sir William Johnson, superintendent for Indian affairs in the Northern Department, wrote to the Board of Trade that this was a "gross
error": "Each nation is perfectly well acquainted with its exact original
bounds; the same is again divided into due proportions for each tribe
and afterward subdivided into shares for each family.... Neither do they
ever infringe upon one another or invade their neighbor's hunting
grounds."[2]

Lord Shelburne, the man in charge of formulating policies for the
lands ceded by the French, recommended that the Appalachians become
the western boundary line between English settlements and a vast Indian reserve. He made one exception: a small reserve in the Ohio Valley
set aside for veterans such as George Washington.

But before Shelburne's reforms could be implemented, the new king
replaced him with a less sympathetic minister, Wills Hill, Lord

Hillsborough. He promptly eliminated any provision of lands for veterans and ordered colonists who had already settled west of the mountains "forthwith to remove themselves." Men such as Washington, who already owned land in the Ohio Valley, now faced losing their property, along with the money they had invested.

The Board of Trade's new policy reflected Hillsborough's analysis that His Majesty's possessions in North America were so many times more extensive than in Great Britain and that "if they were equally inhabited, Great Britain could no longer maintain dominion over them. . . . It is therefore evidently her Policy to set bounds to the Increment of People, and to the extent of the Settlement of that Country."

The Board of Trade reported that the king had personally "approved and confirmed" the principle that the western expansion of the colonies should be limited "to such a distance from the seacoast, as that those settlements should lie within the reach of the trade and commerce of this kingdom." The Crown did not intend to allow settlers to live beyond the reach of British regulators and tax collectors. By limiting westward expansion to the coastal colonies east of the Alleghenies, British policy shifted radically from "salutary neglect" to "the exercise of the authority and jurisdiction" needed to hold the colonies "in due subordination to, and dependence upon, the mother country."[3]

Hillsborough's decree echoed the demands of the extreme voices in Parliament who, even before the French and Indian War, said that "the colonies should be governed like Ireland, keeping a body of standing forces" with "the abridgements of their [the Americans'] legislative powers, so as to put them on the same foot that Ireland stands." (Hillsborough was an Irish peer and a major landholder there, employing thousands of tenant farmers.) His faction also insisted that future royal governors should be appointed by Parliament to make them "independent of the people."[4]

Hillsborough's sweeping Proclamation of 1763, rushed through the Privy Council and signed by the king, also forbade future purchases of Indian lands east of the Proclamation Line and placed the Indians under the British military commander in chief for America.

The North American continent west of the mountains, so hard-won by colonial as well as British troops, now became a vast Indian reserve, its lucrative fur trade to be exploited exclusively by the British. Moreover, ten thousand British troops were to police the settlers as much as the Indians.

At first, George Washington scoffed at the line. Undeterred, he decided to form a corporation, the Mississippi Land Company. He had come around to the belief that settlement should be carried out by corporations, not by individuals. Writing the articles of agreement himself, with three of his brothers and four members of the Lee family, he applied to the Crown for a grant of 2.5 million acres of land at the confluence of the Ohio and Mississippi Rivers. The grant would open up settlement along 210 miles of Mississippi riverfront from the Ohio to the Tennessee Rivers. Each of fifty shareholders stood to receive fifty thousand acres.

If settling on lands now reserved for the Indians posed any ethical impediment to Washington, he dismissed it in his petition to the king. Citing recent Indian attacks in Pennsylvania and Virginia after the Braddock fiasco, he argued that it would be wise "to [get] that country settled as quickly as possible."[5]

His application for a corporate land grant arrived in London just as the king signed the ban on any further migration west of the mountains. The shareholders continued to meet annually, but their petition was hopeless.

Washington considered the Proclamation Line one more blunder by the fledgling postwar British cabinet. He wrote to a fellow shareholder that, because he was a member of the Virginia House of Burgesses, he must keep "his initial reaction a profound secret." As a colonial official, he wrote, "I might be censured for the opinion I have given in respect of the King's proclamation."[6]

Yet the damage had been done. Soon, rather than continue to bend the knee to Englishmen who considered him their inferior, Washington would begin, slowly and carefully, to pull himself away from his sybaritic life and risk everything.

CHAPTER NINE

"WHAT MORE CAN
THEY DESIRE?"

Once it had convinced itself it needed an army to maintain order in America, the British cabinet reshuffled itself again. After an anti-Scottish mob overturned Lord Bute's carriage in the streets of London, he resigned as prime minister. The Queen Mother once again chose a replacement: George Grenville.

As First Lord of the Admiralty, Grenville had sponsored an act of Parliament which, for the first time, allowed Royal Navy ships to assist in enforcing trade laws. And as William Pitt's pinchpenny brother-in-law, Grenville was known for being compulsively frugal, and given to anti-American ranting on the floor of Parliament.

The size of the national debt horrified Grenville. Despite the worldwide spread of the postwar depression, in March 1764 Grenville chose this singularly inopportune moment to press Parliament to pass the American Revenue Act. It was the first law ever enacted in Parliament specifically to raise money for the Crown by taxing American colonists, who, until then, had decided on their own taxes in colonial legislatures. Based on a six-month investigation into smuggling by the Treasury, the act was predicated on the need to defend the colonies. The report induced Parliament to extend the Molasses Act of 1733 and double the duty on refined foreign sugar.

New tariffs affected almost every American. Duties on goods from competing empires were doubled. The House of Commons imposed new or steeper tariffs on the importation of foreign textiles, coffee, indigo, Dutch rum, and Madeira and Canary Islands wines—the favorites of Americans. Further stifling American trade, the act drew a long list of raw materials that could be exported only within the British Empire, including iron, hides, whale fins, potash, pearl ash, and raw silk.

To James Otis, the lawyer who had argued vociferously against the writs of assistance in Massachusetts, this new law was a dangerous experiment, a test of colonial resistance on the road to incrementally increased demands. If Britain could impose taxes on Americans "without consent, they cannot be said to be free. His barrier of liberty being once broken down, all is lost."[1]

Worse for American colonists, in the midst of the postwar depression, and just when Parliament was on the point of presenting America with the bill for defeating the French, Grenville pushed through another onerous piece of legislation, mandating that all fines and taxes henceforth be paid in sterling or gold.

Such a requirement placed great strain on America, where sterling and gold were both in short supply. The colonies had no banks and no intercolonial currency. In a barter-and-credit economy, colonists had improvised alternative forms of currency. Decades earlier, Massachusetts, facing a serious cash shortage, had devised a solution, only to see it end in disaster. In 1740, merchant Samuel Adams Sr. had helped to create a land bank, granting mortgages based on the valuation of developed land and issuing paper currency. But rival merchant Thomas Hutchinson, at that time a member of the Governor's Council, persuaded the royal governor to press Parliament to outlaw the bank. The Board of Trade in London ordered the bank's organizers to buy back all the money they had issued with silver and gold.

Adams was fortunate to escape a jail sentence, but he lost his life's savings. He could no longer afford the expenses of his son's education at Harvard. The son, Samuel, was forced to wait on the tables of his wealthier classmates; humiliated, he learned to despise Hutchinson, the pro-British faction, and the British in general.

After Harvard, Sam Adams considered a law career but instead went into business. His job as a clerk in a countinghouse lasted only a few months; he was too preoccupied with politics. His father somehow scraped together £1,000 (roughly $150,000 today) to help him found a political newspaper; it folded within a year.

Then the elder Adams's friends in the caucus appointed young Adams as Boston's tax collector. He proved reluctant to collect the taxes of ordinary citizens, concentrating on wealthy merchants. When he resigned, collections had fallen behind by £8,000 (about $1.2 million today).

Regardless, his father made him a partner in the family's malt business, which supplied the town's breweries. Inheriting the business and a fine house, Sam neglected both as he plunged ever deeper into politics—and debt. His second cousin John Adams said that Sam "never planned, laid a scheme, or formed a design for laying up anything for himself or others after him."[2] Nevertheless, Sam Adams emerged as the opposition's leader in Boston's town meeting when Parliament passed the Currency Act of 1764, which outlawed all colonial currency.

The act especially targeted Virginia, which had for more than a century paid its clergy with tobacco. According to legislation passed in 1748, the colony's established Anglican clergy were paid sixteen thousand pounds of tobacco per year. In New England, clergy were paid with firewood: a popular preacher stayed warm by his fire in the winter and bartered extra cordage for other necessities; an unpopular one was left to shiver by a cold hearth.

When Virginia's tobacco crop failed in 1758 during a long drought, the price of tobacco shot up from two to six pennies a pound, tripling clergy salaries. After protests by parishioners, the assembly passed legislation allowing debts incurred in tobacco to be paid in a new paper currency. The House of Burgesses issued £250,000 (roughly $37.5 million) in legal tender currency. The Two Penny Act set the pay of clergy at two cents a pound, the old rate. Virginia continued to issue paper money until 1764, when King George III vetoed the law and substituted the Currency Act.

In a debut court appearance, Patrick Henry defended the Two Penny Act, arguing that "the King, by disallowing Acts of this salutary nature, from being the father of his people, degenerated into a Tyrant and forfeited all rights to his subjects' obedience."[3]

The royal veto left Americans with no banks, no currency, and none of their own coinage. In a system of credits, many colonial financial transactions were by barter—surplus grain harvests bartered for livestock was commonplace. George Washington's tobacco crop, shipped to his broker in England, was credited to his account and bought, in exchange, a wide range of manufactured goods, from furniture to clothing to luxuries, including a growing list of commodities—such as hats and woolens—that colonists were forbidden to produce. All fees to the Crown and its representatives, including from the recording of deeds, customs duties, and even marriage licenses, had to be paid in specie, the gold or silver coins of nine nations, including British pounds sterling and Spanish dollars. Debts owed to British citizens could also be paid by credits for raw materials shipped to England by colonists.

By passing the Currency Act, Parliament radically extended British home government control over its colonial governments regardless of their ancient charter privileges. To Americans already struggling with a sharp postwar business decline, the deflationary Currency Act, shrinking the cash supply, and the strict enforcement of higher import duties threatened to ruin the colonial economy.

The Boston town meeting in May 1764, with the effects of collapsing American trade visible along its dying waterfront, denounced taxation by Parliament without representation and urged united opposition by the colonies.

Sam Adams regarded the stream of new regulations imposed by each session of Parliament as an alarming infringement of colonists' rights. He foresaw the consequences of taxing colonists without their representation in the House of Commons:

> If our trade may be taxed, why not our lands? Why not the
> product of our lands and everything we possess or make use

of? This we apprehend annihilates our charter rights to govern and tax ourselves. It strikes at our British privileges
which, as we have never forfeited them, we hold in common
with our fellow subjects who are natives of Britain. If taxes
are laid on us in any shape without our having a representation where they are laid, are we not reduced from the character of free subjects to the miserable status of tributary
slaves?[4]

In America's first trade boycott, in August 1764, Boston merchants
stopped importing English lace and ruffles. Mechanics followed suit,
wearing only leatherwork clothes tanned in Massachusetts. A non-
importation movement spread south to Virginia, which was reeling from
another parliamentary edict that had shattered George Washington's
and many other Virginians' visions of wealth. French and Indian War
veterans had been promised land grants as recruitment bounties; Washington expected fifteen thousand acres. Their plans for a landed future
were dashed when the royal Proclamation of 1763 closed the frontier.

It was the currency crisis that first alarmed Washington. With hard
money scarce and paper money illegal, Washington, like other planters,
was forced to rely on further borrowing or fall even deeper in debt to
British merchants. He warned that British merchants' insistence on re-
payment in sterling would "set the whole country in flames."[5]

When Indians attacked the frontier, this time the Crown refused
military assistance, leaving Virginia's militia to fight alone. Burgess
Washington was given the task of finding some way to pay the soldiers.

As the depression deepened, British merchants refused to extend
Americans further credit. In response, the Massachusetts Assembly
organized the first intercolonial protest movement by establishing a committee of correspondence to link with the other provincial assemblies.

Perversely, as the protests metastasized, Parliament retaliated, passing the Stamp Act of 1765, the first excise tax ever imposed on the American colonies.

Intended to raise £60,000 annually (roughly $9 million today), the tax, taken together with projected customs duties, was supposed to yield one-third the cost of the military garrisoning of the colonies.

The tax stamps had long been required in Britain on bills of lading, dice and playing cards, mortgages and liquor licenses, wills, legal papers of all kinds, insurance policies, printed pamphlets, newsprint and newspaper advertisements, almanacs, pamphlets and broadsides, calendars, surveying documents, and even college diplomas.

The paper on which legal documents were written would have to be purchased from England with the stamp already embossed on it, and stamped paper was outrageously expensive. The contracts of apprentices and clerks required costly stamps roughly equivalent to a 5 percent wage tax.

At a time when roughly half of Harvard's students were on scholarships, the tax stamp for each diploma cost £2 (about $300 today). Cash-strapped William Paterson, a future congressman and coauthor of the Constitution, could not afford the requisite stamp when he graduated the College of New Jersey (present-day Princeton). He had to go on working in his father's store for another two years before he could practice law.

While cash was scarce and unemployment high, the stamp tax required purchase in gold or silver. The burden fell heaviest on colonists with the greatest clout—merchants, lawyers, ship owners, tavern owners—overnight broadening the base of opposition to parliamentary power.

In New Jersey, penniless lawyers shut down the courts rather than conduct any business requiring the obnoxious stamps. They could not afford to advance specie to buy stamps for legal papers when it often took years before they were paid by equally cashless clients.

Like other Southern planters, George Washington was hit hard by the new levy. For every deed he recorded or lease he executed, for insurance on crops he shipped to England, for every document he filed in court, he was required to come up with four shillings in gold or silver coins—what he paid a farm manager for a week's wages.

After a day surveying his fields or poring over his ledger books,

Washington liked to relax by playing cards or rolling dice with guests at his Mount Vernon gaming table. Now, every pack of cards required a one-shilling stamp and every pair of dice a ten-shilling stamp—enough to buy a barrel of fine Madeira or a pair of workhorses. Every page of the *Virginia Gazette* filled with letters and essays protesting the tax had to bear a one-penny stamp.

As Washington rode into Williamsburg for a session of the House of Burgesses, he had to coax his horse through knots of rough-hewn up-country farmers in buckskin leggings and hunting shirts who had ridden all the way from the Shenandoah Valley. They were in an ugly mood. It was they who would be the most affected by any new tax: they bartered for everything they hunted or grew. Every loan for seed money, every lease, and every lien against future harvests already required gold or silver for courthouse fees. Where were they supposed to come up with more sterling?

In the four months since a ship had brought news of the latest tax, Washington had stayed on the political sidelines, but he was growing more and more agitated by a system binding Americans ever more tightly to England. It had taken him a long time to begin to question British policies toward the American colonies. But now he protested the stamp tax to the London commission merchants who sold his tobacco and bought all the goods he was not allowed to produce.

He felt he was being robbed by middlemen and now by stamp men. Punitive British levies would only drive Americans to make themselves less dependent on imports from England, develop their own crops, and manufacture goods for their own markets. Calling the tax stamp an "ill-judged measure," Washington for the first time publicly criticized British trade policy:

> What more can they desire? All taxes which contribute to lessen our importation of British goods must be hurtful to the manufacturers of them. . . . Our people will perceive that many luxuries, which we have hitherto lavished our substances to Great Britain for, can well be disposed with while

the necessaries of life are to be procured for the most part within ourselves. . . . Great Britain may then load her exports with as heavy taxes as she pleased but where will the consumption be? . . . There is not money to pay the stamp. . . . Who is to suffer most in this event, the merchant or the planter?[6]

British merchants could have answered Washington's rhetorical question: Exports to America dropped by 15 percent between 1764 and 1765.

On the motion of James Otis, the Massachusetts Assembly proposed an intercolonial meeting to seek relief from the odious levy. Delegates from nine colonies converged in New York City in October 1765, the month before the Stamp Act was to take effect, for the Stamp Act Congress.

Of the twenty-seven delegates in this first intercolonial congress, ten would later serve in the First Continental Congress. Virginia, North Carolina, and Georgia could not send representatives because their royal governors had refused to convene assemblies that could elect delegates; New Hampshire sent no delegate but afterward approved the Congress's resolutions.

In the moderately worded Declaration of Rights and Grievances, authored by Philadelphia lawyer John Dickinson, the delegates asserted they possessed all the rights and liberties of the king's subjects in Great Britain. Most notably, the declaration held that there could be "no taxation without representation" expressed personally or through their own elected representatives.

It was impossible that colonists be physically represented in the House of Commons because they were three thousand miles away. Therefore, the Stamp Act Congress concluded, a tax could be imposed on them constitutionally only by their own elected legislatures, the only bodies legally able to impose an internal tax.

The Congress, reasserting trial by jury as an inherent right to all British subjects, protested Parliament's extension of Admiralty courts onto

America's shores, empowering them to try a case anywhere within the British Empire. Marine cases could now be decided by judges instead of juries, an innovation that allowed judges and naval officers to pocket the fines they levied. Before adjourning, to underscore their resolve, the delegates voted to support continuing the boycott on English goods.

On November 1, 1765, the day the Stamp Act went into effect, virtually all business in America was suspended; by then, no tax stamp could be found. In every colony, the royally appointed stamp commissioners—each of whom had posted a £3,000 bond (about $450,000 today)—had been intimidated into resigning. When Parliament ignored the Stamp Act Congress's petitions, riots broke out in virtually every coastal town where unemployment was high.

Some merchants did not join the protest movement voluntarily. Those who resisted faced the wrath of the Sons of Liberty, a new and potent political force. In Boston, Sam Adams organized a crowd of waterfront toughs who, after consuming a gill or two of rum, chased the newly appointed stamp commissioner, Andrew Oliver, through the streets. Ransacking his home, they roared on to attack the mansion of his brother-in-law, Thomas Hutchinson, recently appointed royal governor. Hutchinson and his family barely managed to escape while the Sons used blocks and tackles to pull down his mansion.

Not even Benjamin Franklin proved immune. In Philadelphia, one faction besieged his home, suspecting that Franklin, still Britain's deputy postmaster general for America, had invented the hated stamps. (He had in fact arranged the appointment of a friend as Pennsylvania's tax commissioner.) Deborah Franklin wrote to her husband in London that only the existence of another, pro-Franklin mob of eight hundred tradesmen and mechanics had ensured her protection.

Far from having created the crisis, Franklin was in London relentlessly lobbying Parliament to repeal the odious legislation, maneuvering himself into the position of primary spokesman among the sixteen colonial agents in England. Under an assortment of pseudonyms, Franklin bombarded the London newspapers with letters. He distributed hundreds of copies of a cartoon he had drawn and published in his *Pennsylvania Gazette* depicting a dismembered British Empire against a backdrop of idle ships.

In the *London Chronicle*, he published his 1754 correspondence with Massachusetts governor William Shirley, who had privately told Franklin long ago that the Crown already was planning to make sure colonial assemblies had no power.

Taxing the colonies without representation in Parliament, Franklin told English readers, was like "raising contributions in an enemy's country." Americans already paid heavy indirect taxes. Existing British laws restrained American trade with other countries and banned colonial manufacturing, keeping prices high in America. British merchants and manufacturers benefited, enabling the British to pay their own taxes out of American pockets.

By risking their lives and fortunes to settle new colonies and defend them against Britain's enemies, Americans had extended British dominions, vastly increasing the mother country's commerce. Yet now they were being asked to forfeit their natural rights as Englishmen.

Traveling widely in the British Isles with his son, Franklin had learned that the American boycott was making Englishmen suffer, too, as exports dropped off precipitously. Franklin spearheaded a committee that visited thirty towns, circulating petitions to British merchants to demand that Parliament repeal the act. By January 1766 the petition of London merchants was attributing bankruptcies to the loss of the American market.

In February, sitting as a committee of the whole, Parliament summoned colonial agents to testify. Franklin stood at the bar, answering 174 questions he had carefully planted among pro-American members, asked in rapid succession to allow no unfriendly line of questioning. On March 4, 1766, the House of Commons voted to repeal the Stamp Act by a lopsided 275–167 vote.[7]

The news of repeal raced toward Boston aboard a ship owned by John Hancock. Perceived in London to be the wealthiest American merchant, Hancock had joined the boycott, allying himself with Sam Adams. On Repeal Day, Bostonians poured from their houses, firing guns in the air and shouting Hancock's name.

Marching with the Sons of Liberty to the debtors' prison, he paid off the debts of all its inmates. Setting off fireworks, he uncorked 250 gallons of Madeira wine for the crowd; inside his mansion, he provided "a grand and elegant Entertainment to the genteel part" of the town.

While Franklin had successfully organized resistance in England against Parliament's introduction of an unpopular new tax in America, John Hancock had emerged in Boston as a hero of the anti-tax radicals, bringing to Sam Adams's protest movement the support of New England's greatest fortune.

CHAPTER TEN

"Half of England Is Now Land-Mad"

With the repeal of the odious stamp levy, many American colonists turned their backs on Britain and faced west, looking for ways to profit from the two billion acres vacated by the French.

In Connecticut, the most densely populated colony, speculators with fortunes amassed by supplying the British Army bought entire wilderness townships. With little hard money, Ethan Allen and his brothers acquired two hundred thousand acres of present-day Vermont.

In Britain, it took connections at court to buy titles and emoluments; in colonial America, connections in London brought land grants. From London, Benjamin Franklin entered the race for land grants in partnership with Anthony Wayne of Pennsylvania. They received a twenty-thousand-acre grant in present-day New Brunswick, Canada, to resettle German immigrants from overcrowded Philadelphia.

In spring 1766, Franklin's son, William, appointed as royal governor of New Jersey, formed a partnership with Philadelphia Quaker merchants to provision British garrisons. As Benjamin's twenty-year printing partnership was about to expire, he was increasingly worried about his income dwindling. He wrote to Deborah:

> If I should lose the post office, we should be reduced to our rent and interest of money for subsistence. . . . When people's

incomes are lessened, if they cannot proportionately lessen their outgoings, they must come to Poverty. For my own part I live here frugally.[1] [Actually, Franklin belonged to sixty London eating clubs and ran a hefty balance with a wine merchant.]

The Franklins, father and son, formed the Grand Ohio Company. They petitioned the Crown for a vast tract that would stretch from the Wisconsin River to the Ohio, from the Wabash to the Mississippi. Franklin urged his father to use his connections at court to secure the charter.

Benjamin, while acting as agent for the Pennsylvania Assembly, also served as the Grand Ohio Company's London agent. The Franklins invited a silent partner, Sir William Johnson, superintendent of Indian affairs in America, to suggest the names of influential Englishmen and then lend his weight to the project by writing to them. This would give Sir William "an opportunity of giving your sentiments to the Ministry . . . which will be of infinite service to the Company."

Letters of recommendation from these highly placed contacts were to be sent to Franklin in London "to present his Majesty and Council for their confirmation." Sir William was to lose no time: the sooner he wrote to Governor Franklin, the better, as "one half of England is now land-mad and everybody there has their eyes fixed on this country."[2]

Johnson wrote back to Governor Franklin that he was eager to pursue the scheme, adding, "I am of opinion it would answer better that I recommend it in general terms as an affair I had heard was in agitation."

Johnson then wrote to the chief secretary of state, Henry Conway, in London, enclosing the plan "at the request of several gentlemen of fortune & character." He stressed the benefits of a new colony that would accrue to England, yet he said nothing of the benefits that would accrue to him.[3] Governor Franklin then invited Sir Henry Moore, royal governor of New York, into the scheme.

At this point, Governor Franklin wrote to his father that he thought it made little sense to buy so much land in the Illinois Country unless it was made a separate colony—with the understanding that Sir William Johnson would be its royal governor. Benjamin liked his son's idea of a new colony and was disappointed only that he couldn't nominate more members for the company.

Franklin estimated the new colony would comprise "near 63,000,000 acres—enough to content a large number of reasonable people." Within a year, he succeeded in winning over Lord Shelburne to their scheme. But then Shelburne was replaced by Lord Hillsborough, who was "terribly afraid of dispeopling Ireland."

Every member of every government agency necessary to grease the ways to the Grand Ohio Company land grant plunked down £200 (roughly $30,000 today) a share. The shareholders included three nephews of former prime minister Walpole; the lord chamberlain; the brother of the secretary of the Board of Trade; the lord chancellor; two members of the king's Privy Council; a director of the East India Company; the postmaster general; and the secretary and undersecretary of the Exchequer.

When Franklin again led a delegation calling at Whitehall, Hillsborough opined, "Their best plan would be to purchase enough land for a new colony, 'Say, *twenty* million acres!'"[4]

A majority of the Board of Trade committee that would consider the Franklins' petition also owned shares. They voted to recommend chartering the Grand Ohio Company's grant to the king for his assent. In August 1772, the king's full Privy Council approved creation of a new colony. It was to be named Vandalia, in honor of the German birthplace of Queen Charlotte.

Each Franklin could now look forward to owning 313,142 acres of rich Illinois soil. But they were treading on soil also coveted by George Washington and his close friends, the Lees.

Only months before Parliament had cut off further western expansion, Washington had pledged to pay his share of expenses to secure the Mississippi Land Company grant. When the Proclamation Line was promulgated, salesman Washington told investors that it was only "a temporary expedient to quiet the minds of the Indians."[5]

In London acting as agent for his family's interests, young Arthur

Lee heard of the Franklins' new land company and wrote home to his brother, Richard Henry, about it. The Ministry has "set everything to sale" and "was going to make a grant of *their lands* to a company of adventurers."

Lee, training as a barrister at the Inns of Court in London, immediately presented a petition to the Ministry asking that the disputed lands not be granted to the Grand Ohio Company until the Mississippi Company learned the terms of the Franklins' venture.

The modest request of only 2.5 million acres by the Mississippi Company, Lee pointed out, not only overlapped the lands requested for the Grand Ohio Company but conflicted with the old Ohio Company of Virginia, to which Washington and the Lees still belonged.

From his veranda overlooking the Potomac River, George Washington envisioned linking the Atlantic Ocean with the Mississippi, the Ohio, and the Great Lakes, no doubt picturing the grand trading empire he aspired to create. It was a vision Washington would pursue for the rest of his life. Following Tidewater wisdom, he bought more land and more slaves and traded his tobacco crops for luxury goods to turn his farmhouse into a great manor.

Still, his impeccable records showed declining profits. Few Virginians owned ships; they depended on English mercantile firms to move their goods by sea. Washington calculated that up to 80 percent of the revenue of his crop was being siphoned off by taxes, transportation charges, unloading, weighing, warehousing, and reloading fees at the docks in London, plus insurance in case the ship sank.

The expenses didn't end there. Washington's London broker offered a variety of services for a fee, charging 3 percent interest—the highest allowed by law—to purchase the latest fashions, including Washington's favorite cheeses (double Gloucester and Cheshire) and felt hats and iron tools for the field hands. Since no banks were permitted in British America, the broker also acted as banker, allowing planter-clients to draw bills of exchange that served as certified checks against the proceeds of tobacco sales or expected future shipments.

Along with his 1760 tobacco crop, Washington sent to his London broker, John Washington, a distant cousin, two bills of exchange totaling £869 (about $130,000 today) to help purchase 2,238 acres adjoining his lands; the next year, £259 (about $40,000 today) to buy slaves. These drafts reached London at the same time he sent four bills of exchange payable to Washington by people who owed him money. They were protested—in modern parlance, they bounced.

Suddenly, Washington found himself £1,900 (roughly $350,000 today) in debt and, for the first time, paying interest. He was stunned.

Washington began to research prices for goods in Virginia. He found his English broker was charging an average of 25 percent more for linens, woolens, and even nails of poorer quality shipped from England. In addition to being out of fashion, most of the clothes Martha received from London didn't fit.

Washington had put money aside for several years to replace Martha's open carriage with a luxurious coach sporting his coat of arms on its doors, but it arrived with its plush interior moldy and began to fall apart at the dock. London tradesmen, he finally concluded, were dumping inferior goods they could not sell in England on Americans at exorbitant profits. Brokers "palm off sometimes old, and sometimes very slight and indifferent goods upon us, taking care at the same time to advance the price. We often have Articles sent to Us that could only have been used by our Forefathers in the days of yore."[6]

Needing cash, Washington set his sights on realistic ways to increase his income. At first, he decided to switch from cultivating tobacco to wheat and corn that he could sell directly to neighbors. Then he built a fishing schooner and a brigantine to seine the river for shad, herring, and whitefish that he could deliver quickly to local markets.

He covered his hillsides with peach trees and apple orchards; he ordered equipment to turn flax into rough linen to clothe his farmhands. Soon his wheat crop was outgrowing the Virginia market; he began to sell it in Philadelphia and the West Indies. He stopped buying more slaves in 1762, instead importing skilled weavers and artisans to train his slaves how to make their own clothing and build their own cabins.

By the late 1760s, Washington calculated that he had one hundred slaves idle at any given moment. He began to question slavery on purely economic grounds. He turned to leasing prime riverfront land to immigrant tenant farmers who sold their tobacco to Scottish storekeepers and then paid him their rent in cash. By 1774, he was raking in £8,000 (about $386,000 today) in annual rents, making him independent of English creditors.

At first, few Americans foresaw an intensive struggle over Parliament's disclaimer, at the tag end of the act repealing the Stamp Act, that Parliament would have supremacy in all matters touching its American colonies.

To most London observers, the act merely seemed a face-saving measure, having no weight because the colonies had always had the right by charters granted in the seventeenth century by the Crown to make their own laws and then submit them to the king for pro forma ratification.

Jubilant students at the College of New Jersey celebrated the repeal by planting a double row of sycamore trees—still extant—in front of Nassau Hall. The New York Assembly commissioned the casting of equestrian statues of King George III and William Pitt.

But Jonathan Trumbull, the deputy governor of Connecticut, was disturbed by Parliament's blanket declaration of sovereignty. Trumbull grew even more alarmed when he received instructions from London that American colonists would now be required to provide quarters and rations for British troops. To him, this meant that America, as if conquered, had become an occupied country.

Trumbull had become one of New England's leading merchants and political figures. He attended Harvard divinity school before joining the family business in Lebanon in western Connecticut. His father, beginning as an uneducated farmer, had built an extensive trade in raising beef cattle and hogs, herding them into Boston, where meatpackers exported them to England and Ireland in exchange for luxury goods that he distributed to stores all over Connecticut. Becoming the region's principal shopkeeper, the elder Trumbull dispensed, among other things, a vast assortment of lace and gloves, gunpowder and knives, rum and food-stuffs.

The transatlantic trading company that Jonathan Trumbull and his partners built up dispatched from the port of New London some sixty ships: twelve-ton sloops to haul produce to markets in Boston and Rhode Island; eighty-ton brigantines carrying horses, cattle, and lumber to the West Indies in exchange for sugar and molasses; and two-hundred-ton brigs carrying salted meats and cod to the Mediterranean, and flax-seed, lumber, potash, whale fins, skins, and furs to England and Ireland.

Provisioning Nantucket Island with farm produce, beef, and pork, Trumbull traded them for whale oil, which he then shipped to England in exchange for finery and furniture to sell in his capacious Lebanon emporium, the forerunner of a modern department store and wholesale outlet.

By marrying Faith Robinson, a direct descendant of *Mayflower* pilgrims John and Priscilla Alden, Trumbull entered New England's Puritan elite. He built and lavishly furnished a hilltop mansion where he held social sway, behaving as something like an English country squire. He rode through the countryside in a fine carriage and extended hospitality in fine clothes tailored in Boston from fine English fabrics.

Part of his stature as a rural grandee depended on dispensing credit. By 1764, when Parliament banned colonial currencies, Trumbull's books carried debts of more than £10,000 (about $1.5 million today), much of it too old and uncollectable. Trumbull accepted payment from Americans in livestock, tobacco, firewood, carting, and carpentry, but his British creditors insisted on payment in gold and silver coins.

Parliament's "new Fetters" worried Trumbull. He feared the British would deploy troops to break up protests against the new tax measures. When he first heard talk of separating the colonies from the mother country, he wrote to William Samuel Johnson, Connecticut's agent in London, that he still considered the interests of Britain and America "mutual and inseparable."

As long as the colonies wanted the protection and manufactured goods of the mother country, it wouldn't be in Americans' interest to separate. As long as the colonies provided raw materials, commodities, and services "beneficial to the native country," Trumbull believed that it would always be in the mother country's interest to keep the colonies "dependent and employed. . . . If violence, or methods tending to violence, be taken to maintain this dependence, it tends to hasten a separation."[7]

While Benjamin Franklin angled for massive land grants, and George Washington came to realize how British merchants were exploiting the growing costs to American colonists of the British trade monopoly, Jonathan Trumbull became a reluctant addition to the growing protest movement, expanding his vast network of international business associates.

PART TWO

BREAKING AWAY

CHAPTER ELEVEN

"BONE OF OUR BONE"

As years of unrest rolled on like the menace of a gathering storm, King George III became infuriated by mobs on both sides of the Atlantic. Reshuffling his cabinet yet again, in August 1766 he discarded Grenville and brought back William Pitt, now titled Lord Chatham, as his prime minister.

In turn, Chatham appointed Charles "Champagne Charlie" Townshend, a bibulous rural nobleman who preferred to stay on his country estates experimenting with crop rotation and fertilizing his turnip fields with manure, as chancellor of the Exchequer.

Soon Lord Chatham's health began to deteriorate, and Townshend assumed the role of head of Britain's government. He was notorious for anti-American ranting on the floor of Parliament. Now in power, he was intent on introducing a new tax scheme that would strip the colonial assemblies of their ability to control provincial governments.

As Benjamin Franklin wrote to his son in New Jersey, with Townshend now at the reins, "no middle doctrine can well be maintained. Something might be made of either of the extremes, that Parliament has a power to make all laws for us, or that it has a power to make no laws for us."[1]

But even Townshend's colleagues were surprised when, in June 1767, he announced new duties on American imports of glass, lead, tea, paint, and paper to defray the salaries of civil officers and judges in America. Further, Townshend reorganized the customs service, placing it under the American Board of Customs Commissioners headquartered in Boston, the breeding ground of opposition to British taxes.

To streamline enforcement, Townshend replaced the old Admiralty court in Halifax with local courts in the ports of Boston, Philadelphia, New Orleans, and Halifax. Then he created an office of secretary of state for the colonies. Its first incumbent: the hard-line anti-American Wills Hill, Lord Hillsborough. The Duke of Newcastle, for so long the advocate of "salutary neglect," said that Hillsborough was addicted to force: "The Doctrine of doing everything by Force prevails now Everywhere." After one tense interview, Franklin summed up Hillsborough's view of Americans: troublesome children who must be punished into obedience.[2]

Parliament's application of the new taxes instantly proved disastrous. In less than eight months, a fresh wave of riots broke out and brought on another crippling boycott on the import of English goods. Angry town meetings from Boston to New York City condemned the Townshend duties as a broad-based assault on colonists' rights. A boycott of British luxury goods by Boston merchants took effect on January 1, 1768; Newport, Providence, and New York City followed suit.

Early in 1769, Boston merchants tightened the sanctions to include almost all British goods, allowing only supplies for its Grand Banks fisheries. New York merchants canceled all orders sent to England after August 15, 1768, boycotting British imports until Parliament repealed the Townshend Acts. Tradesmen vowed not to deal with merchants who refused to join the boycott. By autumn 1769, merchants in every other port joined the boycott.

In addition, Virginians banned the importation of slaves from the Crown-owned Royal African Company. And to stimulate domestic wool production and encourage a homegrown textile industry, Virginia planters pledged not to slaughter lambs weaned before May 1.

College students promised to give up sipping imported wines and, at the 1770 commencement of Queen's College (now Rutgers), with Royal

Governor William Franklin on the dais, graduates showed up in home-spun gowns instead of the traditional imported academic robes. House-wives vowed to stop serving tea imported from England and renounced fashionable silks and satins.

Normally, Britain sold fully one-third of its exports in America; tens of thousands of jobs depended on the transatlantic trade. Consequently, the anti-Townshend embargo hit British commerce even harder than the Stamp Act crisis did.

Imports dropped by 35 percent in 1769. In New York, exports also dropped, by 86 percent; in Philadelphia, by nearly half. Overall, British exports to the American colonies plummeted by 40 percent in a single year.

George Washington was incensed that he had lost the right to manu-facture iron, as his father had done. With British law now forbidding the practice, he was forced to import from Britain many essentials his arti-sans could have been trained to produce at Mount Vernon. For the first time, he took a stand publicly, calling for the deployment of America's powerful new economic weapon, the boycott. He urged the "starving" of British trade and manufacturing. Further, he contended that nonim-portation would force planters to live within their means, encouraging domestic manufacturing and employment. And anyone refusing to boycott a broad range of goods "ought to be stigmatized."[3]

The crippling boycott on the import of English goods forced Parlia-ment, in April 1770, to rescind all the Townshend duties with the excep-tion of a token three-pence-in-the-pound (about 2.5 percent) tax on tea. But even that trivial remaining tax violated the very principle Americans were attempting to make the British understand.

Not all Virginians honored these sanctions. Thomas Jefferson was an upstart lawyer in the colony at the time. His father, a surveyor, had mapped Virginia's boundaries. One of eight children, young Thomas had been sent away to a clergyman's boarding school before matriculat-ing in the College of William and Mary. Reading law for fully seven years, he had hung out his shingle as the only lawyer in the Shenandoah Valley qualified to practice before the colony's highest court. On days when the General Court convened in Williamsburg, Jefferson courted Martha Wayles Skelton. Discovering their love of music, he set aside his oath to uphold the boycott on imports and ordered a custom-made, solid-mahogany clavichord from London for his bride-to-be so she could accompany his fiddling.

Outraged by the boycott, an increasingly hostile Parliament shifted customs operations onto American soil for the first time. Crown-appointed agents and informants shared the proceeds of confiscated goods, their raids now supported by Royal Navy cutters. When customs collectors were chased through the streets and threatened with having their houses torn down, they appealed to the Ministry in March 1768 for an armed force to protect them. The fifty-gun frigate *Romney* was dispatched from Halifax.

In June, the customs commissioners received an urgent appeal to send troops to Hancock's Wharf. A crowd had locked a customs official in a cabin of John Hancock's sloop *Liberty* while they unloaded a cargo of untaxed Madeira wine. The customs board ordered *Liberty* seized. As it was towed to an anchorage near *Romney*, a crowd attacked the commissioners. The next day the customs commissioners fled to Castle William on an island in the harbor and appealed to London for troops.

In a showcase trial, John Adams defended Hancock. There was little question of Hancock's guilt, but Adams based his defense on the fact that Americans had not been represented in the Parliaments that had enacted the trade laws and now were being tried by Admiralty courts without juries.

Unable to find witnesses willing to risk testifying, the British prosecutors produced no evidence of illegal activity and ended up dropping all charges, making both Hancock and Adams heroes of a growing resistance movement. Seizure of ships for widespread smuggling became virtually impossible.

On orders from Lord Hillsborough, Sir Thomas Gage, the British commander in chief for America, rotated forces from Canada to Boston.

Into a town of sixteen thousand, he injected four thousand Redcoats to bivouac on the Common. The stench of latrines wafted over the town. As historian David Hackett Fisher points out, Gage chose his troops unwisely, selecting "for that difficult assignment the 29th Foot, a regiment notorious for poor discipline, hot-tempered officers, and repeated violent clashes with civilians in Canada and New York."[4]

Shortly after the Redcoats pitched their tents on the Common, the first serious flare-up occurred. When a butcher taunted a soldier who then knocked him down, his commanding officer applauded the "lesson." But when the local justice of the peace fined the soldier, he refused to pay up. Instead, he slashed the constable who attempted to arrest him.

General Gage's attitude hardened with each fracas. He wrote to his superiors in London, "Democracy is too prevalent in America, and claims the greatest attention to prevent its increase." New England's laws were bizarre, the people litigious, wrote Gage, who was married to the daughter of a wealthy New Jersey merchant. "Every man studies law, and interprets law to suit his purpose." Americans, he concluded, were "already almost out of reach of Law and Government."[5]

By aggressively escalating attempts to extract revenues from British American colonies, Britain's ministers, after a century of failures, had turned modest gains into a fiasco.

At twenty-nine, John Adams had married Abigail Smith just before she turned twenty. Abigail's father, Parson William Smith, had taken five years to make up his mind to permit Adams to marry his daughter. The Smiths didn't see in Adams the best possible husband material. They knew that he had first intended to enter the ministry, Mr. Smith's profession, but had given up because of religious doubts. Young Adams probably didn't confide to Parson Smith what he later wrote to Thomas Jefferson: that he despised "frigid John Calvin" and rigid Congregational mores.

At the same time, Abigail's family believed, as so many people in New England did at the time, that very little social prestige or respect could be found in the legal profession. As Poor Richard wrote to his own son William when he revealed his intent to study law, "God works wonders now and then / There goes a lawyer, an honest man."

Besides, as a lawyer, Adams might not necessarily be a good enough provider for their daughter, since few men in Massachusetts could make a living practicing law. But Adams had gradually emerged as Boston's leading lawyer. With two children, the Adamses moved from Braintree to Boston, settling in a modest house in Brattle Square. He had attracted heightened public attention in 1768 in a showcase trial when he defended Hancock in the Liberty case.

On March 5, 1770, the pent-up tensions of months of clashes between soldiers seeking part-time jobs and the town's unemployed laborers turned into a riot. A crowd gathered at the customhouse and pelted an eighteen-year-old Redcoat with ice. When the main guard arrived under the command of Captain Thomas Preston, the crowd pushed and shoved until the soldiers fired into the mob, killing three rioters outright and wounding two.

To quell the rioting, Samuel Adams, leader of the town's radicals, demanded that Governor Hutchinson withdraw the troops to islands in the harbor. Preston and eight of his men were arrested by town officials for murder. Hutchinson asked the town's two leading lawyers, John Adams and Josiah Quincy, to undertake the soldiers' defense. At their trial in October, Adams won acquittal for Preston and six of his men; two, found guilty of manslaughter, were branded on the hand and released.

Americans came away from the trial with, in effect, their first national holiday, the annual anniversary observance of what became known as the Boston Massacre. Silversmith Paul Revere's shocking engraving of the deadly clash helped etch it into the growing narrative of British oppression of the colonists. On its first anniversary, crowds gathered at Faneuil Hall for Massacre Day and increasingly incendiary speeches.

John Adams emerged from the Preston trial so unpopular that only his cousin Samuel's protection shielded his family from attacks in the streets. Adams moved his clan back to Braintree, to the safety of the family farm. Yet, as Adams emerged as a leading pamphleteer for the protest movement, his practice once again thrived. In 1772, he enjoyed his most lucrative year, trying some two hundred cases in Superior Court, many of them in maritime law, with his regular clients including John Hancock.

Adams also became popular as an orator. In one case, the busy Adams rushed into court before he realized that he had forgotten his notes. While his clerk dashed back to his office to fetch the client's file, Adams improvised before the judge and onlookers. He was still talking when, nearly an hour later, the clerk, breathless, returned. Adams could now sum up—to the applause of the patient jury.

And Adams was finally making enough money to expand the Braintree farm. With his earnings, he bought up neighboring five- and ten-acre plots of salt marsh and upland that he and Abigail and a handful of farmhands could manage themselves, never speculating in western lands.

Only days after Adams won acquittal for Captain Preston in Boston, in Salem, New Jersey, customs collector James Hatton seized a smuggler's vessel in Delaware Bay. An angry mob recaptured the ship, and the Sons of Liberty tarred and feathered him. At the Admiralty court trial, no witness would testify. As Philadelphia's deputy customs collector John Swift explained to the American Board of Customs Commissioners in Boston:

> The hands of Government are not strong enough to oppose the numerous body of people who wish well to the cause of smuggling. . . . What can a Governor do, without the assistance of the Governed? What can the magistrates do, unless they are supported by their fellow Citizens? What can the King's officers do, if they make themselves obnoxious to the people amongst whom they reside?[6]

As the British government employed the Royal Navy to impose an effectual blockade on America's ports, it reinforced troops and customs officers ashore in an attempt to exert more pressure on American merchants. In turn, as they opposed ever more numerous regulations and taxes, the oppressed merchants passed from being considered enterprising businessmen under the century-long British policy of benign neglect to being determined and systematic smugglers. And then, turning to outright resistance, the merchants edged closer to open rebellion against Britain.

Like the Hancocks of Boston, the Browns of Providence, with their merchant empire at stake, were prepared to resort to extreme measures to resist British tax collectors. On June 9, 1772, the customs schooner *Gaspee* ran aground in Narragansett Bay while pursuing a suspected smuggling packet. Sensing an opportunity to inflict vengeance on the hated tax collector, eight boatloads of men attacked the schooner under the cover of darkness. They captured the officer and his crew and torched the ship.

In response, Lord Hillsborough issued a royal proclamation offering a reward of £500 ($75,000 today) for information leading to the apprehension of Brown and his confederates. Hillsborough ordered a commission of inquiry to arrest suspects and send them to England to be tried for treason. But no witnesses would come forward, and no arrests were ever made. Brown would later boast in writing of his exploit.

The threat to remand suspects to England alarmed many moderate Americans, but they found even more menacing to self-rule Governor Hutchinson's announcement that, henceforth, he and all Massachusetts judges would be paid directly by the Crown.

At a stroke, this rendered the colony's administration and judiciary independent of the provincial assembly's power of the purse guaranteed in its royal charter. As angry men all over America read the Crown order, they set up committees to coordinate their protests against British innovations that were endangering civil liberties, including the right to a speedy trial by a jury of one's own peers, as guaranteed since 1215 by the Magna Carta.

To challenge this latest abridgment of the colonists' traditional liberties, Sam Adams called a Boston town meeting. Chaired by James Otis, the meeting authorized a standing committee of correspondence to report "to the World" Sam Adams's "List of Infringements and Violations of those rights."

The town meeting's call for reciprocity with other provinces quickly led ten other colonies to create similar committees. In Virginia, the standing committee of correspondence created by the House of Burgesses included Thomas Jefferson, Patrick Henry, and Richard Henry Lee.

As tensions over heavy-handed customs collection intensified, Hutchinson reported to London that Bostonians were ignoring the last remaining Townshend duty. Eighty percent of the "prodigious" amount of tea consumed by Bostonians, he reported, was smuggled from Holland through the Dutch Caribbean island of St. Eustatius to avoid paying the modest three-penny duty. He warned that if Britain showed no resentment "for so high an affront," it would encourage colonists to adopt measures "to obtain and secure their independence."

At the same time, the Massachusetts Assembly fired off a petition to Benjamin Franklin, now its agent in London, with instructions for him to present it to the colonial secretary, Lord Dartmouth, asking him to rescind Hutchinson's orders. Dartmouth refused to accept the petition: "The King would be exceedingly offended."[7]

It was at this moment that Franklin, reporting to assembly leaders, enclosed letters he said he believed "laid the foundation of most if not all of our present grievances."

Five years earlier, Hutchinson, then chief justice, and his brother-in-law, the provincial secretary Andrew Oliver, had carried on a secret correspondence with Thomas Whately, a cabinet minister and coauthor of the Stamp Act. Hutchinson had castigated "the licentiousness of those who call themselves the sons of liberty," singling out Samuel Adams and John Hancock. Hutchinson urged "an abridgement of what are called

English liberties in the American colonies." Force must be used, he insisted. One result of Hutchinson's and Oliver's letters had been the transfer of British troops from Canada to Boston.[8]

Still the highest-ranking British-paid postal official for America, Franklin never did reveal how he had obtained the incendiary letters. But when he learned of their existence, he evidently asked the disgruntled courtier John Temple, who had recently been fired from the American Board of Customs for his pro-American leanings, to purloin the letters from the home of Whately's brother, who held them after Whately's death in 1772.

The contents of the letters infuriated Franklin. He had never forgotten how, two decades earlier, Hutchinson had haughtily brushed aside his Plan of Union in Albany.

Sending ten of the Hutchinson-Oliver letters to Thomas Cushing, Speaker of the Massachusetts House of Representatives, Franklin noted that he had sworn to Temple they would not be printed or copied but would merely be shown to leading citizens to demonstrate that it was Hutchinson's advice to the Ministry that had led to the British government's recent obnoxious behavior toward Massachusetts.

But to Samuel Adams, it was inconceivable that Franklin would send such incredibly revealing letters if he had not intended them to be made public. He read them to a secret session of the House and had them copied and printed. The House sent off a petition to the king, asking to have Hutchinson, now royal governor, removed from office.

Incredulous that Massachusetts-born, Harvard-educated Hutchinson, once his friend, could have written such appalling statements about his fellow colonials, John Adams exclaimed: "Bone of our bone! Born and educated among us! Vile serpent! Cool thinking deliberate villain!"[9]

Samuel Adams also demanded the impeachment of Andrew Oliver, now Massachusetts's chief justice. When the House granted Adams's call with a vote of 92–8, Hutchinson dissolved the Massachusetts legislature.

Samuel Adams, chairing the Boston town meeting, responded by inviting John Hancock to deliver the third annual Massacre Day oration.

In the most impassioned speech of his life, Hancock, the wealthiest merchant in New England, joined Samuel Adams as the leaders of the resistance movement in Massachusetts.

The arrival of Hutchinson's purloined letters in Boston set off a series of town meetings that effectively triggered the American Revolution. The letters appeared in the August 31, 1773, Boston *Public Advertiser*—just as Bostonians learned from Benjamin Franklin that Parliament was empowering the British East India Company to recoup its losses from Americans' smuggling.

The company's stockholders, including Lord Dartmouth, the colonial secretary, had paid £1,000 ($150,000 today) each for shares in the tea monopoly. In 1773, its share price had plummeted to £160, all but annihilating their investments. Franklin wrote to his son that Americans' refusal to take British-taxed tea was bringing the company "infinite distress." Americans were buying twice as much smuggled tea from the Dutch. As the British East India Company became unable to pay its debts or any dividend, its plunging value annihilated £3 million (about $450 million today). It was the worst British credit crisis in fifty years, touching off bankruptcies and massive layoffs in British manufacturing firms; thousands of workers were either starving or subsisting on charity.

In an attempt to buoy the flagging economy, Parliament voted to amend the tea laws. Parliament had already been allowing the company a "drawback," a refund of 60 percent of the 25 percent import duty it had been paying when the tea came from India to England before transshipment to the colonies. Now, under the revised Tea Act of 1773, Parliament allowed a 100 percent customs drawback on tea exported to America, amounting to a 20 percent price cut, undercutting both legitimate Boston merchants as well as smugglers. The prime minister, Lord North, insisted that the three-pence-in-the-pound import duty still be paid: Americans must pay a duty on tea as a mark of the supremacy of Parliament.

In addition, Parliament allowed the monopoly to export directly from India to the colonies, certain that East India tea could now be sold so cheaply that it would induce the colonists to cease smuggling their tea from the Dutch colonies and instead buy large quantities from the company, thus assuring the company's—and the British economy's—recovery.

Instead of time-honored auctions, the tea was now to be consigned. In September, half a million pounds of tea set sail for American ports. Journeying toward Boston were three ships owned by Nantucket whale-oil exporter William Rotch. The company's Boston consignees, authorized to sell the tea aboard the ships, were two sons and a nephew of Royal Governor Hutchinson. In December 1773, news of the Hutchinson letters, which had been ratcheting up anger throughout the colonies for months, finally broke in the London newspapers. Thomas Whately's brother, a member of Parliament, accused John Temple of stealing the letters and challenged him to a duel, during which Whately was seriously wounded. Benjamin Franklin, to avoid further bloodshed, decided it was time for him to come forward. In a letter published on Christmas Day, he admitted, "I alone am the person who obtained and transmitted" the letters to Boston.[10] When the tea ships had arrived in Boston Harbor, the throng at the town meeting angrily demanded that the cargo be sent back. Hutchinson refused. Shortly after dark on December 16, a week before Franklin's public confession in London, some eight thousand Bostonians—more than half the port's population—gathered around Old South Meeting House. William Rotch reported that Hutchinson was still refusing to allow his ships to clear the harbor and return to England without paying the duty. The lost customs duty would have amounted to £7,000 (about $1 million today) and would have paid Hutchinson's, the judges', and the customs commissioners' salaries.

As if giving a prearranged signal, Samuel Adams proclaimed from the pulpit, "I don't see what more Bostonians can do to save their country!"[11] At these words, a bosun's whistle split the air and a war whoop erupted. Several dozen men, their faces blackened, threw off their coats.

Wrapped in old blankets and carrying hatchets and pistols, they raced through the cold night air to Griffin's Wharf and clambered into three longboats that carried them to the towering tea ships. Leading the raiders over the decks and into the holds were several leading tea smugglers, including John Hancock.

As an estimated one thousand Bostonians watched silently for three hours, teams of the Sons of Liberty, ignoring all other cargo, hoisted 342 lacquered chests of tea topsides, smashed them open, and threw 90,000 pounds of tea, valued at £9,659 (approximately $1.5 million today), into Boston Harbor. The customs officers had vanished. Not a single suspect was ever arrested. No shots were fired. John Adams recorded the scene in his diary: there was, to the protests, a "Dignity, a Majesty, a Sublimity."[12]

CHAPTER TWELVE

"The Prime Conductor"

On the morning of January 11, 1774, Benjamin Franklin called for his slave valet Peter to bring the carriage around for the short drive to Whitehall Palace.

Expecting to testify at a preliminary hearing of the Board of Trade on the Massachusetts Assembly's petition to remove Governor Hutchinson, Franklin was surprised to be told that the committee needed more time to study the charges. The hearing had been rescheduled; he should retain counsel. News of the destruction of property so valuable to British interests had reached London even as Franklin was preparing for the hearing.

Arrival of the news of the Boston Tea Party had led Britain's attorney general to immediately charge Samuel Adams, John Hancock, and the leaders of the Massachusetts legislature with treason. Hutchinson was ordered to bring them to justice by trial, either in Massachusetts or in England.

By the time Franklin returned to Whitehall, the story of the Tea Party had spread throughout London. The episode was a serious blow to the British economy; among its biggest losers were members of Parliament who owned shares in the British East India Company and were furious at Americans, especially their representative, Benjamin Franklin. He had fallen so far out of favor at court after his public admission of stealing the Hutchinson letters that no one warned him that the Crown intended to turn the Hutchinson hearing into Franklin's trial. He would now face Solicitor General Alexander Wedderburn, who for two years had been blocking the Franklins' Vandalia Company land grant.

On the morning of January 20, 1774, Franklin selected a fashionable blue suit of Manchester velvet, ate quietly, and sent for his carriage. As he drove through Whitehall Gate, he was surprised to see so many coaches. In nearly two decades of attending hearings, he had never seen such a crowd there. Alighting, Franklin spotted his radical Whig friends Joseph Priestley and Jeremy Bentham and, shouldering through the crowd, their good friend, Edmund Burke.

The hearing room, the lofty fifteenth-century Cockpit, was crowded with thirty-five members of the Privy Council, an unusually large number, in their ermine-trimmed red robes, arrayed in gilded chairs around the great green-baize-covered council table, many accompanied by their wives. Lady Elizabeth Montagu, in a gold-trimmed red-velvet chair, was chatting with the Duchess of Rutland, Lady Falmouth, Lady Hardwicke, the Countess of Coventry, and the Countess of Marchmont.

Wearing a scarlet cape and a full white wig, Lord Gower, chairman of the Privy Council and a stockholder in the Illinois Company, sat on a small throne under a scarlet canopy. Franklin also recognized Lord Rochford, an Illinois Company shareholder, and Lord Rodney, another major land speculator.

Lord Sandwich, first lord of the Admiralty and a joint postmaster general who did not believe an American should hold high office, sat beside Franklin's nemesis, Lord Hillsborough, and Lord Dartmouth, who had perused Hutchinson's letters and considered this son of a Boston candlemaker supremely impudent.

Protocol demanded that Franklin remain standing. For ninety minutes he stood twenty feet from Wedderburn as the solicitor general launched into a highly colored history of the past decade in Massachusetts, ending with the declaration that there had been no complaint against Hutchinson until Franklin had stolen and published the governor's private correspondence.

Sneering, Wedderburn alluded to Franklin, who had been elected to the Royal Academy for his pioneering experiments with electricity, as "the prime conductor" of secret designs. Nothing could "acquit Dr. Franklin of obtaining the letters by fraudulent and corrupt means. . . . I hope, my lords, you will mark and brand this man." Joseph Priestley later wrote that "Wedderburn's sarcastic wit" caused the councillors to laugh "outright" and thump their canes.[1]

Writing afterward to a friend, Franklin likened the scene to a "bullbaiting." He said he had kept "a cool sullen silence, reserving myself to some future opportunity." By prior agreement, the Privy Council peremptorily dismissed the charges against Hutchinson.

As Franklin left the hearing, he bumped up against the solicitor general. Speaking slowly but loud enough for others around him to hear, Franklin told Wedderburn, "I will make your master a little king for this." The next day, Benjamin Franklin was fired as deputy postmaster general for America.[2]

Even after the First Continental Congress convened in Philadelphia in May 1774, Franklin remained in London for more than a year after his dismissal, enduring abusive anti-American speeches in Parliament, in the homes of friends, and in the newspapers. Distancing themselves, Lord Stanhope and other noble shareholders in the Vandalia Company asked him to resign to protect their investments.

Franklin's firing cast his financial affairs into shambles. With his partnership in the *Pennsylvania Gazette* now expired, his substantial post office income cut off, and his agent's salary from Massachusetts and Georgia in arrears (Georgia's by four years), he was unable to pay the legal fees for his Cockpit defense even as he was sued in civil court for stealing the Hutchinson letters.

His accounts in America were left in confusion after the recent death of his wife, Deborah, and Franklin was unable to collect rents from his tenants. He himself was four years behind in the rent for his stylish London flat.

With no authority from America, Franklin pursued informal negotiations with pro-American members of Parliament, including Lord Chatham, until Hillsborough demanded in Parliament to know why Franklin was still at large. A shocked Franklin discovered that the Ministry had been using his conversations with friends as a ploy to keep him in England while warrants were prepared for his arrest.

Thoroughly alarmed, he gave out the wrong date for his departure and, with his grandson, William Temple, and his slave Peter, on March 20, 1775, secretly sailed for America, leaving so abruptly that he was unable to pack most of his clothes, books, or papers.

In the wake of the Boston Tea Party, Parliament passed a series of Coercive Acts revoking Massachusetts' seventeenth-century charter, banning town meetings, stripping the legislature of its taxing authority, and clamping the colony under martial law.

The Boston Port Act, intended "to starve New England," passed Parliament by a 3–1 vote, cutting off all trade by land and sea and rescinding fishing rights in the Atlantic until Boston repaid the value of the tea. Its port could remain open only to coastal ships delivering fuel and food, but with no commerce, few Bostonians had any money to pay for provisions.

On June 1, 1774, the day the Boston Port Act took effect, church bells tolled solemnly all over New England, shop windows were draped in black, and normal business came to a standstill. Sympathizers in other colonies kept Boston provisioned, driving donated flocks of sheep and herds of pigs from Connecticut across the narrow neck of land connecting the town and the mainland, passing between rows of British cannon. A cargo ship full of rice arrived from South Carolina; Virginia sent money and nine thousand barrels of flour for distribution. Rhode Island commissioned a new meetinghouse to put Boston's unemployed carpenters to work. For the first time, the scattered colonies were uniting in common sentiment.

The same day that Parliament passed the Coercive Acts, it overwhelmingly approved the Quebec Act, replacing the military laws in force in Canada since the end of the French and Indian War with a highly centralized form of civilian government. This further outraged Puritan New England.

The counterrevolutionary act was the personal creation of Quebec's military governor, the French-speaking Sir Guy Carleton. He sought to win over the conquered French *habitants* by honoring their traditions, their laws, and even their Roman Catholicism, to the dismay of some three thousand New England traders and settlers who had flocked in to take over the fur trade.

Considered by Bostonians as a reprisal for the Tea Party, the Quebec Act created a vast new colony entirely unlike any other province. Extending Quebec's borders to the Ohio River deep into territory claimed by Connecticut, Massachusetts, and Virginia, the act was intended to permanently block American westward expansion.

George Washington and other veterans had been promised, and for twenty years had expected, land grants in the Ohio Valley. Benjamin Franklin and his son, William, for the past decade the royal governor of New Jersey, along with the members of Philadelphia and Connecticut mercantile houses, had invested heavily in multimillion-acre colonization schemes seeking grants of land from Vermont to the Mississippi. Now, by an act of Parliament, all of them were cut off from what had become essentially a vast, fur-producing Indian reserve allowed to trade only with Great Britain.

The Quebec Act was widely dreaded as a model of the form of government the British planned to impose on the colonies to the south. It created a single-house legislature with an executive council appointed by the king to advise the royal governor, with no lower house elected by the people.

The act also preserved French land-tenure law and abolished habeas corpus and trial by jury. While Catholicism was still suppressed in Britain, the establishment of the religion in Quebec meant that, for the first time since the Reformation, there would be bishops in the British realm supported by the tithing of the crops and the incomes of all citizens.

Injection of the religious issue brought an immediate and harsh reaction. At Yale College, the Reverend Ezra Stiles, a philosophy professor and its future president, considered the Quebec Act the outstanding grievance against the British government. Thousands of New England troops who had marched at the side of the British to evict the French from Canada felt betrayed.

Protest against the Quebec Act was incorporated in the most radical Massachusetts document, the Suffolk Resolves, which called the new Canadian charter "dangerous in an extreme degree to the Protestant religion and to the rights and civil liberties of all America. . . . We are indispensably obliged to take all the measures for our security . . . to acquaint ourselves with the art of war as soon as possible."

Adopted at a province-wide convention, the Suffolk Resolves declared the Coercive Acts unconstitutional and recommended ignoring them. The convention, in a step little short of open rebellion, urged Massachusetts citizens to form a provisional government until Parliament repealed the Coercive Acts. Meanwhile, citizens were to arm and form their own militias.

Finally, the Suffolk Resolves recommended stringent economic sanctions against Britain. Carried at once to Philadelphia by Paul Revere, the resolves received the immediate endorsement of the First Continental Congress, which ordered them printed and distributed throughout America and Britain.

Outraged at Parliament's heavy-handed reaction to the Boston Tea Party, George Washington soon turned his thoughts to the damage the Quebec Act posed to his heavy investment in the Ohio Valley.

In a letter he had written in 1774, Washington had recorded his excitement at finding in the western lands high-quality hardwoods and coal "of the very best kind" close to waterways.[3] The productivity of his Mount Vernon fisheries allowed him to imagine future catches from inland rivers. He found "River cats" (catfish) so big that their fry could have gobbled up the largest adults in the Potomac. He had scouted the best sites for hunting game—including buffalo—and dreamed of linking inland waterways with transatlantic markets.

Through relatives, he had been surreptitiously buying up the bounty claims of fellow veterans in financial distress. On his way to becoming the most successful of all the western investors, he had already amassed twenty thousand acres along the Great Kanawha River in present-day Ohio.

But Washington had grown incensed at what he considered British machinations to outflank him, especially when he learned of an investment scheme to interpose a new western colony between his Ohio lands and further westward expansion. Fulminating at British overlords' "malignant disposition towards us poor Americans founded equally in Malice, absurdity & error," he did not know that one obstacle to his grand western ambitions was Benjamin Franklin's Vandalia.[4]

Stunned by the Boston Tea Party, Washington, who preferred beer to tea, had nevertheless remained silent, but property had been destroyed; the tea company, he believed, must be compensated for its loss. Despite the fact that the Quebec Act closed off access to his Ohio Valley lands, Washington was unwilling to abandon his grand plan to rent them to the tenant farmers he still expected to come from Germany.

But then a new royal decree declared it a crime for the American colonies to disrupt trade with Britain. Washington realized that, by boycotting British goods, he was making himself liable to arrest and trial in England, "where it is impossible," Washington wrote to his erstwhile neighbor Bryan Fairfax, "that justice shall be done."[5] Now, not only was his financial well-being threatened but so was his freedom.

He called this latest British assault on American rights "the most despotic system of tyranny that ever was practiced in a free government."

Parliament had no more right to "put their hands into my pocket without my consent than I have to put my hands in yours." Americans would never consent to be taxed "without their own consent."

With characteristic understatement, Washington was succinctly encapsulating one of the major causes of Americans' growing resistance to Parliament's usurpation of their cherished charter right to set their own taxes to pay for governors, courts, public buildings, road, bridges—all the expenses of their towns and provinces. He considered it outrageous that Parliament, denying the colonists the right to print their own currency, insisted that taxes be paid in scarce gold and silver in a barter economy. Washington could have gone on for hours, but he summed up the essence of the most serious colonial grievance in a few memorable words. He denounced "those from whom we have a right to seek protection" for "endeavoring by every piece of Art & despotism to fix the Shackles of Slavery upon us." Ironically, he had come to believe that there was a close analogy between Parliament's treatment of Americans and the master-slave relationship. "We must assert our rights," he wrote, "or submit to every imposition that can be heaped upon us till custom and use shall make us as tame and abject slaves as the blacks we rule over with such arbitrary sway."

Espousing a total trade embargo, Washington argued that Americans should "put our virtue and fortitude to the severest test." Economic warfare promised victory without resorting to armed conflict.[6]

While organizing a donation from Alexandria's citizens of £273 (about $41,000 today) in cash and a shipment of wheat and flour for the poor of Boston, he was elected a delegate to the First Continental Congress in Philadelphia, which had been chosen because it was the midway point between the northernmost and southernmost colonies.

Washington arrived in Philadelphia with the Fairfax Resolves he had coauthored with a neighbor, George Mason, calling for a boycott of "all Manner of Luxury and Extravagance" and urging "Men of Fortune" to set examples of "temperance, frugality and industry," to develop domestic manufacturing and wean themselves from dependence on the mother country.

The Fairfax Resolves were a thorough indictment of British policy by a distinguished group of Americans who resented being

> considered as a conquered country. The present inhabitants are the descendants not of the conquered but of the conquerors. . . . Our ancestors when they left their native land and settled in America brought with them (even if the same had not been confirmed by charters) the civil constitution and form of government of the country they came from.

Americans were as entitled to all the "rights, advantages and immunities" of other British subjects as if they had remained in England. Only freely chosen representatives of the people could govern them: this was the basis of the English constitution.

The electrifying Fairfax Resolves were to serve as a prototype for an intercolonial boycott of English trade, explicitly banning the slave trade:

> During our present difficulties and distress no slaves ought to be imported into any of the British colonies on this continent. And we take this opportunity of declaring our most earnest wishes to see an entire stop forever put to such a wicked, cruel and unnatural trade.

Cynically, the Fairfax Resolves proposed abstaining from human trafficking only temporarily, long enough to protest new British rules that they felt demeaned them as slaves, but knowing full well that they would, as soon as the political crisis passed, resume the importation of enslaved Africans to their plantations.

CHAPTER THIRTEEN

"Improving Our Fortunes"

The complete collapse of commerce in Boston thanks to the Coercive Acts left John Adams without any legal work: "I don't receive a shilling a week."[1] He soon found unexpected new employment: The Massachusetts Assembly chose the two Adams cousins among its five delegates to the First Continental Congress in Philadelphia.

Of the seventy-three delegates from thirteen colonies, the majority were lawyers or had studied law, among them several English barristers trained at the Inns of Court in London. Twenty-seven delegates were primarily merchants; virtually all the delegates from Virginia and South Carolina were planters as well as merchants; many were involved in western land speculation.

Soon after delegates divided into committees, Governor William Franklin crossed from New Jersey to collaborate with Joseph Galloway, conservative Speaker of the Pennsylvania Assembly and Benjamin Franklin's longtime chief lieutenant.

Modifying the elder Franklin's Albany Plan of Union, Galloway, supported by Governor Franklin and conservative delegates, called for a grand legislative council elected triennially by the legislatures of all the colonies and meeting annually with a president approved by the king and serving at his pleasure.

Whereas Benjamin Franklin's plan had merely called for a union of all the colonies to facilitate defense against Indian attacks and to adjudicate land claims, the Galloway plan went much further.

At Governor Franklin's suggestion, the American legislature was to be connected to Parliament and would send delegates from America to sit in the House of Commons, providing actual representation of Americans in Parliament and addressing a major cause of the unrest of the 1760s. Either Parliament or the American council could propose laws for the colonies, but both must approve them. The underlying principle of the Galloway Plan of Union was that no law could bind America without her consent.

Pennsylvania's chief delegate to Congress, Galloway had the support of moderates in the Middle Colonies and South Carolina. When Galloway presented the plan to Congress, Samuel Adams introduced a motion to table it, which passed by a 6–5 vote. Soon after it was shelved, a box was delivered to Galloway's Market Street mansion containing a hangman's noose and orders to use it himself or else a mob would; accompanying it was a torn life-insurance policy. Galloway abruptly withdrew the motion and retired to his Bucks County farm.

Adhering to its policy of making unanimous each delegation's votes, the First Continental Congress voted to withdraw Galloway's plan, then voted to expunge it entirely from its minutes.

In its place, Congress drafted a moderately worded Declaration of Rights and Grievances, essentially a collaboration by Jonathan Dickinson and John Adams. It went beyond the assertions of the Stamp Act Congress of 1765 of Americans' right to representation and internal governance to acknowledge that the colonists would "cheerfully consent"—Adams's words—to some limited regulation of their trade. Because the declaration asserted that approval of some measures could be withdrawn, it implied that Parliament did not have authority in all cases whatsoever, as it had ruled after repealing the Stamp Act.[2]

Adams's phrase touched off an acrimonious three-day debate. James Duane of New York insisted that Parliament's authority was a fundamental principle of the unwritten English constitution and could not be withdrawn by any colony: "There must be some supreme controlling power over our trade, and that this can only rest with Parliament."[3]

Samuel Ward of Rhode Island declared that Parliament had no right whatsoever to regulate the colonies' trade, arguing that "one kingdom should not be governed by another," especially since Parliament had become thoroughly corrupt—"subject to the Frowns, Flatteries and Bribes" of a self-aggrandizing Ministry. As a whole, Ward contended, the English people as a result had become "immersed in luxury, riot and dissipation."[4]

When the Declaration was put to a vote, the delegations divided, five in favor, five against, with two delegations, Massachusetts and Rhode Island, split.

According to Congress's rules, Adams's statement of American rights had been defeated. But at dinner at John Dickinson's that evening, the discussion apparently swayed at least one of the guests. The next morning, Congress voted to retain Adams's strong wording.

Along with Congress's assertion of the colonies' rights, the declaration criticized revenue laws imposed by Parliament since 1763: extension of vice admiralty jurisdiction over customs cases, dissolution of colonial assemblies, and the stationing of a standing army in seaport towns in peacetime. Among ten resolutions, the petition enumerated the rights of colonists, including "life, liberty and property," as well as the exclusive power of provincial legislatures "in all cases of taxation and internal polity, subject only to royal veto."

After pledging to continue economic sanctions against Britain until Parliament repealed all thirteen acts passed since 1763 that violated American charter rights, delegates argued for three weeks over what exports, if any, would be exempted.

The Southern colonies, most dependent on exports, won a one-year delay on implementation of the ban. Unsatisfied, South Carolina's delegates, pointing out that 65 percent of their rice harvest and 100 percent of their indigo crop was exported to Britain, while only 5 percent of New England's market was in England, threatened to leave Congress unless their crops were exempted. After two South Carolina delegates walked out, Sam Adams brokered a compromise, exempting rice.

In its first step toward acting as a governing body for all the colonies, Congress drafted the Articles of Association to bind all Americans to uphold the ban on all British imports—including slaves. Congress's members pledged to

> neither import nor purchase any slave imported after the first day of December next; after which time we will wholly discontinue the slave trade, and will neither hire our vessels nor sell our commodities or manufactures to those who are concerned in it.

The Articles of Association for the first time not only required all Americans to honor the sanctions but made violators accountable to the public. Local committees were charged with enforcement: Some seven thousand Americans overnight would become legal enforcers of the embargo. The names of offenders would be published: "All such foes of the rights of British America may be publicly known, and universally condemned as the enemies of American liberty."

Delegates went so far as to pledge that any colony found in violation of the Articles of Association would not only face ostracism but would be publicized as "unworthy of the rights of freemen and as inimical to the liberties of their country."[5]

As historian Richard Beeman put it, "In both its economic and political contexts, the Association was a genuinely radical document. It asked the American people, and American merchants in particular, to make significant sacrifices. At the same time, it asked the American colonies to submit themselves to the authority of a superior entity."[6]

Congress shipped off its declaration to London, where King George treated it with pure contempt. He had already made clear his opinion of the colonies' behavior.

On August 23, the day before the declaration was to be delivered, the king issued his Proclamation Suppressing Rebellion and Sedition. The king believed the imperial crisis had been caused by "many of our subjects in divers parts of Our Colonies" being "misled by dangerous and ill-designing men" who were to blame for "disorderly Acts," the "obstruction of lawful Commerce, and . . . the Oppression of Our loyal Subjects."

The colonies were now in "open and avowed rebellion"; the rebels were "traitorously preparing, ordering, and levying War against US." When Lord Dartmouth finally presented Congress's declaration to the king in September, George III never even looked at it.[7]

Throughout the colonies, objections to the trade boycott had become dangerous for any dissenters. An article in the *New York Journal* illustrates how suppression of dissent became cruel, systematic, and ritualized. In Piscataway, New Jersey, Thomas Randolph, a cooper, "had publicly proved himself an enemy to his country by reviling and using his utmost endeavors to oppose the proceedings of the Continental and Provincial Conventions and Committees in defense of their rights and liberties." His sentence: tarring and feathering. In frigid December weather, the local Sons of Liberty stripped off his clothing, broke open a fresh barrel of pine tar, and, heating it in an iron cauldron until it was bubbling hot and thin enough to spread, applied it to Randolph's head, face, and body with ladles and brushes until all his skin shriveled and blistered, giving off a rancid steam into the crisp winter air. He must have screamed and pleaded for mercy.

Then the Patriots slit open his mattress with their knives and, dancing and cheering around his strange-looking form, sprinkled sharp-tipped goose feathers all over his roasting, stinking flesh. If, as sometimes happened, the sizzling tar ignited a few of the feathers, they could be beaten out readily enough, even though by this time the slightest touch would make Randolph scream again.

As the *Journal* recounted, Randolph was "carried in a wagon round the town. He soon became duly sensible of his offense, for which he earnestly begged pardon and promised to atone, as far as he was able."

After a half hour, Randolph was released and allowed to return to his home. "The whole was conducted with that regularity and decorum that ought to be observed in all public punishments."[8]

At the opening of Parliament on November 30, King George read a belligerent speech from the throne in which he rejected a petition from the City of London beseeching the king to define the terms of a just and honorable peace before unleashing the full force of British arms against the colonists.

George III said he regretted the miseries his subjects had "brought upon themselves by an unjustifiable resistance to the constitutional authority of this Kingdom." He denounced Congress's "most daring spirit of resistance and disobedience to law" and reiterated his "firm and steadfast resolution to withstand every attempt to weaken or impair the supreme authority of this Legislature over all the dominions of [his] Crown." Until royal authority could be reestablished and the "now existing rebellion is at an end, there would be no peace." British arms would force the colonists back into subjection.

A bill to withdraw the troops from Boston and negotiate a settlement of colonial grievances proposed by Lord Chatham went down to raucous defeat, 68–18. When Chatham then called for a repeal of all the acts that had enflamed Americans in exchange for American acknowledgment of parliamentary supremacy, he was again shouted down, 61–31.

In February 1775, the Houses of Commons and Lords declared Massachusetts in a rebellion aided by illegal organizations in other colonies and ratified the king's decision "to enforce due obedience" to Parliament "by the most effectual measures." Adopting the New England Restraining Act, Parliament cut off New Englanders' access to the North Atlantic fisheries, the primary source of the region's sustenance, at the same time restricting its trade.

Some moderate delegates, such as the English-born merchant Robert Morris, had been staving off a decision about independence. Morris, the illegitimate son of a Liverpool tobacco broker, had grown up in Oxford on Maryland's eastern shore. With his partner, Thomas Willing, he had grown rich building ships in Philadelphia and, like his father, cramming them with tobacco from the Chesapeake, selling or trading their cargoes at handsome profits in the Caribbean for transshipment to Europe. The question of loyalties was tortuous. But the king's response to the merchants of the City of London "totally destroyed all hopes of reconciliation," Morris wrote, and made "a declaration of Independency inevitable."[9]

Delegates to the Continental Congress did not learn of the king's refusal to read their petition, or of his Proclamation for Suppressing Rebellion and Sedition, until mid-November, so slow was transatlantic communication. It would be early January 1776 before the king's speech from the throne reached America.

The news evoked a mixed reaction in Congress. John Adams's correspondence contained no hint of the royal rejection, possibly because Congress had passed a resolution on November 9 imposing stricter rules of secrecy signed by every member that provided that "if any member shall violate this agreement he shall be expelled [from] this Congress and deemed an enemy to the liberties of America."

John Dickinson, principal author of the conciliatory petition to the king, could not conceal his disappointment: "Neither Mercy nor Justice was to be expected from Great Britain." It was now too late to turn back: Congress had "drawn the sword and thrown away the scabbard."[10]

In late February 1776, newspapers arrived from London with word that Parliament had passed the American Prohibitory Act. Congress learned that, since New Year's Day, American ships sailing off the British Isles had been subject to seizure. From March 1, the act provided, all colonial ships bound for or sailing from American ports were to be seized and confiscated by the Royal Navy.

While New England ships had already been blockaded, now all the colonies' maritime commerce would be subject to seizure. Parliament had resolved to wage economic as well as political and military warfare.

The trade of the Southern colonies for the first time would be targets. Three weeks later, Congress threw open all American ports to foreign trade.

Driving into Philadelphia in May 1774, George Washington had assured a critic that he had no desire "to set up for Independence," fearing "the horrors of civil discord." After all, his first American forebear had fled the English civil wars of the seventeenth century.[11] But by the time he rode home to Mount Vernon at the end of the First Continental Congress in October, Washington passed militia drilling in every town. He realized, from the mood of the country and of Congress, that not only economic but armed warfare was now inevitable.

Washington could see that a decade of ideological ferment and partisan protests over Britain's fumbling attempts to formulate imperial trade policies had finally boiled over into open rebellion. He set out at once to train militia, at first drilling a single company, then recruiting and training a second company to act as a defensive force for Virginia.

All winter, the drift toward war continued. In the spring, reluctantly laying aside any thought of a visit to his western lands, Washington, preparing to return to Philadelphia for the Second Continental Congress, packed his red-and-blue British brigadier's uniform.

In New England, the resistance movement was winning followers, especially merchants. In Connecticut, the general assembly commissioned two new independent companies, each recruited, outfitted, and paid by wealthy ship owners.

Jonathan Trumbull, now the royal governor, anonymously drafted resolutions for the general assembly, ordering all towns to double their arsenals of powder, balls, and flint. Connecticut also mustered six new regiments of militia, upwards of six thousand men in a colony of one hundred thousand citizens.

The assembly dispatched fast ships to the Caribbean to purchase weapons and gunpowder and ordered all militia to train for twelve days, double the normal term of service, paying them six shillings a day, double the wages of a skilled artisan.

In March 1775, a purge of the leadership of old militia units swept a dozen officers from their posts, including any suspected of being Loyalists, their offices invariably going to the most radical Patriots, the Sons of Liberty. Thoroughly intimidated, more than 1,100 Loyalists from all over New England fled from their homes into Boston, seeking British protection.

Over the winter, George Washington decided to leave the management of his business interests to family members. To his brother, John Augustine, he wrote that he expected a militia command. "It is my full intention to devote my life and fortune in the cause we are engaged in, if need be."[12]

To his longtime friend and neighbor George William Fairfax, who had fled to England, he wrote, "The once happy and peaceful plains of America are either to be drenched in blood, or inhabited by slaves. Sad alternative! But can a virtuous man hesitate in his choice?"[13]

In late April 1775, Washington learned that Lord Dunmore had sent royal marines to seize Virginia's supply of gunpowder at Williamsburg. The next day, a rider dispatched to Mount Vernon brought him the first fragmentary account of fighting in Massachusetts.

CHAPTER FOURTEEN

" 'Tis Time to Part"

In his open two-horse carriage, John Hancock surely made for an impressive sight as he hurtled south toward Philadelphia. It was springtime in New England, and more than a year after he had been selected as a Massachusetts delegate for the Second Continental Congress, Hancock was journeying toward a meeting that would lead to war—and, perhaps, disaster for the colonies. In the carriage with him was his rumpled mentor, Samuel Adams. Hancock's selection to serve beside him was a testament to his high regard at home, earned as much by his considerable wealth as by his fierce patriotism.

Inheriting at age twenty-six from his childless uncle the helm of the House of Hancock, the Bay Colony's largest business enterprise, the hardworking Harvard graduate became New England's leading merchant. John Adams observed that Hancock had become "an example to all the young men of the town. Wholly devoted to business, he was as regular and punctual at his store as the sun in his course."[1]

After a year's visit to London to cement the firm's ties with its brokers, Hancock set Boston's fashions, ordering from London a vast wardrobe of frilled shirts, gilt-edged jackets and breeches, and silver-buckled shoes. And when John Hancock ordered a scarlet velvet jacket, Boston's young blades followed suit.

Hancock employed hundreds of people in retail stores, as well as on

the fleet of ships built to cart whale oil to Britain and return crammed
with Madeira wine, tea, and luxury goods. As his empire grew, Hancock
would typically construct several stores and warehouses at a time, hiring
hundreds of otherwise unemployed skilled workers. Countless New
Englanders depended on him for their livelihood.

Tapping his wealth to bankroll a nascent political movement, Hancock had become the most popular radical leader in Boston, largely because of his largesse. His workers rewarded his generosity by electing
him first as a selectman, then as a provincial legislator, and then—the
city's highest honor—as moderator of the Boston town meeting. He had
emerged as a spokesman for Boston's shopkeepers and merchants. Appointed to the province's general court, he had served on thirty committees, resolving disputes while—or by—hosting lavish dinners at taverns
and at his Beacon Hill mansion. His popularity soared when, after the
Boston Tea Party, he shipped back to England at his own expense all the
tea in his warehouses.

His dedication to the cause had not waned with the threat of war. As
colonel of the city's Corps of Cadets, he had spent £100,000 (about $15
million today) of his own money to purchase cannon, ammunition to
equip the Boston Train Band of Artillery, and uniforms and muskets for
the militia. In March 1775, Samuel Adams selected Hancock to deliver
the annual Massacre Day oration, spotlighting Hancock as an outspoken
critic of the British occupation. At the podium of Faneuil Hall, they had
become visible if unlikely partners in leading the resistance movement
in Massachusetts, the elegantly attired merchant and the rumpled Son of
Liberty.

In April, Hancock had fled Boston with Adams when the British
commander, Sir Thomas Gage, received orders from London for their
arrest on treason charges. They had hidden in a church basement in
Woburn while Redcoats searched for them in Lexington and Concord.
Before they escaped, Hancock had insisted on outfitting Adams in a new
suit; he could not represent Massachusetts in the Continental Congress
in his usual heedless garb.

Hancock's carriage finally rolled into Philadelphia on May 10, 1775, just as Britain's Major General Sir Henry Clinton was installing himself in Hancock's Beacon Hill mansion. Hancock had managed to bring with him to the first meeting of the Second Continental Congress large amounts of gold and silver and letters of credit—including the entire treasury of Harvard College. As the college's treasurer, he had been entrusted to invest its endowment. Fearing it would fall into British hands, he had taken the treasury with him to Philadelphia. He would later return it, somewhat miffed that anyone had doubted he would.

On that same day, on orders from provincial congresses in Massachusetts and Connecticut, Ethan Allen and Benedict Arnold, along with eighty-nine members of the Green Mountain Boys, charged through the gates of Fort Ticonderoga on Lake Champlain, seizing its vital cannon.

John Hancock was not the only businessman to arrive in Philadelphia. Connecticut's delegation to the Second Continental Congress consisted almost entirely of land speculators who were now blocked by royal decree from the lucrative fur trade being taken over by the British. It was Wethersfield merchant Silas Deane who, as secretary of the Connecticut committee of correspondence, had "borrowed" £300 (about $45,000 today) from the colony's treasury to obtain gold and silver coins to finance Ethan Allen's mission to take control of the Lake Champlain forts. Deane obtained the coins from Christopher Leffingwell, whose family managed several flourishing businesses, including the manufacture of paper—a scarce commodity—and chocolates. Leffingwell was the captain of the Norwich Light Infantry, a cavalry unit composed of businessmen and their clerks.

Ethan Allen knew Silas Deane as a fellow shareholder and prime mover in the Susquehanna Land Company, which sought a royal grant to a wide swath of land in northern Pennsylvania stretching from the Delaware River to Lake Erie. With the support of the powerful faction of Connecticut's governor, Jonathan Trumbull, also a Susquehanna Company shareholder, Deane had been proselytizing the company's cause to fellow congressional delegates.

Son of a prosperous second-generation blacksmith who had served in Connecticut's assembly, Deane had attended Yale College on a full scholarship and taught school while studying law. He had married wealthy widows twice: his first wife was a member of the Webb commercial clan; his second, the daughter of former governor Gurdon Saltonstall. Tapping his marital network to become a rich merchant and ship owner, he had entered politics during the Townshend Act protests and had served in the assembly since 1768.

By the time John Hancock reached town, Benjamin Franklin had been in Philadelphia for days, having arrived from his London crossing on May 5. The morning after, the Pennsylvania provincial congress elected Franklin a member of its delegation in the Continental Congress and appointed him chairman of the colony's Committee of Safety.

With Franklin at its helm, Pennsylvania ordered munitions from the French and Spanish West Indies. Once again, Franklin would be in a position to protect his properties, which would certainly be in easy cannon range of British warships. He wrote to a friend in Parliament of finding "the commencement of a civil war with all ranks of people in arms, disciplining themselves morning and evening."[2]

During the first weeks of the congressional session, Franklin was largely silent, seeming to colleagues to be more spectator than participant. After spending most of the past two decades in England, he felt himself a stranger among strangers. But there may have been a deeper reason.

On his third day back in America, disturbed by reports of his son's pro-British activities, Franklin dashed off an angry note to William, decrying his continuance as royal governor of New Jersey. They met briefly when William came to Philadelphia to pick up his own son, Temple, and then again in late May at the home of Joseph Galloway in Bucks County.

Franklin had come to urge his son to resign as governor, and for Galloway, once a close ally of Franklin's, to return to his elected seat in

Congress. Yet, despite his descriptions of his experiences at the hands of the Ministry and his attempts to affect reconciliation between the British government and the colonies, he failed to sway either man. He left heartily disgusted with his son's thoroughly British turn of mind. Their decade-long collaboration for an immense grant of western land—the last remaining bond between them—had become a closed chapter. There was no point to discussing it further.

Father and son would meet only twice more before the Revolutionary War. Congress appointed Benjamin postmaster general, giving him an expense account in lieu of a salary. According to his expense ledger, in August 1775, while escorting four wagonloads of gunpowder to Washington's camp in Massachusetts, Franklin stopped off in Perth Amboy, the provincial capital of New Jersey, and again attempted to persuade William to resign as royal governor.

Knowing that William had no other source of income than his governor's modest salary and fees, Benjamin offered his son the salaried postmastership of Philadelphia—at £320 a year, roughly one-fifth the governor's salary—if he would resign his royal post and return to Philadelphia with him. Years later, a London magazine reported that Benjamin also had offered to sign over his entire estate to his son if he would join the revolutionary cause.

In January 1776, the New Jersey Provincial Congress ordered Governor Franklin placed under house arrest. The elder Franklin was astonished to learn that, the previous June, his son had summoned the New Jersey Assembly into a special session in an attempt to reestablish royal authority. Alarmed, the provincial congress had passed a series of resolutions to overthrow the royal government. Acting in "direct contempt" of the Continental Congress, they declared, "William Franklin, Esquire, has discovered himself to be an enemy to the liberties of this country."

In Philadelphia, the Continental Congress debated whether to jail Governor Franklin. Pleading a cold, Benjamin stayed home, abstaining from the vote. Told of Congress's decision, Franklin wrote to his son-in-law, Richard Bache, recipient of the postal job he had offered William, "I have lost my son."[3]

William Franklin's arrest accompanied the disarming of Loyalists in New Jersey and on Long Island, where they made up the majority of property owners. As a radical provincial government seized power, the threat of a civil war loomed.

CHAPTER FIFTEEN

"UNPARDONABLE REBELLION"

Taking his seat with the Massachusetts delegation in the upper chamber of the Pennsylvania State House for the Second Continental Congress, Harvard-educated John Adams seemed surprised to find men he considered to be of marginal education in the tall Windsor chairs around each delegation's green-baize-covered table. One Connecticut delegate had been a shoemaker before entering radical politics; two Pennsylvanians were plain farmers, another a country doctor.

Adams would soon discover that the majority of delegates were educated and among the wealthiest men in America. They included nine plantation owners and five merchants, men of hereditary landed estates and mercantile fortunes. There was a former royal governor and a judge. There were no Quakers, who refused to take oaths, and no Jews—whose religious beliefs precluded many of the wealthiest Americans from serving in the Congress.

As at the First Continental Congress, the majority were men trained in the law if not practicing it professionally. They had served in legislatures and on high courts, had written the charters of hospitals, colleges, and counties; they were men who were not easily intimidated by the idea of writing a new constitution to frame a new government. Five of them were barristers who had been trained in common law at the Inns of Court in London.

There were also graduates of almost every American college: Yale, Princeton, Harvard, Pennsylvania, and William and Mary. And one delegate was a self-employed retired printer from Pennsylvania who had attended school for only a single year but had received honorary doctorates from Oxford and St. Andrews and was a fellow of the Royal Society of England.

In a letter to Abigail at home in Braintree, where she was milking the cows and managing the hired farmhands, Adams characterized his newfound colleagues. James Duane of New York, collection lawyer turned king's counsel, had a "sly, surveying eye"; John Dickinson, a leading radical pamphleteer, was merely "a shadow . . . pale as ashes."[1]

When Congress convened on May 10, 1775, its presidency had been left vacant by the death of Peyton Randolph of Virginia. In choosing his successor, delegates divided along sectional lines. John Adams mustered support for the candidacy of John Hancock over another Virginian.

To more moderate delegates, Adams could tout John Hancock's qualifications, including his extensive experience in the Massachusetts legislature. Conservatives favored Hancock because of his experience as moderator of Boston's town meeting as well as his wealth and business acumen. Samuel Adams's more radical Popular Party backed Hancock because of his outspoken resistance to the British occupation of Boston. On May 24, Hancock won unanimous election as president of the Continental Congress.

Many conservatives were horrified when they learned of the New England radicals' seizure of the Crown forts on Lake Champlain inside New York province. Until then, Congress had preserved the appearance of acting only on the defensive. Seizing £2 million (about $300 million today) of royal property and taking Redcoats and their families as prisoners complicated affairs. At the New York delegation's insistence, Congress voted to remove the captured cannons to Fort Edward, at the southern tip of Lake George, and take an "exact inventory" so that they could later be "safely returned" to the British.

George Washington was appointed to chair a defense committee after a thorough review triggered six days of debate over general defense preparations, recruitment bounties, and a final attempt at reconciliation with Britain. Congress approved Washington's recommendation to fortify King's Bridge on the Harlem River, erect batteries on either bank of the Hudson, and enlist three thousand volunteers.

As the only delegate in uniform, Washington made a vivid impression. Silas Deane described his "easy, soldier-like air and gestures."[2] John Adams, writing to Abigail, admired Washington's "cool but determined Stile and Accent."[3]

Washington's experience as a military logician led to his next appointment, as chairman of the committee on military supply. As each week brought Washington more duties, President Hancock appointed him to the board of financial estimate—all the other board members were merchants.

In the spring of 1775, Congress could do little more to aid New England than ask interior towns to send gunpowder to the ill-equipped militia barricading the British inside Boston. Washington urged Congress—and Congress heeded his advice—to recruit "expert marksmen" from the backwoods of Virginia and Pennsylvania to march to Boston and be placed "under the senior officer of the army."

But who exactly would take command of a continental army? From which colony would he come? John Adams had been working after hours to gain support for his contention that, unless the leader came from outside Massachusetts, the other colonies would fear New England's domination. To him, the obvious choice had to be a Virginian. Virginians outnumbered Massachusetts and New York men of fighting age five to one; Virginia's troops, crops, and money would be vital.

On May 14, Washington listened as Adams lectured Congress on the need for other colonies to support the New England army. What could be better than to appoint a seasoned veteran who represented all the colonies? On the dais, where he was presiding, Hancock brightened when Adams said he had one man in mind—then reddened when Adams said the man he had in mind came from Virginia.

Thunderstruck, Washington stood up and practically ran from the room. Ushered back in, he was informed that "all America" wanted him. He stayed away the next day, asking his friend and fellow delegate Edmund Pendleton to help him draw up two documents: his acceptance speech and his will. Washington declined Congress's offer of a £500 monthly salary (about $75,000 today), asking only for reimbursement of his expenses.

To Martha, he wrote that he had been "apprehensive" that he might be appointed but that it was "utterly out of [his] power to refuse." It would add to his "uneasy feelings" if she were "complaining at what I really could not avoid."[4] Sending his carriage back to Mount Vernon, Washington purchased five horses and a lightweight phaeton.

Early on the morning of June 23, 1775, escorted by congressmen who got up to see him off, General Washington rode north on the Post Road escorted by Philadelphia's First City Troop, a band playing as they passed still-shuttered shops. Crossing largely Loyalist New Jersey with no armed escort, Washington disguised himself by pulling a purple smock over his blue uniform and donning a hat with a tall plume.

He carried a letter of introduction from President Hancock to Dr. James Warren, president of the Massachusetts Provincial Congress, assuring him that Washington was "a gentleman you will all like."[5]

When Washington reached Cambridge on July 3, he found that nearly four hundred Americans had been killed in the Battle of Bunker Hill. The British had won the field but at the terrible cost of 1,054 casualties, a high proportion of them officers.

Taking command of 14,500 New England militia whom he had to quickly train to be the Continental Army, Washington saw himself—and the British saw him—as the Oliver Cromwell of the American Revolution.

Like Cromwell, he saw the struggle as a civil war, with virtuous American colonists oppressed by a corrupt ministry in the service of an errant king. Like Cromwell, he was a member of the aggrieved squirearchy and of the Continental Congress, which, like Cromwell's Parliament, opposed the wicked ministry and its army by fielding its own army to force reforms.

Also like Cromwell, this descendant of English royalists saw that the army, including its generals, must be subservient to the wishes of elected politicians. The people voted for congressional delegates, not for him. Checking at every step with Congress, Washington set about imposing order and discipline.

In July 1775, a full year before voting on independence, Congress, clearly in defiance of British orders-in-council, resolved that any ship transporting munitions to America from "the Continent" could load and export goods in exchange. Congress appropriated funds for selected merchants to procure gunpowder for the Continental Army—at a 5 percent commission.

In September, Congress created the Committee on Secret Correspondence, empowering its members—merchants John Alsop and Philip Livingston of New York and Thomas Willing and Robert Morris of Philadelphia—to draw £50,000 (about $7.5 million today) from the Continental treasury to buy one million rounds of gunpowder, ten thousand muskets, and forty cannon.

Within days, Congress also created the Secret Committee on Trade, capitalizing on its members' global commercial contacts and their own vast credit. Samuel Ward, a merchant and the former governor of Rhode Island, served as chair. John Alsop, Philip Livingston, and Francis Lewis of New York joined Silas Deane of Connecticut and Robert Morris and Benjamin Franklin of Pennsylvania in the committee's secret proceeding.

Building on Willing and Morris's existing network, Morris singled out twenty-four-year-old William Bingham as the committee's principal agent in the Caribbean. Son of a prominent merchant and holder of a master's degree from the College of Philadelphia (today's University of Pennsylvania), young Bingham owned several ships. He had already worked with Franklin as secretary to the Committee on Secret Correspondence.

In a joint committee appointment, Franklin and Morris commissioned him to sail to Martinique, where he was to pose as a private merchant while cultivating diplomatic connections with the French government for the Committee on Secret Correspondence and purchasing ten thousand muskets for the Secret Committee on Trade. He was also to purchase a shipload of gunpowder under a contract between Willing and Morris and the colony of Virginia and, taking half share for himself, a shipment of linens and other French finery on Morris's private account.

Morris warned Bingham that the risk of capture of these ships was high, but so were profits: "One arrival will pay for 2 or 3 or 4 losses."[6]

Morris had been bracing for the inevitable British reprisal for the Boston Tea Party. Under the terms of the Continental Association's boycott, all imports from the British Empire were to shut down by December 1, 1775. In anticipation, European mercantile houses were tightening credit terms for American merchants. Morris's firm loaded all its ships with cargoes of tobacco, wheat, and flour and, drawing on its network of partners, dispatched between fifty and sixty ships to its network of brokers in Spain, Portugal, Italy, and England.

Morris instructed his correspondents to use the proceeds of the sale of the cargoes to pay all his debts in Europe and to request from banking firms in London and Rotterdam "bills at long sight"—letters of credit with long-term maturation dates that would give Morris credit to draw on in the event of a protracted crisis with Britain. In addition to the first flotilla of merchantmen, by late December 1774, Morris dispatched two fast new twenty-ton vessels that could make two transatlantic deliveries in only four months.[7]

With the British blockade tightening, Morris saw a new commercial opportunity. As he wrote to Silas Deane in France, "The Scarcity of Goods all over this Continent affords a fine opportunity to private adventurers." Foreseeing handsome profits for hard-to-get everyday necessities, he ordered "Woolens & Linens, Pins, needles, etc. etc. suited for the consumption of this country."[8]

Morris had emerged as America's leading capitalist by January 1776, when the Secret Committee on Trade issued its largest contracts, requisitioning $300,000 (roughly $9 million today) in congressional funds to purchase arms, gunpowder, and cloth for uniforms, tents, and sails. While the order was divided among eight contractors, Morris's firm received fully half.

When Samuel Ward died of smallpox in March, Congress voted unanimously to appoint Morris chairman of the Secret Committee on Trade. No one voted against him, even if some members expressed reservations. When Horatio Gates asked John Adams his opinion of Morris, Adams confided, "He has vast designs in the mercantile way and no doubt pursues mercantile ends, which are always gain, but he is an excellent member of our body."[9]

Once George III declared the American colonies in rebellion, the Royal Navy issued orders to its ships' captains "to proceed as in the case of actual rebellion against such of the sea-port towns and places, being accessible to the king's ships, in which any troops shall be raised or military works erected."

In October 1775, Captain Henry Mowat of the HMS *Canceaux* issued an ultimatum to the people of Falmouth, Massachusetts (today the city of Portland, Maine). "After so many premeditated Attacks on the legal Prerogatives of the best of Sovereigns" and "the most unpardonable Rebellion" of the townspeople, he intended to "execute a just Punishment." After negotiations, Mowat agreed to hold his fire until the next morning if the townspeople surrendered their cannon and muskets and gave hostages. When Falmouth sent him only a handful of weapons, *Canceaux* bombarded the town with hot shot. "Hundreds of helpless women and children" fled in wagons with their belongings piled high as flames engulfed the town's structures. Mowat's gunners kept firing until, as he later reported, "the whole town was involved in smoak and combustion."[10]

George Washington rushed news of the raid to Congress, describing the attack on Falmouth as a "horrid procedure" and warning that "the same Desolation is meditated upon all the Towns on the Coast."[11]

In early November, Lord Dunmore, aboard HMS *Fowey*, declared Virginia under martial law and issued a proclamation emancipating all slaves and indentured servants who would flee their rebellious masters and rally to the king's colors. In Norfolk Harbor, the colony's principal seaport, Dunmore assembled a small navy of merchant ships and sloops-of-war. At Great Bridge, twelve miles to the south, Dunmore ordered a wooden fort built to protect Loyalists and Scottish merchants from coastal Virginia and the Eastern Shore of Maryland who sought British protection.

To oppose Dunmore, nine hundred buckskin-clad riflemen from the Virginia and North Carolina backcountry—the British called them "shirtmen"—built a fort. John Page, the second-in-command of Virginia's militia, rushed word to the Continental Congress in Philadelphia that the Virginia troops faced "a body" of armed runaway slaves "headed by Scotsmen and a few regulars."[12]

The night of December 8, Dunmore reinforced his outpost with Redcoats, gunners from British ships, and Loyalist volunteers. The first land battle of the Revolution in the South, the Battle of Great Bridge, broke out the next morning. Only three Redcoats reached the American line. One hundred Virginians poured their fire into them at close range. In all, 102 grenadiers died, a worse casualty rate than at Bunker Hill.

On New Year's Day 1776, Lord Dunmore ordered Norfolk's warehouses destroyed. Virginia's principal port burned for five days. Nine-tenths of the town was destroyed.

Congress did not learn of the burning of Norfolk until January 8, the same day it learned of the king's speech declaring the colonies in open rebellion. To make matters worse, news arrived that a British fleet had departed Cork, Ireland, laden with five thousand Redcoats, its sails set for American shores. The news that black slaves had fought alongside British regulars—40 percent of Virginians were enslaved—sent a collective shudder down the backs of slave owners. The prospect of a massive slave insurrection with blacks supporting the British in a civil war alarmed the planter class, including George Washington.

CHAPTER SIXTEEN

"INDEPENDENCE LIKE A TORRENT"

With the arrival of each ship from Britain, and each dispatch from Washington's headquarters, the drumbeat for independence intensified. Hard on the heels of London newspapers carrying the king's denunciation of the colonists as "traitors" and reports of the burning of Norfolk came Thomas Paine's publication of his pamphlet *Common Sense*.

With its angry rhetoric and clear, blunt language, *Common Sense* flayed the monarchical form of government, attacking George III as "the Royal Brute" chiefly responsible for obnoxious measures against the colonies. Advocating a complete break with Britain on practical as well as ideological grounds, it called for an immediate declaration of independence.

Read aloud in taverns, it became the bestselling publication in America overnight. Within three months, *Common Sense* sold 150,000 copies. Eventual sales of 500,000 copies made it proportionally far and away the most popular work ever published in America. Paine would donate all its royalties to support the Continental Army.

A dismissed former customs officer in England, Paine had arrived in Philadelphia during the First Continental Congress with a recommendation from Benjamin Franklin, who arranged for Paine to edit his *Pennsylvania Magazine*. Paine was soon editing its rival publication, the highly successful *American Magazine*.

But even as Paine urged Americans to rise up against the British, George Washington remained increasingly skeptical about the prospect of equipping an army "without any money in our treasury, powder in our magazines, arms in our stores. . . . And by and by, when we shall be called upon to take the field, shall not have a tent to lie in."[1]

As the colonies girded for war, they searched for weapons in gun shops, trading houses, and private homes, settling for an array of muskets, rifles, fowling pieces, pistols, and blunderbusses. Some volunteers had no weapons at all, possessing only pikes or swords. Washington even considered sending unarmed militia home.

In Pennsylvania, Franklin's Committee of Safety advertised for weapons in the newspapers. In South Carolina, the people of Charleston lacked weapons and ammunition until they broke into royal magazines and took some thousand muskets, then seized a British brig carrying twenty-three thousand pounds of gunpowder. In New York City, the few cannon available lined the parapets of Fort George on the Battery until King's College students, led by twenty-year-old Alexander Hamilton, dragged them away under fire from a British man-of-war to arm the first artillery company in the Continental Army.

Like most of Virginia's leaders, Thomas Jefferson had remained ambivalent about independence as late as the summer of 1775, unwilling to contemplate a total break with the mother country. In August, he wrote to John Randolph, his cousin in England, that he was "looking with fondness" toward "a reconciliation" with Britain and a "return of the happy period when, consistently with duty, I may withdraw myself totally from the public stage and pass the rest of my days in domestic ease and tranquility."[2]

By November, he had shifted his ground and was blaming the king as well as Parliament for the out-of-control pace of attacks and reprisals. Inching closer to supporting independence, he warned Randolph that Americans lacked "neither inducement nor power to declare and assert a separation."[3] The shocking news that the British had burned Norfolk made Jefferson agree with Paine's insistence that the time for talking was over. The specter of British troops seizing his property and sending him in irons to England for trial as a traitor banished any further hesitation.

Jefferson arrived in Philadelphia on May 14, 1776, after an eight-day ride on horseback from Monticello, escorted only by his slave valet Bob Hemmings. In his first year as a delegate, Jefferson had arrived with an entourage of three liveried slaves, a carriage, and four horses, but he had learned that to stable a horse cost nearly double his own lodgings in a boardinghouse.

After one week, he moved to a more commodious two-room apartment at Seventh and Market Streets, only a two-block walk from the statehouse. Jefferson took his seat in Congress just as delegates were concluding an acrimonious debate over John Adams's motion calling on all colonies to establish their own state governments, a step just short of declaring their independence.

At the same time, in Williamsburg, the Virginia Convention was debating a resolution calling for the Continental Congress to vote for independence.

In Philadelphia, the congressional delegations divided sharply, 6–4, with two abstentions. Delegates of New York, Pennsylvania, Maryland, Delaware, and New Jersey insisted they had not been empowered by their provincial conventions to vote for independence.

Dickinson and Wilson of Pennsylvania and Robert R. Livingston of New York, representing colonies with major ports and the bulk of the foreign trade, joined planter Edward Rutledge of South Carolina in professing they were "friends" to Virginia's resolution but opposed adopting it at the time, declining "to take any capital step till the voice of the people drove us into it." Without the public's "power," no declaration would be effective. If such a vote were taken, the Middle Colonies' delegates would "retire" from Congress; their colonies might "secede from the union."

Proponents of an immediate declaration, including John Adams and the Virginians, countered that until all the colonies declared for independence, no European power would negotiate with them or even allow

American ships to enter their waters. Such a split would certainly "discourage any foreign power from [joining] themselves to our fortunes."

John Adams was so confident of an imminent vote on a declaration of independence that, ignoring the congressional embargo on personal correspondence, he wrote exultantly home to Abigail, "Every post and every day rolls in upon us, independence like a torrent."[4]

For the first time, Congress was blaming the king, not just his ministers, for America's grievances, a critical step. Customarily, the king was regarded as being above parliamentary politics. Accusations extended to him only when grievances became so general and his personal complicity so evident that the authority of his government could be questioned.

A public attack on the king was a recognizable constitutional form—an announcement of a revolution. The specific charges by this time included the Prohibitory Act, which removed America from the king's protection, and his refusal to answer Americans' petitions for redress of grievances.

In early May, Congress learned from a Cork newspaper that Britain was sending an additional forty thousand troops to America, including German mercenaries and Scots Highlanders. Obtaining smuggled copies of treaties that documented the king's alliance with German cousins to provide rented troops, Congress ordered the treaties published in Philadelphia newspapers—along with alarming news from Canada.

A two-pronged American invasion there had ended in disaster, with nearly a thousand men killed or captured. Its joint commanders were among the casualties: General Richard Montgomery had been killed; Colonel Benedict Arnold seriously wounded. Thousands of reinforcements rushed from Massachusetts were dying of smallpox. On May 24 General Washington returned to Philadelphia from Cambridge to report to Congress that he expected a massive counterattack on New York, where he could muster, at most, only seven thousand troops fit for duty.

On Friday, June 7, 1776, a courier arrived in Congress with word that Virginia's convention had resolved unanimously to instruct its delegates "to declare the United Colonies free and independent states." Richard Henry Lee rose and read aloud, "Resolved, That these colonies are and of a right ought to be free and independent states, that they are absolved from all allegiance to the British Crown and that all political connection between them and the state of Great Britain is, and ought to be, totally dissolved." John Adams seconded the motion.

But royal governments were still functioning. The Continental Congress was meeting on the ground floor of the Pennsylvania State House; upstairs, the Pennsylvania Assembly was still in session.

Conservatives strenuously disagreed with Adams and Lee. According to notes Adams kept, Duane of New York demanded to know, "Why all this haste? Why all this driving?" Duane considered the May 15 Virginia resolution "a machine for the fabrication of independence." James Wilson of Pennsylvania rose to add his objection: "Before we are prepared to build a new house, why should we pull down the old one and expose ourselves to all the inclemencies of the season?"

In a speech, John Dickinson, who was married to a wealthy Quaker, warned the New England delegates they would have "blood on their hands" if they precluded the possibility of peace. Adams jumped to his feet and disagreed vehemently with Dickinson, who pursued Adams from the chamber and angrily demanded to know why "you New England men oppose our measures of reconciliation." Dickinson threatened, "I, and a number of us, will break off from you in New England."[5]

Infuriated by Dickinson's "magisterial" tone, Adams characterized Dickinson as a "piddling genius" in a private letter intercepted by the British and widely published in Loyalist newspapers. Adams wrote to Abigail, "We are not on speaking, nor bowing terms, for the time to come."[6]

At an impasse, on June 11 Congress finally decided to postpone the vote for twenty days to allow reluctant delegates to write home for new instructions. Meanwhile, to avoid a further loss of time, Congress appointed a five-man committee to draft a declaration of independence, its members Jefferson, John Adams, Franklin, Robert Livingston of New York, and Roger Sherman of Connecticut.

Even as they met for the first time to discuss guidelines, dispatches from the warfronts ratcheted up the pressure. Washington reported that a British fleet of 132 ships had sailed from Halifax bound for New York; another fleet of 53 ships was sailing into the waters of Charleston, South Carolina. The defeated Northern Army had evacuated Canada, its smallpox-ridden remnants retreating to Lake Champlain.

When George Washington accepted command of the New England militia besieging Boston, Benjamin Franklin was placed at the head of the committee to draw up his orders, to plan in detail the structure of his chain of command, and to write the declaration Washington was to read to the troops when he formally assumed command.

Drawing on his experience in defending Pennsylvania during the French and Indian War, Franklin wrote to his friend Joseph Priestley in England that he was as busy as he had ever been in his life. His days began at six in the morning with a Committee of Safety meeting; from nine to four, Congress sat.

Franklin's new role reinvigorated his inventiveness. At Bunker Hill, British bayonets had proved devastatingly effective; since American rifles had octagonal barrels, bayonets could not be affixed to them. Thus, Franklin proposed adopting the pike, a short-handled spear used by naval boarding parties. Next, he championed the reintroduction of the English longbow to mitigate the acute shortage of muskets and gunpowder. If his ideas seemed unconventional, it was because, as he grew more implacably opposed to all the talk of accommodation with the British, he looked more and more for chinks in the armor of the superior British forces.

Turning once again to Philadelphia's naval defenses, Franklin's defense committee ordered the construction of twenty-five row galleys—fast, maneuverable fifty-foot boats powered by two dozen stout oarsmen. With auxiliary lateen-rigged sails, they could race up to larger ships and intercept landing craft by sweeping them with shot from small bow- and stern-mounted swivel guns, which he had seen in Scotland.

But it would take more than spears and rowboats to stop huge British men-of-war with heavy cannons and contingents of marines. Franklin had just the idea. The Delaware River was dotted with mid-river islands that made it difficult for men-of-war under full sail to rake the Philadelphia waterfront with broadsides. To enhance these natural defenses, Franklin suggested planting obstacles just below the water's surface. Similar defenses had turned back a British attack on France during King George's War.

Organizing Philadelphia's militia, Franklin selected officers for the armed boats, obtained medicine for the troops, sent gunpowder from the city's magazine to the New York Committee of Safety, and requisitioned some of the lead captured by Allen and Arnold at Fort Ticonderoga.

At the same time he was serving on the committee to import gunpowder, he coauthored a petition to Congress to excuse conscientious objectors to war from military service in exchange for fixed fines in gold, sorely needed for defense. Franklin's defense project deeply impressed his colleagues. His utility multiplied his authority.

Like Washington, Franklin declined a salary but not an expense account. The appointment also gave him control of the gathering, transmittal, and interception of all intelligence.

Congress also commissioned expert printer Franklin to oversee the engraving of Continental money to replace British coins bearing George III's likeness. He arranged the appointment of his son-in-law, Richard Bache, as congressional commissioner of the first American mint.

Traveling with a congressional delegation to Washington's camp at Cambridge, Massachusetts, during a four-day council of war, Franklin advised Washington on the reorganization of the army.

With New England militia enlistments soon to expire, Washington urged recruitment of a better-disciplined, better-supplied Continental Army of twenty thousand men signing up for one-year hitches. The council also formulated articles of war and drafted guidelines for prisoner exchanges and for disposing of the prizes captured by privateers already harassing British supply lines.

Visiting Watertown, Franklin turned over to the Massachusetts Assembly £100 (about $15,000) he had received from friends in England to aid Americans wounded at Lexington and Concord and for the widows and orphans of those killed by British troops. The assembly responded by paying him his four years' overdue stipend as its agent in London.

And, at a dinner, Franklin met Abigail Adams. America's first postmaster general agreed to deliver a letter to her husband. In it, she described Franklin, "whom . . . from my infancy I had been taught to venerate. I found him social but not talkative, and when he spoke something useful dropped from his tongue. He was grave, yet pleasant and affable."[7]

When he returned to Philadelphia, Franklin was assigned to the five-man Secret Committee on Foreign Affairs, the forerunner of the State Department. To facilitate establishing communications "with our friends in Great Britain, Ireland and other parts of the world," Franklin arranged two swift packet vessels. In July 1775, Franklin wrote to Joseph Priestley that Congress had not yet "applied to any foreign power for assistance, nor offered our commerce for their friendship." But the news that the king had hired troops from Hesse and Brunswick removed any doubt that Congress must seek foreign aid.[8]

When the Second Continental Congress adjourned on August 1, 1775, Franklin was selected to serve on its most powerful committee: the standing committee to rule until a new Congress could be elected. Benjamin Franklin had become the king's most resourceful, formidable, and pervasively rebellious subject.

CHAPTER SEVENTEEN

"A Free and Independent People"

Thomas Jefferson and his bride, Martha, were honeymooning at his Albemarle County farm in 1773 when they received word that Martha's father had died. As her one-third share of John Wayles's fortune, Martha Jefferson inherited eleven thousand acres in five counties, along with 135 slaves. Her father left some £30,000 in assets, but he also left £10,000 in debts to British merchants, including a recent consignment of slaves who could not be sold under the Association boycott. Of the balance, Thomas Jefferson was to receive £6,600 (roughly $1.5 million today). He also held his father's shares in the Loyal Company, rival to the old Ohio Company, which he had acquired after surveying the Shenandoah Valley.

It was enough money to make Jefferson feel he could afford a life of comfort, and at last he believed it was safe to abandon his never-profitable law practice. In June 1774, Jefferson ran an ad in the *Virginia Gazette* chastising "the unworthy part" of his law clientele who had not paid their bills. After six years of fruitless drudgework, he had been paid only £797 of the £2,119 he was due. At age thirty-one, Jefferson walked away from the courtroom.

Instead, he decided to devote himself to a life of researching history and international law, writing political philosophy, and improving his landed estates. Atop his mountain, he began to write *A Summary View of the Rights of British North America.*

A neophyte burgess from the westernmost county, he took it upon himself to draw up instructions from the Virginia Convention to its delegates in the First Continental Congress. Couched in the terms of resolutions, he offered for the first time a detailed compendium of America's grievances against king and Parliament. Jefferson sent a copy to Patrick Henry, but Henry apparently never read it. The copy Jefferson dispatched to Peyton Randolph, presiding over the convention, met a better fate. Randolph "laid it on the table for perusal."

One delegate recollected hearing Jefferson's resolutions read aloud and "applause bestowed on most of them." But Jefferson's resolutions were not adopted; there were still many delegates who recoiled at the armed revolt implicit in his ultimatum.[1]

Some of Jefferson's admirers put his *Summary View* through the press in Williamsburg. Before the end of 1774, it was reprinted in Philadelphia and read by members of the First Continental Congress, then reprinted twice anonymously in London, where Jefferson overnight became known as the most radical writer in America.

As historian Pauline Maier put it, *A Summary View* became the first sustained piece of political writing that subjected the king's conduct to direct and pointed criticism. Jefferson's writing ability was so well known to the Continental Congress by the time he was elected in 1775 that, when he arrived in Philadelphia, one of the youngest delegates at only thirty-three, Samuel Ward of Rhode Island, greeted him as "the famous Mr. Jefferson."[2]

When the committee appointed to draw up the declaration met, it voted that Jefferson should be its draftsman. To rivet the attention of the Declaration of Independence's intended audience—the free populace of the thirteen mainland British colonies—Jefferson laid out his major premise: that the step America was taking was necessary, coming reluctantly after many attempts at reconciliation.

Asserting the rule of right reason that philosophers since Thomas Aquinas had taken volumes to argue, Jefferson plunged on to posit the doctrine at the heart of the English revolutions of the seventeenth century, that, as John Knox had put it, "resistance to tyranny is obedience to God." Steering clear of overt antagonism to the idea of kingship in what was sure to be scrutinized throughout a world ruled by monarchs, Jefferson contended that Americans had the right to revolt against a bad king, a tyrant.

In language usually reserved for common criminals, he enumerated eighteen charges intended to prove George III had been guilty of tyranny over his American colonies.

In effect, Jefferson was drawing up a bill of indictment against the king. If he could prove his case, there would be no question that Americans had to renounce their allegiance to a wicked ruler and that, therefore, "these United Colonies are and of right ought to be free and independent states."

At the top of the list of America's grievances, Jefferson placed the American colonies' lack of their own currency. He asserted that the king "refused his assent to laws the most wholesome and necessary for the public good." In both draft documents, Virginia's Declaration of Rights and the Continental Congress's Declaration of Independence, Jefferson was referring to the Currency Act of 1764.

In all his harsh indictments of the king of England, Thomas Jefferson, owner of at least 140 slaves, reserved until last his strongest language, blaming George III personally for the slave trade:

> He had waged cruel war against human nature itself, violating the most sacred rights of life and liberty in the persons of a distant people who never offended him, captivating and carrying them into slavery in another hemisphere, or to incur miserable death in their transportation thither.
>
> This piratical warfare, the opprobrium of *infidel* powers is the warfare of the *Christian* king of Great Britain. Determined to keep open a market where *MEN* should be bought and

sold, he has prostituted his negative for suppressing every legislative attempt to prohibit or restrain this execrable commerce.

In every British American colony, slavery was legally protected. In most of largely rural New England, the enslaved made up a small percentage of the population and were economically insignificant.

But Rhode Island, where merchants such as delegate Stephen Hopkins were actively involved in the international slave trade, had a higher percentage of slaves than any other colony in New England. Newport had become the most lucrative slave-trading port in North America. Its merchants, according to historian Allison Stanger, had sponsored at least 934 voyages to Africa, and its ships had procured at least 106,544 people to sell in North America: fewer than half had survived the passage.[3]

In the Middle Colonies, 10 percent of New York's population was enslaved, and 7.5 percent of New Jersey's. While Quakers voiced opposition to the institution of slavery, some 2.4 percent of Pennsylvanians were enslaved. In Delaware, 6.4 percent of the populace was enslaved.

The farther one traveled in the South, where slavery was more important to the economies of the colonies, the greater the percentage of the population laboring in slavery: Maryland, 32.8 percent; Virginia, 41 percent, North Carolina, 33.7 percent. In South Carolina, at 53.9 percent, enslaved blacks outnumbered free whites.

The records of slave ownership among the delegates are incomplete, but the percentage of ownership seems to exceed the proportion in the colonies they represented: the delegates were drawn from the wealthier ranks of society.

Every delegate from Virginia, Maryland, and North and South Carolina owned slaves, most of them in large numbers. With the exception of Christopher Gadsden, a merchant, all the South Carolina delegates owned hundreds of slaves; Henry Middleton held eight hundred. Among Virginians, George Washington, Richard Henry Lee, and Benjamin

Harrison each had two hundred or more enslaved people. Patrick Henry's slaveholdings would eventually increase from thirty in 1774 to one hundred.

Among the New England delegates to the Second Continental Congress, two—John Hancock and Stephen Hopkins—owned slaves. In the Middle Colonies, the New Yorkers had a few house slaves. Pennsylvania delegate John Dickinson had publicly opposed the institution and was in the process of freeing his slaves; Benjamin Franklin owned one house slave and a slave valet.

After Franklin and Adams and the entire committee approved Jefferson's draft, they delivered it to President Hancock. For the next three days, Congress dissected every article.

Jefferson later wrote that he was stunned by his colleagues' "immediate" agreement to cut out entirely his condemnation of the African slave trade. Any reference to slavery "was struck out in compliance to South Carolina and Georgia, who had never attempted to restrain the importation of slaves and who, on the contrary, still wished to continue it," Jefferson wrote. Leading the protesters was the youngest delegate, twenty-six-year old Edward Rutledge of South Carolina, owner of eight hundred slaves.

Jefferson recorded his astonishment at how quickly "our Northern brethren" acceded to Southern objections. Among them were two land-rich New York delegates.

One was James Duane, son of an Anglo-Irish immigrant, who had first married Mary Livingston, daughter of the Hudson River manor lord Robert Livingston; in 1766, her wealthy father, Robert, married Gertrude Schuyler, daughter of Albany land baron Philip Schuyler, making himself even wealthier. These unions had secured for Duane a place in the highest and most influential echelons of New York's landed aristocracy. Duane's father-in-law, Livingston, employed hundreds of impoverished tenant farmers on their vast Hudson River estates. Alexander

Hamilton, Schuyler's future son-in-law, would become Duane's law clerk. Duane would later become the first post-Revolutionary mayor of New York City and the first U.S. district court judge in New York State.

The other land-rich delegate from New York was Robert L. Livingston, the son of Robert R. Livingston, the chief justice of the Supreme Court of Judicature of New York Province, who had assembled the 166,000-acre Livingston Manor, which stretched twenty miles along the eastern bank of the Hudson River, garnering rents from 285 families of first-generation Scottish tenant farmers. As Robert R. Livingston's heir, Robert L. Livingston could expect to receive a royal land grant of nearly one million acres. Independence from Britain would cost him this lucrative grant. Among his cousins were many of the wealthy and powerful land barons of the Hudson Valley, who, collectively, owned four million acres of New York and New Jersey farmland that not only fed New York City but shipped exports all over the Atlantic world. To the slaveholders of the South, there was little difference between the plantation owner and the land baron of the North who collected rents from threadbare tenant farmers.

Throughout three excruciating days of editing, Jefferson sat beside Franklin, "who perceived that I was not insensible to these mutilations."[4] Jefferson later wrote little about the hack-and-slash editing, merely sending off to Richard Henry Lee in Williamsburg a copy of his draft declaration along with the version edited and approved by Congress.

Jefferson didn't take public credit for writing the nation's first and arguably most famous foundation document, because he was not proud of it. Disappointed that he had played no important role in writing the new Virginia constitution, smarting from the thorough vetting of his draft Declaration, Jefferson decided to quit Congress—to him only a temporary meeting of delegates from the British colonies. Far more important to Jefferson was the reshaping of weak old English colonies into strong independent states.

John Adams took quite the opposite view. Once again disregarding the embargo on congressional correspondence, he wrote jubilantly to

Abigail that the day of the signing of the Declaration of Independence "will be the most memorable epoch in the history of America." He predicted that it would be "celebrated by succeeding generations as the great anniversary festival." It was "the Day of Deliverance" that ought to be solemnized with "pomp and parade, with shows, games, sports, guns, bells, bonfires" all over North America "from this time forward forevermore."[5]

As if that were not elegy enough, in a second letter, Adams wrote that in a few days Abigail would see "a Declaration setting forth the causes" of "this mighty revolution" that would "justify it in the eyes of God and man." Adams saw the hand of God in the birth of the new nation: "It is the will of God that the two nations should be sundered forever."[6]

The contrasting reactions of Jefferson and Adams to their declaration of independence from Great Britain foreshadowed a rift that would only widen over time. Jefferson saw Virginia as his country; Adams considered each state part of a new nation.

CHAPTER EIGHTEEN

"Very Useful Here & Much Esteemed"

On the same day the Second Continental Congress formed a committee to draft the Declaration of Independence, it also created a second panel, made up of a delegate from each state and chaired by John Dickinson. Realizing the need for some sort of national government to replace British rule, the committee set out to prepare a provisional constitution for a confederation of states.

One week after Congress promulgated the Declaration of Independence, the Dickinson committee presented draft Articles of Confederation and Perpetual Union.

But Congress, engaged in a spreading war, was not ready for a serious debate on the form and structure of a new national government. It set aside two days each week to hammer out a document, and the fourth and final draft would not be adopted until November 1777. Submitted to the individual states for ratification, it strongly resembled Franklin's 1754 Plan of Union, envisioning a loose-knit group of sovereign and independent states in "a firm league of friendship" for their "common defense, the security of their liberties and their mutual and general welfare."

With a single-chamber congress as its central institution, each state would have one vote in Congress, its contingent made up of two to seven delegates elected by its state legislature. When it came time to enact legislation, the delegates from a particular state were to work out their position on the issue and then cast a single vote on behalf of their state. Delegates could serve only three out of every six years; its president, for only three years, and could not succeed himself.

Congress was to serve as the last resort for appeals of disputes between the states and would have the authority to coin money, operate a postal system, maintain armed forces, and make treaties and alliances.

But the Confederation Congress would lack the authority to levy taxes and regulate commerce. Without taxing power, its revenues were to come from the states, each contributing according to the value of privately owned land within its borders. Troops were also to be furnished according to a formula negotiated annually by Congress. The provisional government lacked a federal judicial system. Any state could block the admission of a new state to the confederation, while Canada could be admitted at any time!

The Articles of Confederation also contained an emoluments clause banning "any person holding any office of profit or trust under the United States" from accepting "any present, emolument, office, or title of any kind whatever, from any king, prince, or foreign state."

Congress defeated Dickinson's most controversial proposal, to define the western boundaries of the states. But no state or combination of speculative investors in Congress was willing to relinquish its claim to a bonanza in western lands.

Maryland, which didn't have any room to expand, insisted that other states give up their claims to lands on the western frontier (today's Midwest). Because their ratification had to be unanimous, it would take nearly five years and two more rejections before Congress finally adopted the Articles of Confederation, in March 1781.

In 1776, all that could be settled was a name for the new entity: the United States of America in Congress Assembled.

On July 4, 1776, John Hancock, president of the Continental Congress, ordered the Declaration of Independence to be read aloud to a crowd in the Pennsylvania State House yard. Dispatch riders hurried printed copies throughout the new states.

In New York City, General Washington welcomed the Declaration's rhetoric as a badly needed tonic for his troops. By the time a copy arrived on July 8, an armada of 150 British troop transports and 30 men-of-war had dropped anchor in New York Harbor; 32,000 Regulars, including 9,000 German mercenaries, had pitched their tents on Staten Island.

Since driving the British out of Boston at cannon point three months earlier, Washington had been amassing Connecticut and New York militia in anticipation of a British counterattack. Now his inexperienced militia faced the largest fleet and most powerful army Great Britain had ever sent from its shores. Washington had the Declaration read aloud to his troops and ordered them back to their billets. Instead, many joined a mob surging through the streets, breaking the windows of suspected Loyalists.

Reaching Bowling Green at the tip of Manhattan, the Sons of Liberty vaulted the fence surrounding the lead equestrian statue of King George III. Looping ropes around the horse and its royal rider, the Sons pulled the fifteen-foot statue to the ground. One man sawed off the king's head; the rest was carted off to Litchfield, Connecticut, where women would convert it into 42,088 bullets.

In April 1775, Congress had voted to allow the exchange with Caribbean islands of cod, lumber, tobacco, and indigo for arms and ammunition. They also commissioned agents to order and funnel supplies from Europe through the West Indies for the Continental Army. Three days after Congress had learned that Parliament had passed the Prohibitory Act embargoing all American trade, Congress dispatched the leading American commercial agent, Silas Deane of Connecticut, to Paris.

Standing for reelection to the Second Continental Congress, Deane had opposed Roger Sherman and Connecticut's conservative assembly faction by supporting the nomination of French and Indian War veteran Israel Putnam as its major general. In retaliation, Sherman, long suspicious that merchant-lawyer Deane had grown rich by manipulating his late wives' fortunes, had marshaled the support of Connecticut's rural majority.

Defeated for reelection, Deane decided to stay on in Philadelphia to serve out his term through January 1776 and continue working with Robert Morris and the Secret Committee. In turn, Morris supported Deane's appointment by Congress to act as America's first diplomat. Franklin, Dickinson, and Morris constituted the secret committee that drew up Deane's instructions and, on March 3, 1776, dispatched him to Paris to act as commercial and diplomatic agent for the Continental Congress.

As historian John Ferling puts it, Deane was "chosen because he knew the mind of Congress." He was "to explore the depth of France's friendship for the American cause." Deane's friend and fellow Connecticut delegate Eliphalet Dyer noted that Deane had been "Very Useful here & much esteemed in Congress."[1]

Franklin and Morris provided Deane with lists of French contacts who could arrange access to the French foreign minister, Comte de Vergennes. Posing as a Bermuda merchant, Deane ostensibly was to discuss commercial ties with France, but his highest priority was to procure uniforms for an army of twenty-five thousand men and "Quantities of Arms & Ammunition," including one hundred cannon. In addition, he agreed to act as commercial agent for Robert Morris at the customary 5 percent commission.

He was also instructed to determine "whether if the Colonies should form themselves into an Independent State, France would . . . acknowledge them as such" and form a military or commercial alliance—or both.

Ever since losing Canada and much of the American West to Great Britain by the Treaty of Paris in 1763, the French foreign ministry had been watching the developing radical movement in the British colonies with keen interest.

To London, Vergennes had posted an observer, merchant

Pierre-Augustin Caron de Beaumarchais, playwright of *The Marriage of Figaro*. At the home of John Wilkes, the radically pro-American lord mayor of London, Beaumarchais was introduced to Arthur Lee of Virginia, whose older brother was a delegate to Congress. The younger Lee was studying law and acting as commercial agent for the Lee family's extensive interests. He had also assisted Benjamin Franklin's colonial agencies.

Beaumarchais informed Lee that on June 10 the French government had approved a gift of one million livres to aid the American revolutionaries. Beaumarchais was to manage the fund by setting up a dummy mercantile house, Roderigue Hortalez et Cie, to mask official French participation. Under international law, to openly supply contraband weapons to the rebellious American colonies would violate French neutrality.

With King Louis XVI's personal approval, the French government employed the pretext of declaring that it was high time to refit its weaponry. Declaring many of its arms and ships "outmoded," the government allowed designated merchants to remove munitions from royal arsenals for a nominal sum to aid the Americans.

In November 1775, a French deputation of merchants from Nantes visited Washington at Cambridge and made arrangements to begin to supply his army with war matériel. By mid-1776, a river of French arms, ammunition, cloth, and quinine was flowing into the Carolinas through the Dutch free port of Saint Eustatius, the first foreign port to salute the American flag.

There, merchants sold gunpowder to the Americans at six times the going rate in Europe. From Jamaica, gunpowder smuggled inside hogsheads that usually carried sugar arrived in Charleston. From Bordeaux, three hundred casks of powder and five thousand muskets sailed on ships flying French colors toward Philadelphia, to be hauled overland to Boston.

By December 1776, Silas Deane would be able to write to Congress that he had dispatched two hundred thousand pounds of gunpowder and eighty thousand pounds of saltpeter from France to Martinique and one hundred thousand pounds of gunpowder from Amsterdam to St. Eustatius for transshipment to the mainland on smaller American vessels.

By the end of 1776, congressional agents were operating openly in all the Dutch, Spanish, and French colonies in the West Indies and in European ports. In early 1777, eight arms-laden French ships would transport two thousand tons of munitions to the Continental Army through Martinique. At every stop, American merchants and their agents, among them Congressmen Silas Deane and Robert Morris, were taking a 5 percent commission of the sale price of the munitions, amounting to millions of dollars in personal revenue over the course of the Revolution.

By December 1776, it had become clear that the Continental Congress needed to maintain a more formal diplomatic presence in Paris. After meeting secretly with a French agent in Philadelphia, the Committee on Secret Correspondence selected one of its members, Benjamin Franklin, to join Silas Deane in Paris. Arthur Lee was to come from London to join Franklin and Deane to form the first American diplomatic mission.

Without informing or inviting Lee, Franklin took along his twenty-two-year-old nephew, Jonathan Williams, to act as the mission's commercial agent. They joined Deane at Passy, a village overlooking Paris, taking up residence in the estate of Jacques-Donatien Le Rey de Chaumont, a government contractor, member of the Farmers-General, and kinsman of France's prime minister.

Franklin would reside there for the next nine years; Chaumont said he would charge no rent but that Congress could show its appreciation by giving him a suitable grant of land.

In March 1775, only three weeks after Congress had learned of the Prohibitory Act's blockade of all American trade, Congress legalized privateering. It was an important move by a fledgling government that had no navy and no ability to impose taxes. The practice would not only raise funds for the war; privateering would also allow entrepreneurs another opportunity to profit.

Congress granted investors commissions to arm their ships at their own expense and to raise crews of seamen who were assured shares in the proceeds of any enemy ship captured intact. A captured ship was sailed to port, where it was auctioned along with its cargo; investors divided the booty with officers and crews according to a formula approved by Congress, reserving a 10 percent cut of the spoils for the commander in chief—George Washington, at the moment—to use for the needs of the army.

In lieu of the enormous expense of building a Continental navy, some 1,697 privately owned vessels were registered by Congress. Of these, 600 carried letters of marque that served as commissions from Congress.

In addition, American agents abroad such as Franklin and Deane would commission some 300 private warships, bringing the total of the United States' commerce-raiding-for-profit vessels to 2,000. After the British evacuated Boston, fully 365 privateers operated from this one port alone. Fitted out, in all, with 18,000 guns, this mercantile armada transported contraband arms and goods while hunting for lucrative prize British merchantmen.

Privateering offered a risky path to overnight wealth—or ruin. Washington's quartermaster general, Nathanael Greene of Rhode Island, invested in privateering voyages. He asked an associate to keep his involvement secret and suggested using a fictitious name. When Congress tried to investigate Greene for allegedly diverting public money to his own business ventures, Washington blocked the inquiry in the interest of military morale.

The Royal Navy not only failed to stop privateering attacks in North American waters but soon faced an official American navy. On the day it received word that the British had begun raiding coastal towns in Massachusetts and Virginia, Congress also learned in a communiqué from General Washington that Parliament was sending five regiments of

Scottish Highlanders and Irish Catholic regulars on a fleet composed of six ships-of-the-line and one thousand marines.

By an overwhelming vote, Congress responded to the threat by authorizing the creation of a naval squadron reporting to its Navy Committee. Congress commissioned Esek Hopkins, a slave carrier and younger brother of Congressman Stephen Hopkins of Rhode Island, to serve as the Continental navy's first commodore; indeed, Stephen Hopkins chaired the committee that appointed him. In October 1775, Congress appropriated £100,000 (approximately $15 million today) "to fit out for sea the first fleet" of four ships. The committee purchased two of the vessels from a member, Robert Morris. The first was the newly launched, two-hundred-ton, 140-foot merchantman *Black Prince*. Its captain, John Barry, called it "the finest ship in America." Refitted with thirty guns and renamed the *Alfred*, it would serve as the flagship of the embryonic Continental navy.

In addition, a second vessel, a brig Morris also sold to Congress, was renamed the *Columbus*.[2] Its captain, Abraham Whipple, the commodore of the Rhode Island navy, was Esek Hopkins's brother-in-law. Hopkins's son John was given the helm of the *Cabot*.

The ships refitted and armed on the Philadelphia waterfront were to act essentially as privateers, their mission to capture enemy shipments of commercial goods and military supplies. By January 1776, when Congress formed the Marine Committee to supersede the Navy Committee, eight ships made up the Continental navy, forerunner of the U.S. Navy.

In the eight-year course of the war, the Continental Congress's small flotilla would capture or destroy 196 British vessels, valued at £6 million (about $900 million today).

American privateers proved even more effective at slowing the British war effort. In little more than the first year of the war, according to the registry kept in Lloyd's Coffee House in London, American privateers captured 733 British merchant vessels valued at £1.8 million ($270 million today), putting them under the auctioneer's gavel in French, American, and Caribbean ports.

Eleven states created their own de facto navies. Governor Jonathan Trumbull signed letters of marque for two hundred Connecticut-based privateering ships. As many as seventy thousand men served aboard privateering ships and shared in the loot. By the end of the war, many crewmen owned their own privateers. The Royal Navy lost one hundred ships in 1778 and more than two hundred in 1779 to the intrepid privateers. The British were eventually forced to build a fleet of frigates just to escort their merchant vessels in slow-sailing convoys.

Meanwhile, American privateers captured more than five hundred vessels, their cargoes valued at an astonishing £66 million ($9.9 billion today).

The proceeds from the privateering hauls would enrich several members of Congress, including Silas Deane, Stephen Hopkins, and, especially, Robert Morris, chairman of the Navy Committee.

At first, Robert Morris abjured personally investing in privateering. He had too many friends in England to take away any of their property. But as the fighting at sea intensified, the British took several of his ships, and he lost "a great deal of property," he wrote William Bingham, "I conceive myself perfectly justifiable in the Eyes of God & Man to seek what I have lost from those that have plundered me."

Building on Willing and Morris's existing network, Morris singled out twenty-four-year-old Bingham as the committee's principal agent in the Caribbean. As a silent partner, he joined Bingham in commissioning the *Retaliation*, which captured thirteen prizes on its first voyage. "My scruples about Privateering are all done away," he wrote to Bingham. It had become his "duty to oppose and distress so merciless an enemy."[3]

No one kept a tally of the full extent of Morris's and Bingham's privateering profits, but Morris had enlisted all his Secret Committee network, sending their ships to Europe and the Caribbean, taking shares in other privateers' cruises. Morris's hauls from the captured ships became legendary among Philadelphians. When the Marquis de Chastellux visited the city, he recorded that Morris was "so accustomed to the success of his privateers that when he is observed on a Sunday to be more serious than usual, the conclusion is, that no prize has arrived in the preceding week."[4]

In France, with Chaumont as his backer, Silas Deane fitted out privateers and sold prizes in French ports, organizing with Chaumont, Morris, and Thomas Walpole in England an international trading company. Their international network included Charles Willing, Morris's partner, in Barbados, where he arranged transshipment of European goods to the American mainland. Morris's associates in Philadelphia had agents in the West Indies and in New Orleans. In an early example of global capitalism, American merchants and their international network of agents burst the bonds of Britain's ancient mercantile system.

To take the helm of the clandestine privateering operation, the French minister of marine, Comte de Sartine, appointed Chaumont, Franklin's landlord, who allowed the American agents to engage in its activities without rivals. Chaumont directed all the company's operations. No prizes could be sold without his approval, and then only on his terms.

Acting as purchasing agents for Congress, Chaumont and Franklin's nephew Jonathan Williams purchased goods captured by privateers. Acting as prize agents, they sold the booty to their associates, including Morris and Deane. Benjamin Franklin would later attest that some transactions reaped as much as an 8,000 percent profit.

Historian Thomas Perkins Abernethy wrote that "Robert Morris thus held the keys to America's foreign trade and through his agents was able to exert a powerful influence upon the foreign policy of Congress."[5]

As the British disembarked in New York City in July and early August 1776, Washington confessed to John Hancock that he had no idea how many troops he had ready for combat. On paper, twenty thousand men were working night and day in searing summer heat to build thirteen cannon-studded forts around Manhattan, on Governors Island, and on Brooklyn Heights. But dysentery had felled thousands of exhausted men.

Early in the morning on August 22, Royal Navy ships moved into Gravesend Bay and began disgorging 15,000 professional soldiers onto Long Island's south shore. Five days later, the British attacked Washington's main force on heavily wooded Brooklyn Heights. In the first pitched battle of the war, one thousand Americans died or were wounded and fifteen thousand were captured.

Three-fourths of the Connecticut militia had already decided to march home by the time the British struck again at Kip's Bay. As British men-of-war shelled them, two thousand men vaulted from their shallow trenches and stampeded up the Boston Post Road without firing a shot.

Attempting to rally them in a cornfield—today's Bryant Park— Washington, swinging his saber and "swearing profusely," struck several officers with the flat of his sword. Three times, he threw his hat on the ground before exclaiming, "Good God, are these the men with which I am to defend America?"[6]

As Washington retreated first north, then across New Jersey to Pennsylvania, his army dwindled to a mere two thousand men. The Continental Congress fled to Baltimore. Delegates could find little time to debate a new form of government.

Benjamin Franklin at sixty, by David Martin

Major General Edward Braddock

Wedding of George and Martha Washington, by Junius Brutus Stearns

John Adams, by John
Trumbull

John Hancock, by John Singleton
Copley
MASSACHUSETTS HISTORICAL SOCIETY

Thomas Jefferson, by Charles Willson Peale
COURTESY OF INDEPENDENCE NATIONAL
HISTORICAL PARK

Robert Morris, by Charles
Willson Peale
COURTESY OF INDEPENDENCE
NATIONAL HISTORICAL PARK

Silas Deane, by William Johnson
COURTESY OF THE WEBB-DEANE-
STEVENS MUSEUM

Arthur Lee, by John Trumbull
BERG COLLECTION, NEW YORK PUBLIC LIBRARY

Pierre-Augustin Caron de Beaumarchais, by
Jean-Marc Nattier

Miniature portrait of Louis XVI, 1784, by Louis Marie Sicardi,
watercolor on ivory

John Jay, by
Gilbert Stuart

Louis XVI snuffbox

Continental three-dollar bill, 1776

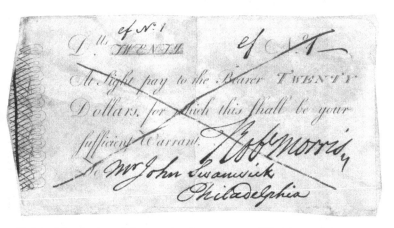

Robert Morris signed thousands of notes to pay Washington's troops when the Continental dollar was virtually worthless.

James Madison, by John Vanderlyn
COURTESY OF THE WHITE HOUSE
HISTORICAL ASSOCIATION

Alexander Hamilton, by
John Trumbull
COURTESY OF THE NATIONAL
GALLERY OF ART

Martha Washington, by Gilbert Stuart
COURTESY OF THE NATIONAL PORTRAIT GALLERY

George Washington and William Lee,
by John Trumbull
COURTESY OF THE METROPOLITAN MUSEUM OF ART

CHAPTER NINETEEN

"For a Little Revenge"

With most of his army fled or dead, Washington paused on September 25 long enough to pen a desperate note to Congress. From the New Jersey shore, he had just seen Lower Manhattan burst into flames. Earlier, Washington had asked Congress for permission to burn the city to deprive the British of shelter. When no permission came, a mysterious fire broke out. Fanned by high winds, it destroyed 493 houses, forcing the British, who accused Washington of ordering it, to spend the winter in tents and cellar holes. In a letter to his cousin Lund Washington, he merely commented, "Providence, or some good honest fellow, has done more for us than we are disposed to do for ourselves."[1]

In his letter, Washington now admonished his congressional colleagues to abandon their fantasy that a soldier could subsist on patriotism alone. "His pay will not support him," Washington insisted, "and he cannot ruin himself and Family to serve his Country, when every member of the community is equally Interested and benefitting by his Labours."

Americans who were willing to fight solely on "Principles of disinterestness" were "no more than a drop in the Ocean," Washington told Congress. The country could no longer fight the war with short-term enlistments of militias, or to finance it with pennies. There must be a total investment in manpower and resources. "This contest is not likely to be the Work of a day; the War must be carried on systematically," he wrote. The army must be established "upon a permanent footing."

Americans had become accustomed to thinking that a well-paid professional army was an anathema. In their writings, Patriot pamphleteers had berated British and German soldiers as mercenaries who fought only for filthy lucre. To admit that Americans needed to be paid to fight somehow diluted their concept of a righteous revolution.

Arguing from personal experience, Washington contended that what motivates men, and especially leaders, was not mere altruism. Nothing was more important than "giving your Officers good pay." That would ensure that they would be motivated both by "Principles of honour, and a spirit of enterprise."

Officers must not just receive subsistence pay but "such allowances as will enable them to live like, and support the characters of Gentlemen." And then they "will not be driven by a scant pittance to the low and dirty arts which many of them practice to filch the Public. Something is due to the Man who puts his life in his hand—hazards his health—& forsakes the Sweets of domestic enjoyments."

If Washington ever had any respect for militia, by now he had lost it. Congress was deluding itself in a belief that a militia not only avoided the hazards of a standing army taking over the country but would save money. "Certain I am that it would be cheaper to keep 50- or 100,000 Men in constant pay than to depend on half the number," he wrote, "and supply the other half occasionally by Militia." Most militiamen were farmers; since most military campaigns overlapped planting and harvest seasons, suspending "farming and manufactures" only added to economic dislocation.

The time militia "spent in pay before and after they are in Camp, Assembling and Marching—the waste of ammunition—the consumption of stores," he argued, "destroys every kind of regularity and economy which could be established among fixed and settled troops. . . . And will in my opinion prove (if this scheme is adhered to) the Ruin of our Cause."[2]

As he was writing to Hancock, Massachusetts and Connecticut, in order to meet their recruitment quotas, were conducting bidding wars, bribing potential recruits with cash bounties. In their place, Washington proposed a national system. There must be pay rates according to rank and enlistment for three years or for the duration of the war.

He proposed a fresh kind of enlistment enticement—land—on a fixed scale, according to rank, in exchange for faithful service for the duration. A beleaguered Congress debated only briefly before acquiescing. From 1777 on, thousands of landless Americans would join the Continental Army, expecting that they or their families would receive from 100 to 500 acres of farmland depending on rank, up to colonel, when the fighting was over. Officers, in exchange for adequate if not extravagant pay, pledged to serve for the duration of the war. Later, land bounties of 850 to 1,100 acres were granted to generals.

Several states offered even higher recruitment bounties. New York offered privates 600 acres; Pennsylvania, 2,000 acres; Virginia, 1,500 acres; and North Carolina, 640 acres, with 12,000 acres to generals.

To Washington, these Continental and state grants underscored the need to organize the lands west of the Appalachians politically. It would be nearly another year of war before Congress, in its second temporary capital at York, Pennsylvania, could pause again to debate the Articles of Confederation.

In August 1777, six coastal states—Pennsylvania, New Jersey, Delaware, Maryland, New Hampshire, and Rhode Island—proposed that Congress be empowered to demarcate the western boundaries of states.

The prospects for approval appeared dim, the stubborn claims to western lands of other states keeping Maryland, which had no room to expand, in opposition. Virginia, the Carolinas, Georgia, Connecticut, and Massachusetts all claimed by their colonial charters that they extended to the "South Sea," which many believed to be the Mississippi River.

Yet the charters of Pennsylvania, New Jersey, Delaware, Maryland, New Hampshire, and Rhode Island confined these colonies to a few hundred miles inland from the Atlantic.

Finally, Congress voted to add a clause to the Articles of

Confederation that Indian tribes could cede their lands to the national government. In November 1778, the Virginia Assembly voided all Native American sales within its charter limits. Pressure from investors in land companies—including the Illinois and Grand Ohio Companies, organized by the Franklins—led Virginia to nullify all Indian purchases in the so-called Northwest Territory.

By 1779, every state had approved the Articles but Maryland, which still refused to ratify until every state ceded its western claims to the Continental Congress. Even when Virginia offered western lands exclusively to soldiers, Maryland remained obdurate.

Virginia remained the pivot of the controversy when Governor Patrick Henry approved sending a small army under George Rogers Clark to seize the Illinois country from the British and their Loyalist auxiliaries, enabling Virginia to claim the territory by right of conquest.

In retaliation for Indian and Loyalist raids, in 1779, Washington had detached a major expedition comprising one-fourth of his Continentals and three thousand New York militia to savage the lands and villages of the Iroquois Confederacy.

Early in 1780, New York's legislature, self-proclaimed overlord of the Iroquois, ceded all claims to its western lands to the Continental Congress. Connecticut, abandoning the claims of the Susquehanna Company to a strip of northern Pennsylvania stretching from the Delaware River to Lake Erie, followed suit in October, relinquishing all its western claims except a three-million-acre tract in northwestern Ohio—the Western Reserve.

Eventually, Governor Thomas Jefferson, Patrick Henry's successor, persuaded the Virginia Assembly to yield its claims to the western lands. Jefferson's proposal stipulated that all speculators' demands be rejected and that the West be divided into new states, to be admitted into the Union on the basis of parity with the old.

Among the Revolutionary leaders who had to abandon their claims to western lands were Washington, Franklin, Jefferson, Richard Henry Lee, Jonathan Trumbull, Robert Morris, and Silas Deane. By this time, according to Commonwealth tax rolls, Governor Jefferson had become the twenty-eighth wealthiest Virginian.

On this basis, in January 1781, Virginia ceded her claims north of the Ohio River, including the bounty lands once promised by the British to George Washington and other Virginia veterans of the French and Indian War.

After three and a half years of political infighting and compromises in Congress, Maryland finally became the last state to sign the Articles of Confederation. Signed while Congress temporarily resided in Trenton, one of nine temporary wartime capitals, the Articles also stipulated that after the war, Congress's assemblages would take place in a new and permanent capital, to be built along the banks of the Delaware River.

Twice in a year, intent on severing New England from the other rebelling colonies, the British had sent combined army and naval forces from Canada to fight their way south to New York City to end the Revolution. In the first invasion from the north, on October 11, 1776, the most important naval battle of the Revolutionary War took place on Lake Champlain.

To block the British, Benedict Arnold built fifteen ships at the southern end of Lake Champlain while the British spent all summer trying to build a superior force just inside Canada. By the time they sailed south, snow covered the ships' decks. In a savage battle at point-blank range behind Valcour Island, Arnold lost only one vessel before escaping at night. In the four-day running encounter that followed, Arnold lost only one more ship before he scuttled eight, carrying his wounded in sails to Fort Ticonderoga. The British arrived too late to attack the heavily defended fort. With thick snow falling, they retreated all the way to Quebec, having squandered a season of war. Their retreat allowed Arnold to dispatch troops to reinforce Washington for his Christmas surprise attack on Trenton. The Revolution clung to life.

Three months later, King George received Major General John Burgoyne at St. James's Palace. Burgoyne had drawn up plans for a march south from Montreal to recapture Fort Ticonderoga and then link up with an army marching north from New York City. By July 1, Burgoyne stood before Ticonderoga's looming walls.

A veteran artillerist instantly grasped the importance of an unfortified hill overlooking the fortress. Overnight the British cleared a path to the summit and hauled up two cannons. Their first salvo convinced the American officers to evacuate the fort or risk losing the entire American army.

When a dispatch from Burgoyne reached London, George III exulted to Queen Charlotte, "I have beat them, beat all the Americans."[3]

Burgoyne had expected to capture the entire American army, but a hard-fought rearguard action allowed all but two hundred Americans to escape.

Now time, not distance, became the enemy: All night, the British could hear the dull thwack of axes and the crash of trees as a growing American army blocked their path, slowing the invasion to a mile a day.

In mid-July, as his army retreated, General Schuyler wrote to Washington of the bleak prospect of stopping the British, who had an army "flushed with victory, plentifully provided with provisions, cannon and every warlike store," while the American army "is weak in numbers, dispirited, naked, in a manner, destitute of provisions, without camp equipage, with little ammunition, and not a single cannon."[4]

Schuyler was unaware that a French fleet, eluding the British blockade by appearing to sail for the Caribbean, had escorted eight supply ships bearing the fruits of Silas Deane's clandestine dealings, in the spring of 1777 delivering guns and ammunition, shoes, blankets and stockings, and tents and tools for the Continental Army. Two of the French vessels, *Amphitrie* and *Mercure*, had arrived at Portsmouth, New Hampshire, their holds crammed with twenty thousand muskets and fifty-two brass cannons. Convoys of oxen dragged them over the Berkshires.

When Burgoyne finally crossed the Hudson, he found the Americans entrenched in elaborate defensive works and armed with French artillery. Most of the Americans' arms at Saratoga were now state-of-the-art French weapons, enabling the Americans to fight the British invaders to a bloody standstill in two battles in which British casualties were double the American toll.

After weeks of waiting, Burgoyne learned that he could expect no help from General Sir William Howe, who had captured Philadelphia and decided to spend the winter in comfort. Surrounded by Americans, his retreat to Canada cut off, Burgoyne surrendered.

Despite the capture of Philadelphia, the loss of an entire army at Saratoga proved to be the turning point of the war, convincing the French that, with their aid, the Americans could defeat Great Britain. While the battles at Saratoga were won by soldiers, their victory would not have been possible without the timely arrival of the ammunition and guns obtained from the French.

Silas Deane later would take his share of the credit: "The purchase, and sending out [of] those cannon, arms and stores, in great degree decided the fate and the independence of the United States."[5]

When news of Philadelphia's loss arrived in Paris, Benjamin Franklin learned that his recently completed three-story mansion on Market Street was not only in enemy hands but was the headquarters of the British secret service. But from the same dispatch, the Americans learned that Burgoyne and his army had surrendered.

When a French official chided Franklin, "Well, Doctor, Howe has taken Philadelphia," Franklin retorted, "I beg your pardon, sir; Philadelphia has taken Howe."[6]

In London, when Lord North learned of Burgoyne's surrender, he panicked. Persuading the king that it was time to offer major concessions to the Americans before they could form an alliance with the French, he dispatched a conciliatory letter to Franklin and Deane in Paris to be carried by a secret service agent, New Hampshire–born Loyalist Paul Wentworth.

Franklin instructed Deane to meet with Wentworth, knowing that the French secret service would report the meeting to Vergennes. At their meeting, Wentworth offered Deane "honors and emoluments" if he cooperated in the reconciliation. Within hours, Franklin heard back from Vergennes. Still cautious, he told Franklin he was reluctant to go to war with England without consulting King Louis's Bourbon uncle, the king of Spain. On the last day of 1777, word came back from Madrid: King Charles III declined to involve Spain in the struggle for American independence.

When Vergennes still remained noncommittal, Franklin agreed to see Wentworth. On January 6, 1778, as they met at the American mission in Passy for two hours, Wentworth handed Franklin an unsigned letter from Sir William Eden, head of the British secret service. A court favorite, Eden declared that Britain was ready to fight for ten years rather than grant American independence. Franklin shot back, "America is ready to fight fifty years to win it."[7]

When Franklin failed to report the meeting to Vergennes, the French foreign minister became alarmed. Convening the king's council of ministers, he expressed his fear that the Americans were preparing to reconcile their grievances with the English king. The French councillors voted unanimously to form an alliance with the Americans.

As the details were being worked out, Franklin sent his secretary, Dr. Edward Bancroft, a boyhood student of Silas Deane's, to London to leak its terms to Franklin's old friend and banker, Thomas Walpole, a partner in the Illinois land scheme. He, in turn, leaked it to Charles James Fox, leader of the opposition. On the floor of Parliament, Fox forced North to admit that he knew the Americans were about to sign a treaty with France.

On February 6, 1778, Vergennes invited Franklin, Deane, and Arthur Lee to the foreign office at Versailles to sign the United States' first international treaty, creating a military alliance between the United States and France against Great Britain. The treaty required that neither France nor the United States agree to a separate peace with Britain. American independence was to be a condition of any future peace treaty. In addition, the treaty was intended to promote trade and commercial ties between the two countries.

When Bancroft asked Franklin why he was wearing a faded, decidedly out-of-Paris-fashion blue Manchester coat to go to the most fashionable court in Europe, Franklin replied, "For a little revenge." It was the coat he had worn when the British had humiliated him at the Cockpit four years earlier.[8]

PART THREE

"THE CRISIS IS ARRIVED"

CHAPTER TWENTY

"DISCORDANT PARTS"

W ith the French now in the war alongside the Americans, the British decided they could not hold Philadelphia, and shifted to a New York–based defensive strategy in the North. A few days before the British evacuation, Joseph Galloway, a onetime political lieutenant of Benjamin Franklin's and the superintendent of police during the occupation, was told that the estimated six thousand Loyalist refugees who had crowded into the city had only to go out to General Washington's camp at Valley Forge and swear allegiance to Congress and they would be safe. Caught between revolutionary fury and loyalty to Britain, many were reluctant to leave, but many of Pennsylvania's most prosperous citizens chose to flee, leaving virtually everything behind. In the ensuing panic, three thousand refugees carried or dragged their belongings across New Jersey, closely pursued by the American army all the way to New York.

Despite his phenomenal success in arranging vital arms shipments, Congress, without explanation, recalled Silas Deane shortly after the signing of the Treaty of Alliance with France.

The three-line letter he received in Paris seemed cordial enough. It merely requested that Deane report in person to Congress in

Philadelphia on "the state of affairs in Europe." What Deane was not told was that Arthur Lee, in letters to his brother, Congressman Richard Henry Lee, had accused Deane of enriching himself through side deals with French merchants and arms suppliers. Lee also alleged that Deane had misdirected payments from Congress to buy goods for his own profit as well as lucrative shares in privateering ships.

Deane had no idea that he had fallen into disfavor with a radical faction in Congress, in part because Deane and Franklin had provided numerous unemployed French, German, and Irish officers seeking high-ranking commissions with glowing letters of recommendation to Congress. While the stream of supplicants included invaluable men like Baron von Steuben and the Marquis de Lafayette, Congress was ill equipped to judge their credentials. As a result, Congress had meted out generalships that made their recipients outrank more deserving and increasingly resentful Americans. So unpopular was one French officer that, when he ignored advice and rode his horse onto a flimsy ferry on the Schuylkill River, it sank—and no American attempted to rescue him.

Among Deane's recommendations was Thomas Conway, an Irish staff officer in the French army married to a French countess but with no combat experience. Soon after arriving in America, Conway, commissioned a brigadier general by Congress, joined a plot to unseat Washington as commander in chief and replace him with Horatio Gates.

Along with a handful of other congressmen, Lee and the Adamses were dissatisfied with Washington's performance. John Adams was certain that Virginians were getting all the well-paying officers' appointments. He wanted to turn military control over to a board of war whose members would be appointed by Congress and who could, in turn, promote political favorites. Gates was to be its president. Washington knew that Gates had remained safely behind the lines at Saratoga but had taken full credit for the victory.

Unaware that Lee, his partner in several land companies, had joined the ranks of his congressional critics, Washington, putting his command on the line, wrote to Lee, "I have undergone more than most men are aware of to harmonize so many discordant parts."[1]

Washington told Lee that Congress's constant and inept interference were beyond his patience. "It will be impossible for me to be of any further service if such insuperable difficulties are thrown in my way."[2]

As he prepared for what he considered little more than a temporary visit to America to report to Congress on European diplomacy, Silas Deane decided to leave his account books and voluminous correspondence behind him in Paris, entrusting them to Bancroft for safekeeping until he returned. It was a decision he would come to regret.

In June 1778, three days after the last British ship evacuated Delaware Bay and sailed to New York, in the first physical manifestation of the Franco-American alliance, a French fleet sailed up the Delaware River to Philadelphia. In the place of honor, Silas Deane, arriving home after three years abroad, sailed on the flagship as the guest of the first French ambassador to the United States, the Chevalier de La Luzerne. When Deane had informed Vergennes that he was leaving France, Vergennes summoned him to Versailles and, to honor his contributions to the alliance, presented to him a snuffbox with a miniature portrait of young Louis XVI, surrounded by diamonds.

Now Deane was stepping foot on his home soil, knowing nothing of the accusations against him until he presented his papers to Congress. For two months, Congress kept Deane waiting for a hearing. In the meantime, he stayed, along with La Luzerne, in the former Penn mansion as the guest of Benedict Arnold, who had been sidelined from combat by his wounds at Saratoga. Arnold was uncomfortably serving as the military governor of Philadelphia, a post that kept him permanently at odds with Congress and, in the aftermath of the British occupation, with radical Pennsylvania politicians.

In August, when Silas Deane finally got his hearing, he was defended by New York delegate John Jay. The day before, Gouverneur Morris had written to Jay, "Your friend Deane, who hath rendered the most essential services, stands as one accused. The Storm increases and I think some one of the tall trees must be shorn of its roots."[3]

Deane had just learned to his chagrin that he could expect no further help from French foreign minister Vergennes, who, on learning of the charges against Deane, instructed his deputy, Conrad Alexander Gerard, against becoming involved.

Denying a charge of financial peculation, Deane presented testimonials from Franklin and Beaumarchais, but having left his correspondence and account ledgers behind in Paris, he was unable to document his expenditures. When he tried to recapitulate his efforts in Paris, he was told to present them in a written statement and then asked to leave the room.

After two roll call votes, he was asked to return a week later. Appearing again, he began to testify but was once more halted and told to return two days later. Then that hearing was postponed. Deane finally got to testify on Friday, August 21. When he completed his statement, he was told to withdraw.

Robert Morris sat through the hearings. It was obvious to him that he himself, as Deane's sponsor and business partner, was the real target. He was already coming under fire for insisting that the American goods, usually tobacco from Virginia, that made up the repayments for the French loan be shipped to his agents in France and not to Beaumarchais.

Beaumarchais had sent an agent, Theveneau de Francey, to Philadelphia to arrange direct remittances, only to discover that no one in Congress would contradict Morris. Francey reported of Morris that, as he was "the only merchant in Congress who has ever conducted large commercial operations, his opinion is law. He has a very great influence and a very great credit. . . . Through his connections in the four quarters of the globe, he has done whatever he pleased. He works for himself in working for the republic."[4]

Nevertheless, Francey went on to accuse Morris of defrauding Congress. According to him, Morris would insure the one-tenth or one-twelfth of a ship's cargo that belonged to him. If the ship arrived safely in France, Morris reaped the profits from his share; if the ship sank or was captured, the entire loss was chalked up to Congress's account, which owed Morris its full value.

Silas Deane never was formally charged or exonerated. Instead, he was offered $10,000 in depreciated Continental currency to settle his accounts, which he refused. Stripped of his diplomatic post, he decided to defend his record publicly.

Breaking Congress's unwritten rule of silence, he counterattacked the Lees in the *Pennsylvania Packet*, for the first time revealing to the public the sharp divisions within Congress. The Lees retaliated by accusing Deane of damaging the American cause, which until then had depended on the appearance of unanimity.

Tom Paine, who had remained silent for a year while employed as the paid secretary of the Committee on Foreign Relations, in an eight-part newspaper series denounced Deane for attacking the Lees. In point of fact, it was hardly an unbiased opinion. Paine's employer, as chairman of the Committee on Foreign Relations, was Richard Henry Lee, brother of Arthur Lee, Deane's accuser.

Paine challenged Deane's statement of his accounts, suggesting embezzlement, and called on each state to examine any mercantile connections between their congressional delegates and Deane.

Turning his sharpened quill to Morris next, Paine called into question Morris's motives for giving no public accounting for the Secret Committee's secret expenditures. Morris, in an "Address to the Public," refused to defend the details of his transactions or give the names of his agents but revealed that he had shared in three joint ventures with Deane: one ship had arrived in France safely, one had been captured, and a third never sailed.

In disgust at the treatment of his partner by Congress, Robert Morris decided, after serving three years in Congress, to resign, to settle the accounts of the Secret Committee, and to ask Congress to appoint a replacement. Silas Deane, left without a congressional commission or salary, decided to return to Paris to assemble his records in an attempt to clear his name.

Visiting Philadelphia, George Washington became disheartened by the Lee-Deane imbroglio and its fallout. To his friend Benjamin Harrison, he confided that he feared the nation was "on the brink of ruin."

> Party disputes and personal quarrels are the great business of the day whilst the momentous concerns of an empire, a great and accumulated debt, ruined finances, depreciated money and want of credit are but secondary considerations and postponed from day to day, week to week, as if our affairs wore the most promising aspect.

He chastised Congress for the "idleness, dissipation and extravagance [that] seem to have laid hold of most of them," adding that "speculation, peculation and an insatiable thirst for riches seems to have got the better of every other consideration."[5]

Stripped of his diplomatic post, Deane departed for Paris to meet with an auditor appointed by Congress. Morris provided him with a letter of recommendation to his old friend Benjamin Franklin:

> I consider Mr. Deane as a martyr in the cause of America. After rendering the most signal and important Services, he has been reviled and traduced in the most shameful manner. But I have not a doubt that the day will come when his merit shall be universally acknowledged.[6]

Deane set out with high hopes, including a contract to supply masts to the French and Spanish navies. He also carried a sheaf of Continental Loan Office bonds to sell on commission to French investors. He sailed in a French convoy aboard the ship *Jane*, which he co-owned with Morris. But ill fortune seemed to follow in Deane's wake: the ship sank, and its valuable cargo was lost. Arriving in France, Deane learned that French investors, shying away from American ventures because of the continuing devaluation of the Continental dollar, would not buy the bonds.

In Paris, Deane learned that all the ships carrying supplies from France to America in which he had invested had been intercepted by the British. Historians have come to believe that Dr. Bancroft, his trusted colleague, in his absence had provided vital information on the ships' movements to his British employers. Deane was financially ruined. He would spend the rest of his life in poverty in Europe. He never did discover that Bancroft, all along, had been a British spy.

It would be sixty years before Deane's family was finally compensated for some of his losses. In 1841, a congressional audit ruled that the Continental Congress's case against him had been "erroneous and a gross injustice" and paid his granddaughter $31,000 (equivalent to $1 million today).

Deane's accuser, Arthur Lee, never did reveal to Congress that he, too, had accepted a diamond-encrusted snuffbox when his posting in the American mission in France ended, just before he returned to Philadelphia and took a seat in Congress as a Virginia delegate.

The Deane affair revealed to the public for the first time the fissures in the carefully cultivated mask of revolutionary ideological unanimity in the Continental Congress.

CHAPTER TWENTY-ONE

"The Pests of Society"

Once Congress ratified the treaties of alliance with France in May 1778, it became an entirely different kind of war. In French uniforms with French weapons and trained during their winter encampment at Valley Forge by Prussian drillmaster Friedrich von Steuben, Washington's reinvigorated army pursued the British as they retreated to New York City, fighting them to a draw in one-hundred-degree heat in the Battle of Monmouth.

For the next five years, the American Revolution became just one theater in a worldwide struggle between Britain and allied American, French, and Spanish forces. The British, attempting to cut off further French aid to Washington's forces, curtailed offensives on land, retreating to their main base at New York and launching sporadic attacks on Connecticut, Georgia, and, in their only major victory, Charleston, South Carolina.

Washington concentrated on defending a strategic quadrant bordered by the northwestern New Jersey foothills, the Hudson Valley, Massachusetts, and Rhode Island, only once mounting a major offensive to crush the pro-British Iroquois Confederacy. In the South, savage guerrilla warfare raged between Loyalists and Patriot neighbors.

Washington's main task shifted from countering the annual British attempts to divide, conquer, and crush American forces to finding enough money to continue to fight at all. He was beginning to suspect Robert Morris of "engrossing," the morally dubious practice of buying up vast amounts of wheat and other scarce supplies and holding on to them until prices rose.

During the winter of near starvation for his army at Valley Forge, Washington had written to his former aide-de-camp Joseph Reed, now president of Pennsylvania's Supreme Executive Council, that he was "well disposed to . . . bringing those murderers of our cause—the monopolizers, forestallers, and engrossers[—]to condign punishment." Washington bemoaned the failure of several states to "hunt them down as the pests of society, and the greatest enemies we have to the happiness of America."[1]

Washington decried what he called the tendency of merchants like Robert Morris to profit from the war. Writing to his kinsman General Andrew Lewis, Washington blamed "want of virtue," which he "dreaded more than the whole force of Great Britain.

> Certain I am, that, unless extortion, forestalling and other practices which have crept in, and become exceedingly prevalent and injurious to the common cause, can meet with proper checks, we must inevitably sink under such a load of accumulated oppression.
>
> To make and extort money in every shape that can be devised, and at the same time to decry its value, seems to have become a mere business and an epidemical disease, calling for the interposition of every good man and body of men.[2]

The arrival of French ships off the American coast only added to food shortages. French sailors and soldiers had to be fed. Philadelphia's waterfront warehouses bulged with grain, but most Americans could not afford it because French commissary officers were paying inflated prices in gold. By 1779, prices were rising at the rate of 17 percent a month while Continental currency had depreciated to one-fortieth of its 1776 value.

Many Philadelphians were confounded by unaffordable provisions in a region of agricultural abundance. Organizing into political clubs such as Joseph Reed's Constitutional Society, they blamed inflation on wealthy merchants. They accused Morris and other merchants of manipulating commodity markets and refusing to accept Continental currency—of buying up grain and holding it in their warehouses for hard-money payments by the French. This practice, known as forestalling, finally made revolutionary tempers boil over.

On July 4, 1779, General John Cadwalader, leader of the conservative Republican Society, tried to give a speech at the statehouse opposing price controls. Radical militiamen armed with clubs shouted him down and broke up the meeting. Cadwalader's speech encouraged conservative merchants to resist. Eighty merchants protested to Pennsylvania's Supreme Executive Council that any attempt to compel a trader to accept less for his goods was an invasion of property rights.

In response, the radicals decided to round up and drive out of the city the Republican leadership. Seeking a scapegoat, they settled on James Wilson, signer of the Declaration of Independence and lawyer to many Loyalists.

Getting wind of the plan, the merchants armed themselves and, reinforced by the elite cavalry of the First Troop Philadelphia City Cavalry, gathered at Wilson's three-story brick mansion, dubbing it Fort Wilson. Across town, at Paddy Byrne's Tavern, radical-led militiamen decided to capture Fort Wilson.

When only the banging of a drum and shouting followed, the First City Troopers went home for dinner, leaving Wilson and General Thomas Mifflin to drill about thirty Republicans. Wilson and Morris appealed to the Supreme Executive Council for protection. Two Republicans ran to the city arsenal and grabbed armloads of muskets, stuffing their coat pockets with cartridges.

A crowd of about two hundred, including many Pennsylvania German militiamen equipped with two field artillery pieces, surrounded Wilson's house. Forty Republicans retreated inside, where the military governor, Benedict Arnold, shared the command with General Mifflin.

The radicals, giving three cheers, charged the house, and Captain

George Campbell leaned out a window and fired his pistol. The militiamen returned fire; Campbell fell, dead. From a third-floor window, Arnold blazed away with his pistols. Four militiamen were killed, a dozen wounded; inside, three more men had been hit.

German artillerymen dragged up a fieldpiece as a militiaman battered in the front door with a sledgehammer. When the militia hurried upstairs, Colonel Stephen Chambers fired, wounding one. Another rushed Chambers before he could reload, dragged him downstairs by the hair, and ran him through with a bayonet. Now heavy firing came from the staircase, upstairs windows, and cellar windows. The radicals retreated, then rallied, surging in again as Arnold directed the fire from upstairs.

At this moment, Pennsylvania president Joseph Reed arrived, a pistol in his hand; at his side was erstwhile portrait painter Captain Charles Willson Peale. Continental Army troopers galloped up, slashing at the rioters. Reed ordered everyone, inside and outside, arrested. The Republicans, able to post bail, were immediately released; the militiamen were incarcerated in Walnut Street Prison, surrounded by cannon and the First City Troop.

The next day, as more militia marched toward the city, Reed and the First City Troop rode out to intercept them. Reed promised to request that the Pennsylvania Assembly grant amnesty to the militia. He explained away the bloodshed as one of the "casual overflowings of liberty." James Wilson went into hiding in New Jersey.[3]

As the fifth year of the Revolution began, Continental currency had depreciated so badly that Lieutenant Colonel Alexander Hamilton, Washington's principal aide-de-camp, could not afford to buy a horse. His old gray mare had been wounded in the Battle of Monmouth, yet army regulations, which he had written himself, barred him from borrowing a mount except for military use. As Washington put it, "Even a rat in the shape of a horse is not to be bought at this time for less than £200" (about $40,000 in depreciated Continental currency). Hamilton's monthly pay: $60 Continental.

That winter, the price of a season ticket to dances arranged for officers in Washington's camp was a virtually worthless $400 Continental. Forgoing a horse, Hamilton bought the dancing ticket and made ends meet by taking all his meals at Washington's mess table and investing his small inheritance in privateering ships.

In September 1778, Congress appointed John Adams as Silas Deane's permanent replacement in Paris with orders to assist Franklin in negotiating a peace treaty with Britain. Adams's appointment ended a six-month impasse in Congress over the terms Americans should propose: independence, minimum boundaries, complete British evacuation of American territory, the right to fish on the Grand Banks—a mainstay of New England's economy—and free navigation of the Mississippi for frontier settlers. Writing to General Philip Schuyler, his future father-in-law, Alexander Hamilton asserted that the root cause of American financial insecurity lay in the states' refusal to grant to Congress, in the Articles of Confederation, the power to tax, leaving Congress and its armies at the mercy of annual requisitions that the states either could not or would not honor.

For instance, Pennsylvania's Conestoga wagons were vital to supplying the armies and transporting war matériel, but Washington had to plead for them each year, and Pennsylvania rarely met its quota. Virginia manufactured cannon and gunpowder, but Governor Jefferson insisted that much of its output go to support Virginia's own garrisons in the Illinois country while providing little support for Continental armies north or south.

With no power to tax, Congress continued to print millions of deflated Continental dollars and had borrowed so heavily in Europe that its credit was exhausted—and then Congress resorted to expropriating, confiscating, and forcing the sale of Loyalists' properties.

Paper money issued in 1777 purchased goods valued at $16 million; by 1779, it took $125 million in Continental paper to purchase $6 million worth of supplies.

Hamilton contended that the nation's poor financial condition was primarily caused by an insufficient supply of stable currency. The crisis worsened as the injection of French gold to purchase provisions from Americans made farmers and manufacturers increasingly reluctant to accept virtually worthless Continental currency. The only cure, Hamilton contended, was to create a national bank.

In "The Continentalist," a fifteen-thousand-word letter printed as a four-part series in the *New York Packet*, the twenty-four-year-old Hamilton argued that Congress must be granted a reliable source of revenue. The "separate exertions of the states will never suffice." All the states' resources "must be gathered under a common authority with sufficient power to carry out the steps needed to preserve us from being a conquered people."

Calling for fiscal reform, Hamilton proposed that a national bank be funded half by foreign loans and half by private subscriptions that could be paid off with Continental letters of credit—fiat money—offered at a depreciated value to make it profitable for merchants to accept them.

Congress could use foreign loans to buy half the national bank's stock. In turn, the bank would help finance the national government by making direct loans to it. The bank would facilitate taxation by increasing the supply of money in circulation that would result from normal business activity. Congress needed to borrow $5 million or $6 million annually. Any nation at war, Hamilton argued, is obliged to borrow money, both at home and abroad. The United States could not be an exception.

To secure foreign loans, Congress would need sure sources of revenue to pay current interest, and each year set aside the funds to retire the principal. Hamilton predicted that with adequate taxes as national resources, the public debt would be wiped out in twenty years.

Hamilton's proposal contained many of the principles that underpinned his workable plan a decade later for a national bank.

In March 1779, twenty-nine-year-old James Madison arrived in Philadelphia to take his seat in the Third Continental Congress. The son of a wealthy planter and the close friend and political lieutenant of Thomas

Jefferson, Madison brought with him £2,000 in Virginia Land Office currency, some Continental paper money, and a few gold Spanish milled dollars.

His Virginia pounds declined in value every week; he had to either spend them with the few merchants who would accept them or exchange them for Continental dollars at a terribly unfavorable rate. The bill for his boardinghouse alone came to a staggering $21,373 in Continental dollars for the first month; his haircut and shaves cost him $1,000.

In April, Madison was forced to take out a loan of $8,000 in Spanish dollars from the federal treasury so that he could pay his bills in non-inflated currency. Still, Congressman Madison, deeply embarrassed, had to write home to his father for assistance.

Madison wrote to Jefferson that the treasury was "empty," the government's credit "exhausted," and his private credit extended "as far as it will bear," and that because of the "improvidence of Congress," the army faced an "immediate alternative of disbanding or living on free quarter [confiscation]."

The American economy was grinding to a halt by the spring of 1780. After the army's worst winter, George Washington faced a mutiny. Because of the latest drop in value of the Continental dollar, supplies stopped reaching the camp at Jockey Hollow in Morristown in the northwest New Jersey mountains. Washington cut rations to the near-starvation level of one-eighth for the next six weeks.

On May 25, the Connecticut regiments paraded under arms in protest, demanding a full ration and their five months' arrears in pay. At least twice before, finding enough money to pay his troops had nearly scuttled Washington's ambitious plans. In 1775, Connecticut troops had refused to march with Arnold into Canada until they could send money home for their families' subsistence. And gold coins raised by fining Philadelphia Quakers for refusing to attend drills had reached Washington just in time to pay his men before they consented to cross the Delaware at Christmas 1776.

This time, Washington called out the Pennsylvania Line to break up the protest at gunpoint. To Joseph Reed, Washington encapsulated his army's desperate condition:

> I assure you, every idea you can form of our distresses will fall short of the reality. All our departments, all our operations, are at a standstill; and unless a system, very different from that which has for a long time prevailed, be immediately adopted throughout the states, our affairs must soon become desperate beyond the possibility of recovery.
>
> If you were on the spot, my dear Sir, if you could see what difficulties surround us on every side, how unable we are to administer to the most ordinary calls of the service, you would be convinced that these expressions are not strong enough, and that we have everything to dread. Indeed, I have almost ceased to hope.

On the first day of 1781, as the war dragged on and the Continental dollar became all but worthless, the appearance of recruiters paying $25 in gold to new recruits provoked 1,500 veterans of the Pennsylvania Line to take up their arms, kill one officer, and wound several others before marching off to Philadelphia to confront Congress.

Making camp at Princeton, they elected negotiators to parley with Pennsylvania officials. Despite concessions, half the Pennsylvania Line quit the service. Three weeks later, when the New Jersey Line also mutinied, Washington attacked their camp and ordered the mutineers to execute their leaders.

Washington's desperate act underscored how near to collapse the American Revolution had come for want of enough money to pay his troops even a fraction of their back pay.

CHAPTER TWENTY-TWO

"For Want of Pay"

As the financial crisis came to blows, a growing nationalist faction in Congress displaced the faction for states' rights, which they believed were seriously weakening their chances of prevailing against Britain.

The nationalists, led by Philip Schuyler and inspired by Alexander Hamilton's writings, proposed Robert Morris for the powerful new post of superintendent of finance.

Since 1776, Morris had advocated scrapping Congress's committee system of administration and replacing it with departments of war, marine, treasury, and foreign affairs under individual executives. In February 1781, in the wake of the mutiny of the Pennsylvania Line, years of objections to centralized authority came to an abrupt end.

To pull back the Confederation from the brink of collapse, Morris was to be given extraordinary powers: as the most important administrator, he would be responsible for every facet of government except the army.

As the central government consisted of only one legislative chamber and no other member had the political support or the money to take control, Morris would be given powers more like a modern president's. (One French official on the scene estimated Morris's net worth at £8 million—about $1.2 billion today—making him the first American billionaire.) At first, Morris was reluctant. Urging him to take on the daunting task, Hamilton wrote,

> You may render America and the world no less a service than the establishment of American independence! 'Tis by introducing order into our finances—by restoring public credit—not by gaining battles that we are finally to gain our object.[1]

Few in Congress could doubt Morris's qualifications. It was he who had raised the money to pay Washington's troops before they would attack Trenton in 1776. When Morris's wife, Mary, organized a women's door-to-door charity drive to raise money to purchase supplies to send to Washington's army, Morris had stepped in to manage its funds. Not only that, he chipped in £10,000 (about $1.5 million today) of his own money and tapped other wealthy Philadelphians for donations. Even Tom Paine contributed $5,000 in depreciated currency. (Morris later returned it.)

But Morris could see another possibility, a more lasting institution. At a series of meetings, Morris proposed that subscribers make installment deposits until the fund reached a goal of £300,000 ($15 million today). In return, subscribers would receive interest-bearing notes equal to their subscriptions to be redeemable in six months. The funds would purchase three million daily rations and three hundred hogsheads of rum for the Continental Army. Morris named his creation the Pennsylvania Bank, in effect the first bank in the United States.

The fund quickly filled with ninety-two subscribers. Within a week, Congress had approved the plan and pledged the credit of the United States to the "effectual reimbursement and indemnity" of the subscribers. Within two months, Washington wrote to Morris that the bank was now his principal source of supplies.

Morris's proven business acumen and personal wealth promised to bring stability to the new post of superintendent of finance.

Alexander Hamilton, Morris's staunchest advocate, had only high praise for America's leading businessman. "Mr. Morris certainly deserves a great deal from his country," Hamilton wrote. "I believe no man in this country but himself could have kept the money machine a-going."[2]

Nevertheless, Samuel Adams led the opposition to conferring so much discretionary power in one man. James Madison countered by leading the nationalists in pressing Congress for Morris's appointment, portraying him as the embodiment of a stronger, more centralized government. On February 20, 1781, with only Samuel Adams still dissenting, the Confederation Congress elected Morris as superintendent of finance.

Before he would accept the post, Morris had a few stipulations. He refused to give up any of his commercial partnerships; instead, he would put his private business in the hands of third parties. But to take control of a growing bureaucracy and cut expenses, he insisted on "absolute power" over officials he deemed deleterious or "unnecessary." He would take responsibility for future congressional financial affairs but not for its past debts.

Once again, Samuel Adams opposed bestowing so much power, but after a monthlong stalemate during which the fiscal crisis did not go away and neither did Morris, Congress capitulated to Morris's terms and he accepted the post.

Only three days later, Morris submitted his plan for the Bank of North America. The keystone of his administration, it would immediately restore the credit of the government and bring back into circulation the nation's private wealth.

A private bank with only a modest capitalization of $400,000 (about $6 million today), the Bank of North America would offer shares at $400 (about $6,000 today) each in gold or silver coin with a projected dividend of 6 percent. The bank would lend money to Congress and receive its deposits; its banknotes would be usable to pay taxes. Making commercial loans payable in thirty or sixty days, it would provide loans in the form of notes that would circulate as paper currency backed by the bank, not the government, replacing the virtually worthless Continental currency.

Each shareholder would have a single vote in electing a board of directors. Its first directors were to be George Clymer, a signer of the

Declaration of Independence, and John Nixon, both directors of the Pennsylvania Bank. Morris could own shares in the national bank but could not serve on its board.

Addressing one of the leading causes of the American Revolution, Morris was creating a national bank in a nation that had never had one before—after every other form of monetary exchange had failed. Mixing private and public finance, Morris sought to make private credit the foundation stone of public finance.

Proselytizing his grand innovation to John Jay, Morris said that he hoped

> to unite the several states more closely together in one general Money Connection . . . and attract many powerful Individuals to the cause of our country by the strong principle of Self Love and the immediate sense of private Interest.[3]

To Franklin in Paris, Robert Morris put his philosophy more succinctly:

> I mean to render this [bank] a principal Pillar of American credit so as to obtain the money of individuals for the benefit of the union and thereby bind those individuals more strongly to the general cause by ties of private interest.[4]

With the war in the North deadlocked, the fighting had shifted to the South—to guerrilla warfare between Loyalists and Patriots, and to hit-and-run British raids. One man-of-war sailed up the Potomac to Mount Vernon. Advised by Washington's cousin, Lund, its manager, that the farm was the property of Washington, the ship's captain said he would not sack the home of such a distinguished gentleman but would accept a sizable gift of, say, Washington's livestock and crops and his choice of twenty-two slaves. After torching neighboring farms, the British sailed away without doing any permanent damage to Mount Vernon.

Governor Jefferson was less fortunate. Lord Cornwallis's eight-thousand-man army bivouacked on three of his farms on their slow march to Yorktown. Helping themselves to food and drink at Monticello, they did no permanent damage. But at Elk Hill, Cornwallis's headquarters for ten days, his army harvested what corn they needed, then burned the rest of Jefferson's crops and his barns and his fences, and took away all his livestock. They rode off on Jefferson's best horses, including his highly valuable prize stud, and cut the throats of any horses too young for service. Leaving Jefferson's farms devastated, they carted away thirty slaves. Jefferson would later insist that he had lost a fortune greater than his entire debt, all the principal and interest, that he owed to his British creditors. British commanders, with the help of Loyalists, had familiarized themselves with the names and addresses of the signers of the Declaration of Independence and paid special attention to their homes. When the British occupied Princeton, New Jersey, they chose as their headquarters the splendid mansion of Richard Stockton. They not only damaged the house but splintered trees and fences into firewood and stole the livestock, including Stockton's prize Arabian horse.

Before abandoning their occupation of Philadelphia, they ransacked Benjamin Franklin's house and threw Benjamin West portraits of Franklin and his wife on the pile in one of their carts.

After Congress at last adopted the Articles of Confederation, in June 1781, it voted to entrust the peace talks in Paris to a commission of emissaries rather than to prickly John Adams alone: his distrust of the French government's intentions was making negotiations difficult, even if the puritanical Adams was enamored of French manners: "The politeness, the elegance, the softness, the delicacy is extreme."[5]

Adams had also openly criticized Franklin's participation in Paris literary salons and his "constant dissipation," which Adams considered harmful to the smooth running of the mission and dangerous to the American cause.

By this time, Congress deemed only two objectives essential:

independence and sovereignty. All other matters were left to the commissioners' discretion to negotiate without binding instructions.

This shift came on the advice of La Luzerne, the French minister to the United States. No action should be taken without the "knowledge and concurrence" of the French, who were surprised by the discord within the American mission.

The French, no doubt aware there were British spies attached to the American mission, secretly investigated Franklin and found him clean, literally: the French secret police, marveled at the cleanliness of his linen underthings.[6]

Before serious negotiations could begin, Franklin met alone with Richard Oswald, Britain's emissary, while Adams went off to the Netherlands to obtain Dutch recognition of American independence and secure a $2 million loan ($300 million today) from bankers in Amsterdam.

John Jay, of New York, the newest addition to the American negotiating team, had learned that a French official had secretly gone to England to persuade the British to confine the United States to narrow territorial limits and to deny traditional fishing rights off Canada. Jay sent his own secret negotiator to London to persuade the prime minister, Lord Shelburne, to acknowledge American independence as a precondition to any settlement. Shelburne won the war-weary cabinet's agreement, and in September 1782, negotiations in earnest finally began.

An immediate sticking point was the treatment of the Loyalists. At first, Franklin insisted that there could be no provision for the Loyalists. All the negotiators undoubtedly were aware that Franklin's son, William, had become the president of the Loyalists and now was in exile in England, pressing the British government for reparations.

The French insisted that Loyalist refugees must be compensated: no royal government could sit by without providing for the faithful adherents of their king. The British tried to defuse the issue by suggesting that reparations for Loyalist losses could be made from the proceeds of the sale of British-held Canadian frontier land.

When Franklin flatly rejected that idea, the British suggested that France and its ally, Spain, give up Florida and New Orleans and turn them into Loyalist refuges. British negotiator Oswald requested either a large tract of land for the Loyalists (such as what is now the entire state of Maine) or blanket amnesty and "strong recommendations" to the states that they compensate Loyalists. Franklin countered that *all* of Canada would have to be ceded to the United States in exchange for compensating the Loyalists. Pointing to the map, he said bluntly, "We would not have them for neighbors!"[7] In the resultant Article 5 of the treaty, the American commissioners pledged that Congress would "earnestly recommend" to the state legislatures full restitution of the rights and property of the Loyalists.

In fact, Franklin knew full well that, under the Articles of Confederation, which he himself had drafted, no state would be bound by this "recommendation." In London, Loyalist refugees saw British accession to this wording as a complete sellout of their rights.

When a fourth emissary, John Laurens, joined Franklin, Adams, and Jay, the quartet decided to disobey Congress's instructions to consult with the French, and they themselves drew up a treaty. Signed by British negotiator Oswald on November 1, 1782, it recognized the independence of the United States.

In settling boundary lines, Franklin unrolled a 1756 map he had printed during an earlier war. With a northerly boundary line dividing Canada and Maine (still part of Massachusetts) at the St. Croix River, it ran along the 45th parallel through the Great Lakes to the Mississippi, then south to New Orleans and the boundaries of Spanish Louisiana and Spanish Florida. (Spain would obtain Florida in the final treaty.) The British signed away the rights to all land between Canada and the Gulf of Mexico, between the Atlantic and the Mississippi.

Franklin's stubborn negotiating had added to the territory of the United States one-fifth of the continent—the rich lands from the Appalachians to the Mississippi so long coveted by speculators like himself and settlers. Adams had held out until he could be assured of New England's right to fish off Newfoundland and Nova Scotia and to dry and cure their catch on the shores of the Maritimes. British forces were to cease hostilities and be withdrawn "with all convenient speed." One key provision, almost an afterthought, was that all debts due to creditors by citizens of either country were validated and their courts made accessible for collection.

Without a single change, the draft articles the American commissioners hammered out in daily meetings at the Hotel du Roi on Paris's Right Bank would be approved by Congress and become the definitive peace treaty.

On the last day of 1782, Robert Morris ushered into the Office of Finance in Philadelphia a grim delegation of Continental Army officers who had ridden through snow and high winds from Washington's headquarters on the Hudson. General Alexander McDougall and four fellow officers had come to demand back pay before the army was disbanded. Officers' compensation alone was $5 million in arrears (about $150 million today). Among the petitioners were General Henry Knox, the chief of artillery, and thirteen other ranking officers from the Continental Lines of five states. Washington had read the petition before the delegation left camp and had "no objection." The petition read: "We have borne all that men can bear. . . . Our property is expended, our private resources are at an end." Asking for years of back pay, the petitioners did not try "to conceal the general dissatisfaction which prevails and is gaining ground in the army, from the pressure of evils and injuries" that through seven years of war had made their condition "wretched."[8]

"The uneasiness of the soldiers for want of pay is great and dangerous; any further experiments on their patience may have ill effects," the petition warned.[9]

If the war ended and the soldiers weren't compensated, they could refuse to disband. Congress would then have to contend with ten thousand armed, hungry, and angry men.

The soldiers' petition called for a written commitment to pay, in hard currency, at some future date, a variety of debts, including compensation for years of short rations and reparation for past payments made with depreciated currency. But the officers' delegation made it clear that the soldiers would no longer wait for an immediate cash payment. They re-fused to go home with nothing more than one more promise from Con-gress.

According to Congressman Madison's notes, Morris met in his office one week later with congressional delegates from every state and in-formed the committee that "it was impossible to make any advance in pay in the present state of finances."[10]

He painted a dire picture. The government's bank had called in its loans; Congress was overdrawn on the French treasury by 3.5 million livres (about $20 million today) and, Franklin had warned, the French would extend no more credit. Morris had overextended his own credit and now demanded that Congress sign off on his own overdrafts.

On January 7, the full Congress authorized Morris to go on over-drawing its French account: France would have to cover the overdrafts or risk throwing the Americans back into the arms of the British. After the vote, Madison bemoaned to a colleague that "such a proof of our poverty & imbecility could not be avoided."

With the new nation on the brink of bankruptcy, it was left to Morris to come up with a plan to satisfy the army. Meeting with Hamilton, Madison, and John Rutledge of South Carolina at the Finance Office, Morris decided he could scrape together a month's pay, $250,000 dollars (about $7 million today), using a combination of bills of exchange and notes drawn against his own accounts.

Summoning General MacDougall and his colleagues, Morris said he would provide them with a month's pay, but only one week at a time, so that the soldiers would not consume it in one celebratory visit to the camp commissary.

By March 1783, Morris, working with Washington and with a New York contractor, came up with a scheme that allowed regimental pay-masters to turn the Morris notes into payment for the troops to take home with them—partly in cash and partly in clothing and supplies, but not in liquor.

At this critical moment, a ship arrived from France carrying $120,000 (about $1.8 million today) in silver coins just as Captain John Barry fought his way from Havana through the British blockade with $75,000 (about $1.1 million today) in Spanish dollars.

Before Washington would release his troops for their long journeys home, he demanded that every soldier receive an "absolutely indispensable" additional three months' pay from Congress:

> To be disbanded at last, without this little pittance . . . like a set of beggars, Needy, distressed and without prospect . . . will drive every man of Honor and Sensibility to the extremest Horrors of Despair.[11]

But, Morris explained tactfully in a letter to Congress, there was no money in the Treasury. The only solution he could offer was to issue $500,000 (about $15 million today) in notes, backed by his credit. After huddling once more with Hamilton and Wilson, Morris decided to issue the soldiers their pay in notes redeemable in six months.

Ordering 15,000 sheets of paper, Morris told the government's printer to stamp each one with the watermark "National Debt." In the first week of June 1783, Morris, working until late at night, personally signed six thousand individual notes in denominations of $5 and $100.

Able to distribute Morris's notes, promises of eventual payment, to his troops, Washington could now safely disband his rebellious army, freeing to it go home with dignity and seek out the land they had been promised as the bounty for their recruitment.

While Washington awaited arrival of the definitive peace treaty from Paris, he turned his mind and his pen toward the new nation's future. In a circular letter to every state's governor, he called for unity in a "respectable and prosperous" civilian government that would provide "the unbounded extension of Commerce."

To achieve this, he laid down four principles: government "under one Federal head," a "Sacred regard to Public Justice," a military "Peace Establishment," and the "mutual concessions" by the states that would be necessary for "general prosperity."

For American independence to be acknowledged internationally, he insisted there must be "complete justice to all Public Creditors." All debts, domestic and foreign, including to the troops, must be honored to avoid "a National Bankruptcy with all its deplorable consequences."[12]

A year later, when Robert Morris resigned as superintendent of finance, he echoed Washington's advice on the paramount importance of establishing the "public credit." "The payment of debts may indeed be expensive, but it is infinitely more expensive to withhold payment." To preserve America's hard-won liberty, its citizens must now unite. Otherwise, "our independence is but a name."[13]

After spending eight years and seven months in the saddle, and occupying 280 temporary headquarters, George Washington stopped off at Annapolis to resign his commission to the Continental Congress. Soon afterward, he arrived home at Mount Vernon in time for Christmas 1783.

Thanks to his creative collaboration with Robert Morris, Washington had been able to pay his troops the money they had earned in blood and sacrifice—and banish his own nightmare of a general revolt.

CHAPTER TWENTY-THREE

"The Most Sordid Interest"

The Revolutionary War left the new nation broke. When Washington sent an aide, Tench Tilghman, to carry the news of the British surrender at Yorktown to Congress in Philadelphia, Tilghman had to shell out his own travel expenses, only to find that the United States Treasury had no money left to reimburse him. Shamefaced congressmen took up a collection.

In Princeton, Washington attended the first postwar commencement of the College of New Jersey, which Hamilton's artillery had shelled during the war. Washington wanted to make a substantial donation. But since Continental currency was virtually worthless, he was mortified to have to resort to giving British gold coins bearing the image of King George III.

And when Thomas Jefferson took his seat in the first postwar meeting of Congress in October 1783, he had to borrow money from fellow delegates James Madison and James Monroe, as Virginia had not reimbursed his expenses for four months. "In the meantime," Jefferson reflected, "some of us had the mortification to have our horses turned out of the livery stable for want of money."[1]

Ignoring their military failure in the Revolutionary War and the consequent treaty of peace, the British Parliament ratcheted up efforts to eliminate American commercial competition. In an obvious attempt to destroy the American merchant marine, Britain re-invoked the colonial-era Navigation Act of 1756, requiring that all goods transported between British possessions or to and from England must be carried on British ships—"English goods in English bottoms."

Banning long-existing trade between New England and its Canadian neighbor, the Navigation Act also barred long-flourishing commercial ties with British Caribbean colonies. Moreover, Britain insisted that its treaty allies, Spain and Portugal, embargo American trade and forbid trade with any of their colonies. Britain also prohibited vital exports from England to the United States, including sheep, wool, and woolens.

All the while, in violation of the peace treaty, Britain refused to remove its troops from fortified trading posts around the Great Lakes and along the Canadian-American frontier, on the grounds that Americans were refusing to honor the treaty by paying off their prewar debts to British merchants as they had been contracted—in silver or gold, not depreciated Continental currency.

By the time France had become a U.S. ally, the problem of the Loyalists had transformed the Revolution into a civil war. In addition to Loyalist enlistments in the British Army and Navy, the British had formed fifty-five regiments of Loyalist Provincial Corps along with nineteen thousand integrated into the Regulars. In all, nearly fifty thousand Americans served under the royal standard, including twelve thousand blacks.

About 20 percent of the white male population were active Loyalists; 40 percent of the Yale College graduating class of 1758 had joined Loyalist units. In New York, this number included many tenant farmers who preferred to remain British subjects. Many Dutch farmers in New York and New Jersey preferred monarchy.

Early in 1783, many towns in New York State adopted resolutions forbidding Loyalists to settle within town limits. Statewide, Loyalists were also barred from practicing the legal and medical professions, from voting, from holding office, and from serving on juries. More than one-fourth of the prewar population had been driven out; in all, thirty-five thousand Loyalists sailed out of New York Harbor in 1783, roughly equal to the seaport's prewar population, bound for Nova Scotia or England. Thousands more fled overland to the Canadian province of Upper Canada, today's Ontario, where seven hundred Loyalist refugees would ultimately settle modern-day Toronto.

Even before the British evacuated the city in November, wealthy Loyalist exiles hired lawyer Alexander Hamilton because of the tolerant views he had expressed in the press. When the New York Assembly passed the Trespass Act, allowing lawsuits for damages to the property of Patriots seized or used by the British or Loyalists, Hamilton alone spoke up: "We have already lost too large a number of valuable citizens."[2]

Hamilton worried that the flight of the Loyalists would seriously weaken the new nation's economy. At the same time, it was hard for Hamilton to refute the accusation that he was cynically arguing from self-interest, especially after so many Loyalists, including scores who had already fled, were paying his annual £6 retainer ($900 today).

In all, Hamilton defended sixty-four cases brought against Loyalists. The most important civil case pitted the fragile young American democracy against international law. Under New York's Trespass Act, defendants were prohibited from pleading that they had acted under orders of the occupying British. The act also denied defendants the right to appeal to a higher court.

Passed while Hamilton was in Philadelphia serving in Congress, by New York legislators seeking to obstruct ratification of the peace treaty, the Trespass Act openly violated the law of nations by contravening the very peace treaty that granted American independence. It ignored, as well, the recommendation of Congress to the individual states.

Hamilton decided to make the suit of Mrs. Elizabeth Rutgers against Loyalists Joshua Waddington and Evelyn Pierrepont the test case. A seventy-something widow who was the aunt of New York's attorney general, Egbert Benson, Mrs. Rutgers had fled the city when the British conquered it in 1776, abandoning substantial property, including a large brewery and alehouse.

Loyalists Waddington and Pierrepont had refurbished the gutted buildings and made, as one historian put it, "a whopping profit through-out the war," escaping to England with their earnings at war's end. The brewery had burned mysteriously, possibly torched by an anti-Loyalist mob; it lay in ruins when Mrs. Rutgers returned to the city. She sued under the Trespass Act for £8,000 (about $1.2 million today).

The central point of the case was the fact that the Loyalist brewmas-ters had taken over the brewery under British Army authority. As Ham-ilton knew from reading his Vattel, an occupying army had the right to use all property in any enemy territory it held. Under the general amnesty extended by the peace treaty, Mrs. Rutgers had no right to any compen-sation.

In the crowded city hall courtroom on June 29, 1784, Hamilton's ar-gument before the Mayor's Court followed three major points. First, the Trespass Act violated the laws of war. New York's own constitution em-braced English common law, incorporating it as part of New York's laws. Common law included the law of nations.

In his second argument, Hamilton pointed out to the court that, un-der the Articles of Confederation, Congress alone had the power to enter into peace treaties. The law of nations demanded a general amnesty. Congress, by ratifying the treaty, had accepted the general amnesty. Ar-ticle 6 of the treaty expressly forbade further confiscations or prosecu-tions of anyone on either side.

Third, Hamilton argued, the Mayor's Court had to decide whether New York's Trespass Act conflicted with any higher law. The state law, he argued, violated the law of nations, the peace treaty, and the mandate of Congress. Therefore, the city court must declare the state law null and void.

In his written opinion, Mayor Duane—Hamilton's law preceptor and a former member of Congress—conceded Hamilton's entire line of reasoning and ruled in favor of Waddington and Pierrepont. Mrs. Rut-gers was entitled to only £800 as rent for the first two years of the war, not £8,000 in damages.

Hamilton won his case by arguing, for the first time, the principle of judicial review that would eventually grow into the establishment of the

United States federal judiciary, including the Supreme Court. For the moment, he made it quite clear that one of the principal defects in the Articles of Confederation was the lack of any judiciary.

He also argued successfully that international treaties must be considered the law of the United States. Only a supreme international tribunal, and not any state law, could invalidate them, and none existed. It was Hamilton's detestation of war profiteering and now confiscations that drove him to break publicly with many of New York's wealthy Patriots.

In particular, he decried the behavior of signer of the Declaration of Independence and former New York delegate to Congress Robert L. Livingston, a Hudson Valley land baron.

In 1779, Hamilton had written to John Jay, "Never was there a greater compound of folly, avarice and injustice than our [New York's] confiscation bill."[3] In 1783, Livingston had echoed Hamilton's view: "I seriously lament with you the violent spirit of persecution . . . unmixed with pure or patriotic motives."

Yet, in 1784, Livingston was writing to his friend John Jay in Paris to arrange credit for him in Europe of £6,000 to £8,000 pounds ($900,000 to $1.2 million today) so that he could buy up confiscated Loyalist estates in New York. The state was auctioning off large blocs at public auction at a time when only the wealthiest had any cash. To Hamilton, this was "the most sordid interest."[4]

To many New York landowners, Livingston could justify his speculations by pointing out that his already vast landholdings had been seriously damaged by Loyalist and British troops during the war, that his tenants were now behind on their rents, and that he had not been paid his salaries either as a state official or as a member of Congress.

Ironically, Livingston's scheme fizzled, because many European bankers were cool to the idea of being repaid with depreciated American currency. Dutch bankers twice turned down Jay's requests on Livingston's behalf. In New York, Livingston could borrow only about $12,500 (about $187,000 today), of which $2,000 ($30,000 today) was a personal loan from Governor George Clinton himself. Livingston bought several brick townhouses in New York City.

He was not the only signer benefiting from postwar land speculation. In Philadelphia, James Wilson, director of Robert Morris's Bank of North America, borrowed nearly $100,000 (about $1.5 million today) on dubious security.

In March 1784, Hamilton drew up the charter for America's second bank, the Bank of New York, originally capitalized at $125,000 (about $1.87 million today). Taking a leading role in setting up the institution, he became one of its original directors. Hamilton steered many of his wealthy in-laws and Loyalist clients to BONY. Blocked from getting its charter from the state legislature, Hamilton persuaded his codirectors to open the bank anyway.

Hamilton's deepening involvement in banking only soured him on financial speculators he thought were weakening the national government. The bulk of his law clients were businessmen, and he could see that the actions of the individual states were undercutting the reputation of the Confederation in Europe.

Watching as the vital trading networks of his youth withered and died, Hamilton groped for an answer, seeking the solution in books. Able to sight-read French, he devoured the three-volume memoirs of Jacques Necker, France's reformist finance minister, just delivered to him from Paris by his close friend and fellow Revolutionary War veteran the Marquis de Lafayette.

Late in 1784, Lafayette returned to America for a tour of the new nation, escorted by an entourage of young French aides and liveried servants. In planning the sojourn, Lafayette had written to George Washington, the general whom he had served faithfully during the war, describing himself as "your adopted son."[5] But, after a two-week visit to Mount Vernon, he declined Washington's invitation to accompany him to the Ohio Valley, where the retired general was having trouble collecting rents on his thousands of acres of lands.

While Washington headed west, Lafayette, eager to see the young nation he had fought for, journeyed south and then north. Traveling with James Madison, Lafayette arrived in New York City, where Congress was meeting, for an emotional reunion with Hamilton. Carrying the pollen of revolutionary ideas, Lafayette also brought news from Mount Vernon of a plan—the joint thinking of Washington, Jefferson, and Madison—to organize a company to develop an inland waterway.

The plan was for the Potomac Company to link the Potomac by a series of canals, roads, and inland waterways to the Ohio River in order to open up the Old Northwest and make it possible, as Washington had long dreamed, to bring the harvest of the interior—including the coal deposits he had discovered in present-day West Virginia—across the Atlantic to European markets.

Washington desperately needed to collect the rents owed to him in the Ohio Valley. His reduced farm income and losses from the British raid on Mount Vernon had left his finances in a "deranged state."[6] He had heard that squatters were laying claim to his western lands, building houses and barns, and he intended to pressure them to pay up. He especially wanted to collect the income from a gristmill he had built (at present-day Perryopolis, Pennsylvania) that was, by all accounts, the most successful west of the Alleghenies. He intended to auction it off during his visit.

Following the route he had taken so long ago with British general Braddock, Washington and his party on the fourth day out passed the Great Meadow, where he had surrendered Fort Necessity. The stockade was now in ruins, but the land under it would fetch good money as pastureland. On the fifth day, they reached Warm Springs, Virginia, where Washington commissioned construction of a five-room house and carriage house as a summer retreat near mineral springs.

Turning to business, he called on his heavily indebted western partner, Gilbert Simpson, who owed him £600 ($90,000 today); Simpson could offer only £30 ($4,500), a female slave, and some wheat. (Washington later learned the woman was not a slave and released her.) And the mill on which Washington had lavished £1,200 (about $180,000 today), a fortune at the time, had been so poorly maintained, it was now inoperable. No one bid at auction.

Angrily, Washington called a meeting of his Scots-Irish squatters. When several insisted they had improved his lands by their hard work and wanted some credit for their years of effort, he flew into a rage. Unaccustomed to anything but deference, Washington brandished deeds with pre-Revolutionary royal government seals on them.

When the settlers offered to buy the lands, Washington refused to sell them individual plots. They would have to pool their resources and buy him out or rent the land from him. When the settlers refused to pay him and said he would have to evict them, Washington rode off to the courthouse in present-day Uniontown, Pennsylvania, and began the process of ejecting squatters he found everywhere on his lands.

With much of America's capital lost with the flight of the Loyalists, and with no stable currency and restrictions on international trade imposed by the British as a worldwide postwar depression set in, Americans were discovering that their independence was only partial. They still lacked economic independence and agency.

CHAPTER TWENTY-FOUR

"HEAVEN WAS SILENT"

No sooner had the British and French sailed home at the end of the American Revolution than a postwar depression set in, sparking growing political discord as well as economic hardship.

What none of the Founding Fathers had divined was that the imperial crisis that began with protests over illegal searches and seizures in Boston in 1761, and had led to a startling military victory two decades later, constituted only the first phase of a protracted ordeal to achieve true independence. While the Treaty of Paris of 1783 halted the overt conflict of the Revolutionary War and granted the United States political autonomy, it did not guarantee American economic independence and agency. Britain immediately set out to deny the United States' sovereignty through unrelenting attempts to stifle American trade and starve her former colonies.

With public credit destroyed, Continental currency in free fall following the exodus of British and French gold, and the army disbanded, unemployment became widespread. Every state attempted to save itself by counteracting the general business malaise, but none succeeded.

In New York, Governor George Clinton and his upstate constituency, mostly farmers, distrusted and resisted the calls for stronger national solutions to interstate problems coming from Alexander Hamilton and New York City merchants, putting them down as too pro-British.

Wielding growing power as a populist, Clinton refused the call of Congress for a special session to consider customs duties to support the government.

Spite was growing sharper among the states, especially between New York and New Jersey. New York demanded a customs duty on every boatload of firewood needed for heating and cooking in New York City; the British had cut down all the trees. Every vessel of more than twelve tons had to be entered and cleared at the customhouse as if it had arrived from a foreign port. Pinched New Jersey boatmen put pressure on their legislature to tax New York for the lighthouse at Sandy Hook, which belonged to New York City.

Connecticut exacted heavier customs duties on imports from Massachusetts than those from Britain. When a Revolutionary War general wanted to cross Virginia from Maryland to Kentucky, he was refused entry until he obtained a passport.

During the years of active warfare, the states had been united in name only. Now the quarrel among them only weakened American prestige abroad. In the eyes of Europe, America was thirteen banana republics. When Jefferson attended the weekly diplomatic receptions at Versailles, he stood at the rear of the line, waiting his turn for a brief visit with the foreign minister, his place determined by the French view of the relative importance of the nation.

Every attempt to promote a coherent policy toward international trade had been blocked piecemeal for five years. States competed with one another. Under the Confederation's rule of unanimity, one state could block any measure.

An initiative to grant Congress even limited control over commerce by allowing it to prohibit ships and goods from countries that had not signed commercial treaties with the United States had failed. Eleven states agreed; New York and Rhode Island, with their vital ports, balked. Two years later, Rhode Island acceded, but New York still refused.

Further complicating the adoption of the Articles of Confederation had been the attack on British forts at Kaskaskia and Vincennes in the Illinois country by George Rogers Clark in 1779 in an expedition supported by Virginia and Pennsylvania investors in the Indiana Company. When the company attempted to sell lands without clear titles, Virginia set up a land office and put lands in western Virginia and south of the Ohio River—the old Ohio Company claim—on the market.

This set off a row in Congress that further intensified the rivalry between states. Blocking the ceding of western lands to Congress as proposed by Franklin and Dickinson, Maryland—whose governor and most influential politicians were members of the great land companies— refused to sign off on the Confederation until Virginia ceded its claims to the territory north of the Ohio.

When, during Governor Jefferson's tenure, Virginia finally ceded its claims, Maryland gave in. But then the New Jersey delegation, thoroughly in the grip of land speculators, led a movement that blocked the cession for three more years. Historian Thomas Perkins Abernethy records that "every time the issue came up in Congress, a delegate from Virginia sprang to his feet and demanded that each member, on his honor before voting, declare whether or not he was personally concerned in the land companies."[1]

Virginia's cession of its claims to western lands finally made it possible for each state to fix its western boundary line. It put an end to speculation in three major land companies—the Indiana, Vandalia, Illinois, and Wabash land companies—effectively bursting the speculative bubble.

In March 1784, at a poorly attended Confederation Congress meeting in Annapolis presided over by Richard Henry Lee of Virginia, Congressman Jefferson presented a plan to establish a government for the Northwest Territories. He proposed dividing the territories into fourteen new states.

Once settlers adopted the constitution and laws of any original state and their population equaled the least populous state, the territory would be admitted to the Union on an equal footing with the original states. Congress adopted Jefferson's Land Ordinance of 1784—all but the final article: "That after the year 1800 of the Christian era, there shall be neither slavery nor involuntary servitude."

To Jefferson, owner of 204 slaves, the abolition of slavery had become a matter of overriding national urgency. He believed that it must be settled by Congress in advance of any further western settlement. In the Land Ordinance, he included an article stipulating the abolition of slavery on all federal lands. It passed. But the next day, when Jefferson attempted to make the ban extend to the existing thirteen states, the delegates deadlocked.

In a fiery debate, most of the Northern states supported abolition, but when it came to a final vote, the Southern delegates, including Confederation president Richard Henry Lee and the rest of Jefferson's fellow Virginians, voted against it.

Jefferson needed the votes of seven states to carry the measure; he could muster only six. John Beatty of New Jersey had a cold and stayed in his lodgings; the majority of New Jersey delegates voted against abolition. The defeat of Jefferson's motion by a single vote sickened him. He wrote to his closest friend, Madison: "South Carolina, Maryland and !Virginia! voted against it."[2]

Years later, Jefferson would write to a French historian,

> The voice of a single individual would have prevented this abominable crime from spreading itself over the new country. Thus we see the fate of millions unborn hanging on the tongue of one man, and Heaven was silent in that awful moment.[3]

Jefferson would go on waiting for "a god of Justice" to free his own slaves.

And when word arrived that John Jay was resigning as minister to France, Jefferson, whose wife had died after giving birth to a sixteen-pound baby, once again resigned in disgust from Congress to join Franklin and John Adams in Paris.

For the next five years, Jefferson would travel widely in Europe, establishing consulates to assist in spreading America's international trade.

CHAPTER TWENTY-FIVE

"I Shall Not Rest"

By the summer of 1786, the postwar depression had reached such a critical stage that no sector of the American economy remained immune. International trade had all but stopped. Farmers could not pay their taxes or their loans and faced widespread foreclosures.

Scottish merchants who operated a thousand country stores had cut off further credit—even refusing to supply seed to farmers—and were suing to collect their debts. The only import-export trading, what little remained, was between Britain and the United States, but it had dropped by 30 percent in one year. Farm wages had declined by 20 percent in five years.

Several states continued to run their printing presses, producing ever-less-valuable currency. And several states had passed "stay laws," stopping collections of debts run up by the vicious combination of a money shortage, high taxes, and insistent creditors.

In Virginia, planters' debts to British merchants amounted to ten times all Virginia currency in circulation. Writing from Paris, Thomas Jefferson resorted to selling off land and slaves to pay his debts to British merchants. When his tenants failed to pay the rent on his Elk Hill farm for the fourth consecutive year, he put it and its complement of enslaved workers on the auction block. But the sale produced no cash: the buyers could only afford to give him bonds against future harvests. The

proceeds of the slave auction, he wrote to his cousin, were "miserable,"
the slaves "averaging only £45 a piece" (about $7,000 today).[1]

In June 1784, James Madison, chairman of the commerce committee of
Virginia's House of Delegates, sponsored a resolution that paved the way
for a joint Virginia-Maryland jurisdiction of the Potomac. Everyone
knew George Washington was behind it.

At Washington's invitation, commissioners from Maryland and Virginia gathered in the new dining room at Mount Vernon in March 1785
to iron out growing trade problems in the Chesapeake Bay region. Washington was not a delegate but, as president of the newly incorporated
Potomac Company, he agreed to preside over the meeting.

The conference came as a result of Washington's years-long efforts to
gain public support for what he called his "grand design," a 190-mile
combined Potomac waterway and canal to link the Ohio Valley with the
Atlantic Ocean. Reports of canal-building projects in New York and
Pennsylvania had added fresh urgency to the meeting.

For thirty years now, Washington had been aware of the riches of the
American interior; no man sought to be the Apostle of American Im-
provement more than Washington. He saw the opening of the over-the-
mountain West as the key not only to prosperity but to survival as a
nation. To establish better communications with the West was even
more critical now than it had been before the Revolution. Thousands of
settlers were moving across the Alleghenies to farm the fertile lands of
the Ohio and its tributaries. European rivals of the new nation were
eager to alienate these pioneers from the United States.

As Washington saw it, on all sides the Confederation was surrounded
by enemies. The British still had not relinquished seven of their forts
around the Great Lakes, and many Indian tribes remained loyal to them.
On the west bank of the Mississippi and in Florida, Spain was working
through its Indian allies to woo away the trade of the settlers.

What was worse, from Washington's standpoint, was that the individual American states, instead of cooperating, were competing and

placing obstacles in one another's paths. No better example existed than Washington's renewed Potomac waterway project.

Even before the war had ended, Washington had turned his mind back to the enterprise that had led him to send off work parties at his own expense to begin to clear a better roadway to his thirty-three thousand acres of western lands.

In January 1783, a recently migrated Irish engineer named Christopher Colles wrote to Washington to offer his services in removing obstacles to navigating the upper Ohio River in western Pennsylvania. By blasting away only "two or three miles" of rapids, Colles claimed, he could open the river for shipping all the way from Fort Pitt down the Ohio to the Mississippi.

Washington had tried to woo Colles to his Potomac River project, but Colles had found work rebuilding New York City's water system and had also proposed a canal between the Hudson River and Lake Erie to a far more receptive New York legislature.

Washington remained convinced that the Potomac waterway was likely to succeed, but it would have to be a private venture. Colles had approached Congress with his own Ohio River proposal, but, as Washington predicted, Congress declined to act on it. By the time Washington hosted the conference at Mount Vernon, the Maryland Assembly was moving ahead with its own project—in direct competition to Washington's Virginia-based Potomac Company.

Even as Washington had waited for the definitive peace treaty to arrive from Paris, in the summer of 1783 he made a sortie up the Mohawk River—the route to the interior that Colles proposed—with several of his generals.

Only Washington's shocking lack of cash and the dilapidated condition of his Mount Vernon farms seems to have made him postpone his plans for a western tour. To the Marquis de Chastellux, he confided, "I shall not rest contented till I have explored the western country and have traversed those lines which have given bounds to a new empire," though his "private concerns" beckoned him back to Mount Vernon.[2]

In Virginia, Washington's partners had gone ahead without waiting for the signed peace treaty. News from Paris that the British would be ceding the vast territory between the Alleghenies and the Mississippi to the new nation was enough to touch off a fresh speculative fever.

Like Washington, many Virginians believed that if they could channel trade between the Chesapeake and Europe into the interior by way of the Potomac, Virginia could become the commercial capital of the nation. As early as autumn 1783, Congressman Jefferson had been appointed head of a committee assigned to draw up plans to situate the new capital of the Confederation's government. He proposed the shores of the Chesapeake.

George Washington's plan was only one element in a blueprint for extending the influence of his native state, already the largest and by five times the most populous. Jefferson had written to Madison in February 1784 that Virginia should press its claims to the west bank of the Kanawha River in present-day Ohio as a buffer zone against Indian attacks on Virginia.

In the same letter, Jefferson urged Madison to support the Potomac waterway in the Virginia legislature. The waterway "between the Western waters and the Atlantic of course promises us almost a monopoly of the Western and Indian trade." He pointed to a Pennsylvania plan to build a canal along the Schuylkill River as an argument for Virginia to act fast.

He urged Madison to introduce a "particular" Virginia tax of £10,000 ($1.5 million today) a year to open up the Potomac and the James Rivers. To guarantee public support, Jefferson suggested Washington as chief executive of the project:

> General Washington has [the] Potomac much at heart. The superintendence of it would be a noble amusement in his retirement and leave a monument of him as long as the waters should flow. . . .
>
> He would accept of the direction of it as long as the money should be employed on the Potomac. The popularity of his name would carry it through the assembly.

Jefferson did not have to persuade Washington of the economic merits of the scheme. The grand project would not violate his declared intention to "quit all public employment." Jefferson was quick to add that he himself did not own "one inch of land on any water either of Potomac or Ohio." Jefferson insisted that his "zeal in this business is public and pure."[3]

To Jefferson, it went without saying that Washington was out of public office and was free to benefit handsomely. At first, Washington responded that, because of interstate rivalries and problems of legislative funding, he doubted a special tax had a chance despite the "great and truly wise" nature of such a policy. Then Washington quickly reversed himself and agreed to superintend the Potomac project. His brief retirement was over.

In the spring of 1784, Madison arranged to have himself appointed chairman of the commerce committee of the Virginia House of Burgesses. On June 20, he then had himself appointed to a commission to negotiate with Maryland to pave the way for joint waterway jurisdiction. Washington's old friend, former congressman Thomas Johnson, pushed a similar resolution through the Maryland Assembly.

All that summer, taverns and drawing rooms buzzed with excited rumors about the waterway. By fall, when Washington visited Seneca Falls on the Potomac on his way west to inspect his Ohio Valley lands, workers were already building huts on both sides of the falls.

On his return, he sent a long report to Virginia governor Benjamin Harrison with a formal petition for incorporation of the Potomac Company. On October 15, 1784, he sent Thomas Johnson incorporation papers to push through the Maryland legislature. For the first time, Washington voiced his growing anxiety over the problems he saw ahead for the new nation:

> The want of energy in the Federal government, the pulling of
> one state and party of states against another and the commo-
> tion amongst the Eastern people have sunk our national

character much below par and has brought our politics and credit to the brink of a precipice. A step or two further must plunge us into a sea of troubles, perhaps anarchy.[4]

The more Washington wrote about it, the better the idea of a Potomac waterway seemed to him, not just as a moneymaking scheme at which the company could secure "a large portion" of the fur trade of the Great Lakes region but as a "necessary step for the well-being and strength of the Union." To Jacob Read he wrote, "It is by the cement of interest that we can be held together."[5]

Against criticism of the waterway as a "utopian scheme," Washington countered that the national government should at least be surveying its vast new western territories so that the West could be opened up to even larger numbers of settlers and traders.

Writing to Richard Henry Lee, he urged Congress "to have the western waters well explored, the navigation of them fully ascertained, accurately laid down and a complete and perfect map made of the country."[6] But Washington's most powerful congressional ally, Jefferson, had already left for Paris as one of the new trade ministers to Europe, and Congress for the first time ignored Washington.

As if on a military campaign, Washington pursued his Potomac project, appearing at the Virginia House of Burgesses on November 15, 1784, when it convened with a "numerous and respectable" group of Virginians and Marylanders who told anyone who would listen that their canal-building project was "one of the grandest chains for preserving the Federal Union."[7]

These same gentlemen helped draft the requisite legislation and sent it to Washington, who forwarded it to commerce committee chairman Madison, stressing that he had grown impatient with the "limping behavior" of the two state legislatures to fund the project. He had decided, he told Madison, that the Potomac project "had better be placed in the hands of a corporate company."[8]

The company was to be capitalized at $1 million (about $150 million today), to be sold to shareholders. Washington's proposal sailed through the two legislatures in a single day: on January 25, 1785, Virginia and Maryland adopted identical bills. Washington triumphantly relayed the news to President Lee in Congress, and Madison passed the word to Jefferson in Paris.

So confident were the lawmakers on both shores of the Potomac that each state bought 50 of the initial offering of 220 shares. Virginia also voted to grant 50 shares to Washington for his efforts. But Washington remained cautious about public opinion. While he needed the money—he wrote to George Fairfax in England that the stock would provide "the greatest and most certain" foundation for his income—he wanted to be "as free and independent as the air" and feared that he would be accused by some of having "sinister motives."[9]

To Jefferson, he wrote that he wanted public opinion to believe he was superintending the project with no other motive for promoting it than the good of two publics—Virginia first, the United States second. Finally, Washington persuaded the Virginia Assembly to earmark the profits from his shares for the education of the orphans of Revolutionary War soldiers.

Washington's public-spirited gesture did not hurt the sale of Potomac Company stock. As Washington bought shares, he urged old friends and colleagues to join him. He pressed Robert Morris, who had held the franchise for American tobacco to France since the peace treaty, to build a large warehouse in Alexandria, adding, "Had I an inclination and talents to enter into the commercial line I have no idea of a better opening to make a fortune." His project would inspire others, eventually bringing "navigation to almost everyone's door."[10]

Visitors to Mount Vernon found themselves a captive audience to a dinner-table sales pitch. One dazed German visitor reported that Washington had bored him for two days with facts and figures.

On May 17, 1785, many of Virginia's and Maryland's wealthiest citizens gathered in Alexandria for the company's organization meeting. At a midday banquet, Washington called the meeting to order and read a brief report on the commercial and political significance of the waterway.

He then called for an election of officers. Daniel Carroll of Carrollton, one of the wealthiest men in America, was chosen as chairman. When the share subscription book went around, 403 shares worth £40,300 (about $6 million today) were pledged. The members then moved on to elect a president and board of directors: Washington was unopposed for president.

Two weeks later in the first board meeting, held in secret in a private room at Alexandria's City Tavern, the board decided to start work immediately, employing two crews of fifty men each to clear two stretches of the river. The directors also decided to begin collecting the money pledged for shares to cover the costs.

Negotiations between the two states' commissioners were scheduled for March 1786. As he was not a delegate, Washington saw fit to invite the commissioners to his newly renovated Mount Vernon. There, the conferees learned from Washington that Americans were snatching up the subscription to shares at double the expected pace. Two hundred and fifty shares were needed to launch the project; five hundred had already been sold. And Washington still expected to hear from foreign investors. He had asked Jefferson to sound out the financial markets in France, Holland, and England.

Washington had left little choice for the commissioners but to iron out their differences. The talks quickly hit a snag, however. Maryland's delegation refused to discuss anything until Virginia agreed to forgo collection of tolls at the entrance to Chesapeake Bay.

Virginia's delegates countered that toll collections must be allowed only at the sites of the waterfalls being removed from the river itself and be collected along a toll road that was to replace the old Braddock Road. They had instructions not to yield on this key issue, but rather than see the talks collapse, they decided to ignore their instructions: Access to the Chesapeake would remain free.

With Washington as silent witness, negotiations went on for eight days. An agreement allowed joint commercial and fishing rights in

Potomac Tidewater region. But then Thomas Stone of Maryland insisted on a resolution calling for a joint application to Congress for permission to build a small, independent navy in case the federal government failed to protect the waterway. (There would be no federal navy until 1797.)

Stone suggested that the same application to Congress should also seek approval for joint Virginia-Maryland regulation of state currencies and import duties to be reviewed at annual meetings. The Mount Vernon conference exposed numerous weaknesses in the Confederation government that the delegates could see must be repaired. Stone also proposed that the commissioners invite delegates from Pennsylvania and Delaware to their next meeting in May 1786 in Annapolis. Finally, delegates from the Virginia legislature suggested expanding the invitation to include delegates from every state. The delegates agreed unanimously.

The commissioners' agreement would become known as the Mount Vernon Compact, the first serious critique of the Confederation government. In later years, Madison considered the talks at Mount Vernon as the first step on the road to creating a new constitution for the United States and establishment of a stronger, more centralized national government.

Not everyone was applauding Washington's messianic devotion to his latest cause. Baltimore merchants were laughing at him, and he knew it. He told an English visitor, "They know it must hurt their commerce amazingly."[11]

A side effect of his single-minded campaign was to remind the leaders of Congress that he had not lost his edge as an organizer and inspirer of men, matériel, and money. Richard Henry Lee, president of Congress, wrote to a friend in Virginia, "You all know his persevering spirit and attendant character . . . [T]hese qualities promise success to the Potomac project."[12]

But serious problems emerged before Washington and the company's directors could visit the worksites that summer. There was trouble finding workers, as most able-bodied men in the region were busy with harvests. But finding willing laborers was easier than getting subscribers of stock to pay up. Even after Washington and the board issued repeated calls and Washington threatened legal action, many stockholders paid little or nothing on their pledges. In private, Washington laid the blame on a weak Confederation government and the resultant shortage of cash.

In the spring of 1786, Alexander Hamilton decided it was high time to throw in with Washington and Madison to rescue the nation from the petty jealousies of its member states. Running to represent New York City in the New York Assembly, he cobbled together a nationalist slate that won the state's legislative election and appointed him as its delegate to the Annapolis Convention.

But when the convention opened on September 11, delegates from only a handful of states—Virginia and the Middle States—appeared. Not even Maryland sent a delegate to the conference in its own state capitol.

After three days—when the other states' delegates still had not arrived—Hamilton, with Madison's support, seized on the broader powers that New Jersey's legislature gave its delegates to press the convention to call on Congress and the state governors to authorize a wider conference that would go beyond studying impediments to trade.

In a circular letter, Hamilton cited "important defects in the system of the federal government" that were causing "embarrassments which characterize the present state of our affairs, foreign and domestic."

The Annapolis delegates called on Congress to authorize a new convention to meet in Philadelphia in May 1787 "to render the Constitution of the Federal government adequate to the exigencies of the Union."[13] And then he moved to adjourn the Annapolis meeting before any more delegates arrived.

CHAPTER TWENTY-SIX

"THE IMPENDING STORM"

Only two weeks after the Annapolis Convention ended so abruptly, debt-ridden farmers in the Berkshire Hills of western Massachusetts, mostly veterans of the Revolutionary army, revolted. Many of the region's farmers could not pay their debts to storekeepers or to tax collectors; they faced eviction from their farms with their families or imprisonment.

Under Massachusetts's conservative new constitution, written by John Adams and adopted in 1780, participation in both voting and office-holding had become limited to men who owned certain levels of property. John Hancock had no trouble qualifying to serve as governor by owning the minimum of £1,000 (equivalent to $150,000) worth of property. In several western towns, however, not a single citizen was qualified to hold statewide office.

Wealthy Boston merchants had taken control of the state legislature and, supported by a new law, allowed landed interests to make loans to farmers at usurious interest rates, which they could no longer repay. The assembly also had shifted the tax burden from wealthy bondholders to impoverished farmers, many of whom were eking out a living on land that they had received in lieu of army pay.

Bankrupt farmers were being thrown into debtors' prisons by the hundreds. The rebels, as Massachusetts politicians were quick to denominate them, became especially bitter because the legislature had adjourned without heeding their petitions for "stay" laws to prevent even more foreclosures.

At a town meeting in Worcester on August 29, 1786, discontent boiled over. Angry calls for action triggered a Hampshire county convention of fifty towns one week later. In a tense gathering, town delegates condemned the Massachusetts Senate, the lawyers, the high cost of obtaining justice, the entire tax structure, and the lack of paper money.

Daniel Shays, a subsistence farmer who had attained the rank of captain in the Revolutionary army, had received his veteran's land grant and held town offices in Pelham. He led an angry crowd of 1,500 armed men to the Northampton County court, where judges were assembling to sentence debtors.

To Shays and his neighbors, the new property taxes and restrictions on voting and office-holding mirrored the major abuses under British rule that had brought on the Revolution. Shays strode up to the courthouse door and delivered a petition, demanding that the judges cease the proceedings.

The next week, an even larger crowd forced the closing of the courts at Worcester. At Concord and Great Barrington, crowds barred judges and lawyers from entering the courthouses and, chasing away the sheriffs, stopped the sheriffs' sales.

Four days after the Northampton protest, Governor James Bowdoin issued a proclamation condemning Shays for introducing "riot, anarchy and confusion." Bowdoin dispatched six hundred militiamen to guard the state supreme court in Springfield. Shays assembled an equal number of armed men and, on September 26, confronted the state militia, forcing it to flee. The supreme court adjourned.

Commissioned by the Confederation Congress to investigate the protests, Henry Knox, a major land speculator, reported that there were at least fifteen thousand "wicked and ambitious men" under arms "determined to annihilate all debts public and private" and threatening "to overturn, not only the forms but the principles of the present constitutions."[1] In fact, at most, Shays led no more than two thousand men at any one time.

Receiving a copy of Knox's report, General Henry "Light-Horse Harry" Lee, a protégé of Washington's, wrote to him "in dire apprehension" about "the malcontents" who had as their object "the abolition of debts, the division of property and re-union with Great Britain." Lee asked Washington to use his "unbounded influence" to restore "peace and reconciliation."[2]

Washington responded that "the picture you have drawn" of "the commotions & temper" was to be "lamented and deprecated:

> Mankind, left to themselves, are unfit for their own government. I am mortified beyond expression when I view the clouds which have spread over the brightest morn that ever dawned upon any country.

Washington refused to use his influence: "Influence is not government."[3]

In Congress, after reading Lee's report that the Shaysites "profess only to aim at a reform of their constitution and of certain abuses," James Madison wrote to his father that he was apprehensive that there would be "an appeal to the sword."[4]

No doubt Washington and Madison were aware that Congress had no money to pay federal troops to put down a rebellion. Realizing that Congress would do nothing, Governor Bowdoin raised £20,000 (roughly $1.2 million today) from private donors and hired a force of 4,400 men, mostly unemployed Bostonians—the largest armed force mustered in the United States since the Revolution.

To Congress, civil war appeared imminent—a war between the unemployed and the disenfranchised veteran. Alarmed at reports that armed rebels were about to seize cannon from the federal arsenal at Springfield, Congress did the one thing it had clear-cut authority to do under the Articles of Confederation: It voted to raise a Continental force and commissioned General Benjamin Lincoln, Washington's second-in-command at the end of the war, to confront the Shaysites.

As snow blanketed the Berkshires, Captain Shays gathered his own army of about 1,200 men. The day after Christmas 1786, he led a march to Springfield to join forces with other insurgents under the command of Luke Day. They aimed to intimidate the small force of militia guarding New England's federal arsenal in West Springfield.

As they rushed to seize guns from the arsenal before Bowdoin's militia could reinforce it, Shays and Day made the classic mistake of keeping their forces divided, straddling the Connecticut River. When Shays proposed a joint attack, Day replied that he would not be ready to attack for another two days. Making matters worse, Day's message was intercepted.

Still expecting Day's reinforcements, Shays pressed the assault the next morning. The Shaysites marched within one hundred yards of the arsenal before its cannons unleashed a volley of grapeshot. Four Shaysites dropped dead; the rest fled.

When Lincoln and his Continentals arrived, Shays and his followers retreated toward the hills of Vermont. Hard-marching all night, Lincoln surprised Shays at dawn on February 4, 1787. With the temperature hovering at twenty degrees below zero, in a running battle on snowshoes in waist-deep snow, Lincoln captured 150 insurgents. The rest escaped, with Shays and his aides disappearing across the Vermont border to seek sanctuary. Protected by officials of the independent republic who refused to arrest them, Shays and his core followers built a mountain fort near Sunderland, in Vermont's southwest corner.

Hastily convening, the Massachusetts Supreme Court attainted four thousand Shaysites of treason, outlawing them and seizing their lands. But in its spring 1787 session, the Massachusetts legislature offered pardons to all Shaysites except their four leaders.

Shocked by the uprising, and unable to remain in his Beacon Hill mansion with his gouty foot elevated, John Hancock returned to politics. Reelected governor in a landslide, he pardoned all the Shaysites. Hancock induced the legislature to repeal direct property taxes, lower court fees, and exempt clothing, household goods, and the tools of the trade from seizure for debt.

Even though Shays's tax revolt had been put down quickly, it thoroughly alarmed Washington and some other American leaders who were becoming convinced that the fragile Union was on the verge of collapse. In Virginia, Richard Henry Lee worried that "the contagion will spread and may reach Virginia."[5]

Learning of Shays's revolt at his post in Paris, Thomas Jefferson took an opposite view, writing to Abigail Adams:

> The spirit of resistance to government is so valuable on certain occasions that I wish it to always be kept alive. . . . I like a little rebellion now and then. It is like a storm in the atmosphere.

And when he learned that the Shaysites had surrendered, Jefferson wrote to John Adams advising amnesty: "God forbid that we should ever be 20 years without such a rebellion. The tree of liberty must be refreshed from time to time with the blood of patriots and tyrants."[6]

Following hard on the heels of the Massachusetts rebellion, in February 1787, speaking before the New York Assembly, Alexander Hamilton demanded his state support the introduction of federal customs duties.

Overcoming the objection of Governor Clinton that a federal customs service would intrude on New York's sovereignty, Hamilton, in a brilliant compromise, proposed that New York appoint tax collectors to collect duties, then turn the money over to the federal Congress. Emboldened, Hamilton then pressed for the appointment of a New York delegation to the May convention in Philadelphia.

For nearly five years in retirement, George Washington had refrained from using his influence to make political pronouncements. But now he wrote to Madison of the need to "rescue the political machine" from "the impending storm." Without "some alteration in our political creed," without a "liberal and energetic Constitution" that would be "well-guarded & closely watched," Washington wrote, the thirteen individual states "would pull each other apart."[7]

While Congress had approved a convention only to make moderate modifications to the Articles of Confederation, Washington, stunned by Shays's Rebellion, was convinced that only a thorough overhaul would do. Now he was willing to lend his influence to bring about sweeping changes.

CHAPTER TWENTY-SEVEN

"Plain, Honest Men"

O n a sweltering afternoon in early May 1787, George Washington arrived in Philadelphia escorted by its elite First City Troop, their white breeches, high-topped boots, and round, black, silver-rimmed hats adding a celebratory note to the opening of the Constitutional Convention. As the cavalcade cantered toward the imposing redbrick statehouse, cheering pedestrians lined the chestnut-tree-shaded streets.

Before the deliberations got underway, however, Washington intended to pay a visit to an old friend. His carriage rattled down cobbled Market Street to Benjamin Franklin's handsome brick townhouse, where the elderly statesman's daughter, Sarah, ushered him into the tree-shaded courtyard. More than three decades had passed since they had first met on the march to the Monongahela; a decade and a revolution since they had last spoken on the siege lines outside Boston. Now there was time for a leisurely visit before the convention officially opened.

Franklin welcomed Washington into the new three-story wing he had added to his house, its first floor devoted to meetings and the collections of his American Philosophical Society. The other two stories housed his handsome library.

The once-poor printer's devil was proud of his rare books; the centerpiece, one that Washington would surely admire, was a priceless history of American horticulture with illustrations in color, one of only twelve copies printed. Franklin had been invited to subscribe to it when Pope Pius VI relinquished his right to a copy. Franklin showed Washington a fine edition of *Don Quixote* and the first edition of Thomas Paine's *The Crisis*, which was written on a drumhead before Washington's epic Christmas 1776 attack on Trenton; Washington had ordered it read aloud to his troops.

A man who had despised governors and worked against them half his life, Franklin now served as president of Pennsylvania's Supreme Executive Council. A man who had once run advertisements in his newspaper for slaves, Franklin had freed his last slave when he was elected president of the Pennsylvania Abolition Society.

It would take another two weeks before a quorum of delegates allowed the Constitutional Convention's proceedings to begin on May 25. Those from Pennsylvania and Virginia had been first to arrive; Rhode Island sent no delegation at all. Several Revolutionary War leaders, including Patrick Henry, boycotted the convention; neither John nor Sam Adams attended; Jefferson remained at his diplomatic post in Paris.

The delegates ranged in age from twenty-six-year-old Jonathan Dayton of New Jersey to eighty-one-year-old Franklin, so feeble from gout and kidney stones that some days he had to be carried in a sedan chair by prisoners from Walnut Street Prison. He often seemed to be asleep, partially because he had to be dosed with laudanum (a combination of opium and honey) to ameliorate his pain. One fellow delegate uncharitably described him as "a short, fat, trenched old man in a plain Quaker dress, bald pate and short white locks"; another noted "an activity of mind equal to a youth of twenty-five years of age."[1]

Among the fifty-five delegates, the average age was forty-two years. Twenty-nine delegates were college-educated; thirty-four had trained at law; the rest were merchants, farmers, or planters. Thirteen were country lawyers, combining farming with quarrels over property lines and deeds.

Eight derived the bulk of their income from mercantile clients engaged in interstate and international commerce. Seven were merchants, four owned ships. Ten received their principal income from public offices.

All the delegates were white males; twenty-five owned slaves, from a single household servant to three hundred fieldworkers. Most were already well-known public figures: thirty-nine had served in Congress. Seven had been state governors; eight had signed the Declaration of Independence; and fifteen had written their states' constitutions. Of nineteen Revolutionary War combat veterans, several bore the scars of battle. Five had served under Washington at Valley Forge. Two were college professors who had founded state universities; seven delegates were immigrants. The wealthiest by all accounts was, of course, British-born financier Robert Morris.*

Not all the delegates were flush with cash. While more than half of them owned public securities, their holdings were bonds purchased from individual states to help finance the war, which by now were heavily depreciated. Typical was Nicholas Gilman of New Hampshire, a Revolutionary War veteran who had owned and operated a general store before taking a seat in Congress. His securities, with a face value of $1,000 (about $29,000 today), were earning only $10 a year (about $290). If he had cashed in his bonds at the start of the convention, he would have received only $125 ($3,625).

Even more strapped was Jacob Broome of Delaware, a farmer whose harvests brought him an income of a mere $733 that year. By thrift, he had managed to invest in public securities. One certificate bore a face value of $38.80 ($1,131 today); the other, $2.78 ($80).

Yet worse off was David Brearley, a Revolutionary War veteran and

---

*Morris had only grown richer since the end of the war. In peacetime, he held a virtual monopoly on the nation's tobacco trade, with a three-year contract to export 20,000 thousand-pound hogsheads of tobacco to France annually in his own fleet of ships. For France, the reward for supporting the American Revolution had been direct access to the sweet tobacco grown around the Chesapeake to turn into snuff. The French were addicted to their pinch of snuff; no longer would they have to pay British middlemen to acquire it. The new middleman was Robert Morris.

now chief justice of the Supreme Court of New Jersey. He had at risk one Continental Loan Office certificate with a face value of $12.45 ($361 today); its market value was a paltry $2.49 ($72).

The delegate with the most at stake in the securities market was Elbridge Gerry of Marblehead, Massachusetts, a merchant who had grown rich by privateering. His investments had a face value of $50,000 but were currently worth one-fifth of that amount (roughly $300,000 today). Gerry was one of the five delegates who stood to gain the most in the securities markets but would either refuse to sign the Constitution or would walk out of the convention.

Edmund Randolph, holder of $13,800 in securities, was George Washington's personal lawyer. He had been his aide-de-camp in the Revolution and attorney general of Virginia. He would refuse to sign the Constitution because he thought it lacked sufficient checks and balances.

John Ten Eyck Lansing, an Albany lawyer and Speaker of the New York Assembly, held $7,000 in securities; he was a close ally of Governor Clinton's, a principal opponent of a federal government. Lansing would walk out of the convention at midpoint because he objected to the idea of a federal constitution.

John Francis Mercer, a Maryland planter, also held $7,200 in certificates; his brother Hugh, Washington's close friend, had been wounded at Fort Necessity and, after acting as the Ohio Company's agent in London, was bayoneted to death in the Battle of Princeton. Despite his own close friendship with Washington, John Mercer also declined to sign.

Luther Martin, also with $7,200 in securities, was a veteran and close friend of James Madison's. One of the nation's most successful lawyers, he opposed a federal government and refused to sign the Constitution because he objected to counting slaves for purposes of representation in Congress.

So great was the disparity between the wealthiest and the average delegates that if these five largest stakeholders had sold their securities on the Philadelphia market as the convention opened, their combined proceeds could have purchased all the securities held by the remaining five delegates.[2]

It was Robert Morris, head of the host Pennsylvania delegation—a man who had come close to holding presidential power as superintendent of finance during the war—who nominated George Washington to preside over the Constitutional Convention.

Washington had once been critical of Morris's financial dealings, yet now he accepted the nomination and took his place at the dais. The retired general was himself land rich but cash poor. He may have owned an estimated fifty-one thousand acres of riverfront property from the Chesapeake Bay to West Virginia, tended by three hundred slaves and as many tenant farmers, but he had been forced to borrow from a wealthier neighbor to pay for his trip to Philadelphia.

Among Washington's colleagues from the Tidewater area, the diminutive, thirty-six-year-old James Madison positioned himself facing the convention's new president at the center of an arc of green-baize-covered tables, where he could hear all the speakers and keep impeccable notes. Accomplished at compromise, Madison, as Governor Jefferson's floor manager in the Virginia House of Delegates, had negotiated Virginia's cession of western lands, setting the example for the other states that had finally brought the Confederation to life. After a ten-year legislative struggle in Virginia, Madison had also won adoption of Jefferson's statute on religious freedom, ending state subsidies for the support of clergy and establishing the doctrine of separation of church and state.

Joining Franklin and Robert Morris at Pennsylvania's table was Morris's business partner Gouverneur Morris, a playboy and gifted writer. Flanking them were Scottish constitutional expert James Wilson and merchant-banker George Clymer.

Like Franklin and Wilson, twelve of the delegates had acquired significant amounts of undeveloped land. On paper, Wilson, president of the Illinois-Wabash Company, owned an empire, but he had so many far-flung speculations that he had become bemired in debt. On a more modest scale, Franklin owned three thousand acres in Westmoreland County, in northeastern Pennsylvania.

Even more delegates were speculating in western lands, the names of some fourteen land companies doubtless quite familiar to them. The old Ohio Company had drawn young Washington to fight the French before he joined Richard Henry Lee in founding the more ambitious Mississippi Company. In the 1760s, Franklin and his transatlantic partners had invested heavily in the Indiana Company, the Vandalia, and the Grand Illinois Company, all seeking massive land grants from the Crown, all aborted by the break with the mother country. Other delegates held shares in the Loyal Company, the Burlington Company, the Greenbrier Company, the Transylvania Company, the Illinois-Wabash Company, the New Wales Company, the Susquehanna Company, and the Yazoo and the Military Adventurers Companies.

For forty years, investors in these companies had been buying land on paper with depreciated currency and holding it with the hope of great future profit. On his latest western trip to buy up shares from veterans, Washington was amazed to hear speculators talk of five hundred thousand acres as they had once talked of a thousand.

Whether they were invested in the securities markets, in trade, or in land, the majority of delegates believed they had to decide just who would vote and who would serve in office and govern the vast new country. The common Enlightenment belief held that property gave a man a stake in society.

Most states required property ownership to qualify to vote. Virginia required twenty-five acres of cultivated land or five hundred undeveloped acres. In Pennsylvania and New Hampshire, the sons of property owners were exempt.

The qualification for holding office was even steeper. Under the 1780 Massachusetts constitution, drafted by John Adams, John Hancock had no trouble documenting that he owned property valued at £1,000 (about

$150,000 today) to qualify to serve as governor. In South Carolina, it took even more—£10,000 ($1 million today) to demonstrate a right to preside over the state. To run for a seat in the state assembly of New Jersey required property worth £500 ($75,000 today) for the lower house, £1,000 ($150,000) for the state senate.

In the debate over who should vote the president, Gouverneur Morris posited that it should be the freeholders of the country. Richard Henry Lee of Virginia defined who should elect as "the solid, free and independent part of the community," as "the men of middling property, men not in debt on the one hand, and men on the other content with republican government and not aiming at immense fortunes, offices and power."

But who should rule the vast new nation? Should holding the highest office in the land require owning even more property? John Jay of New York believed so: The "people who own the country ought to govern it."[3]

Edmund Pendleton rose first, presenting a proposal of fifteen resolutions that had been drafted by James Madison. Known as the Virginia Plan, it went beyond merely revising the Articles of Confederation; it proposed an entirely new national government.

Proposing a bicameral legislature with proportional representation of the states, a lower house elected by the people, and an upper house elected by the lower house from nominees proposed by the state legislature, Virginia's plan called for a chief executive to be chosen from the national legislature, a judiciary with a supreme court, inferior courts elected by the legislature, and a council of revision with veto powers.

After two weeks of intense debate, William Paterson of New Jersey, leading the opposition to the Virginia Plan—which had become known as the large-state plan—introduced the smaller states' plan. Paterson's nine resolutions called for equal representation of the states in both houses of Congress.

The New Jersey plan stressed retaining the Articles of Confederation but would grant to Congress what it lacked: the powers to tax and to regulate foreign and interstate commerce. The plan called for a plural

executive, not a single chief executive, without veto power, and a supreme court to be appointed by Congress. The treaties of the United
States and the acts of Congress were to be the supreme laws of the states.

The lines were now drawn between delegates content with amendments to the Articles of Confederation and advocates of scrapping the
Confederation entirely and drawing up the framework for a new form of
national government.

It was Alexander Hamilton who had urged George Washington, his former commanding officer, to attend the convention and lend his weight
to the movement for reform. Setting aside his lucrative law practice,
Hamilton himself had joined, enjoying the support of a coalition of New
York City merchants and wealthy Hudson Valley landowners led by his
father-in-law, General Philip Schuyler.

Hamilton had been appointed to the convention by New York governor George Clinton, now serving his sixth term. Clinton represented
mechanics, artisans, and upstate farmers who favored the Confederation's policies of paper money and no taxation. His appointment of
Hamilton was hardly in line with that support, but he had assured that
the ambitious young economist would be outvoted by his two other ap-
pointees, Robert Yates and Robert Lansing.

In Alexander Hamilton, fellow Northern delegates saw not only a
former congressional colleague, New York City's leading lawyer, and a
spokesman for major landowners, Loyalists, merchants, and bankers but
also an outspoken nationalist. Southerners saw him through a different
prism: as an abolitionist. He was well known to be the co-founder and
chairman of the Society for Promoting the Manumission of Slaves.
Never forgetting his boyhood apprenticeship in the Caribbean, where he
had been required to wash and oil the bodies of slaves as they came off
the ships from Africa to be auctioned into lifelong bondage, Hamilton
was raising money to buy and free enslaved people.

Hamilton had never owned a single slave, but he knew Governor
Clinton owned eight. He had written and published a petition to the

legislature that alluded to the slave trade with "the Southern States" and called on New York to ban further importation of slaves from Africa to end "a commerce so repugnant to humanity and so inconsistent" with revolutionary ideals. The bill had passed, over the fierce opposition of representatives of slave-owning Dutch constituents. Only Quakers had freed all the slaves they owned in New York; many New Yorkers, anticipating further reforms, had sold their slaves to the agents of Southern planters.

On the morning of June 18, after several days of intense debate over the New Jersey plan, Hamilton asked President Washington for the floor. He rose and, without consulting his notes, began a speech that would unfurl for six uninterrupted hours. He felt, he began, that he was obliged to declare himself "unfriendly" to both the Virginia and New Jersey plans, yet was "particularly opposed" to Paterson's small-state plan. No amendment of the Articles that left the states sovereign "could possibly answer."

He was discouraged by the "amazing" number of delegates who expected the "desired blessings" by merely substituting a weak federal government for a loose-knit confederation of sovereign states. To Hamilton, all the defects lay with the states:

> All the passions we see, of avarice, ambition, interest, which govern most individuals and all public bodies, fall into the current of the states and do not flow into the stream of the general government. . . . How then are these evils to be avoided? Only by such a complete sovereignty in the general government as will turn all the strong principles and passions [to] its side.

Because they were not commercial, small states like New Jersey would only contribute "to the wealth of the commercial ones." And they could never meet tax quotas as qualifications for voting, as the Virginia Plan proposed. "They will and must fail," he argued, and the Union itself would be dissolved.

The only answer, he argued, was to eliminate the cost of state government by "extinguishing" the state governments: "They are not necessary for any of the great purposes of commerce, revenue or agriculture." They should be "abolished." What would work better would be "district tribunals—corporations for local purposes." And he did not believe that "republican government could be established over so great an extent."

Many of Hamilton's auditors reeled at such heresy, but Hamilton raced on:

> In every community where industry is encouraged, there will be a division of it into the few and the many. Hence, separate interests will arise. There will be debtors and creditors. Give all power to the many, they will oppress the few. Give all power to the few, they will oppress the many. Both, therefore, ought to have power, that each may defend itself against the other.

Hamilton then read aloud his own plan of government: a two-house Supreme Legislative Power, a representative assembly, elected by freemen, serving three-year terms, and a lifetime senate—resembling the English House of Lords but not hereditary—to serve "during good behavior." Senators would be chosen by electors. Judges would be elected directly by the people and serve during good behavior.

The governor—Hamilton did not use the word "president"—would be chosen for life; the governor would have veto power over all laws and would be charged with executing them. He would be commander in chief of all the military forces, and he would make all treaties "with the advice and approbation of the Senate." He would appoint the heads of the departments of finance, war, and foreign affairs. The chief executive would nominate all ambassadors subject to Senate approval, and he would "have the power of pardoning all offenses but treason," which would require the assent of the Senate. Hamilton feared that a governor unchecked could be a "monster"; thus, he, as well as judges and senators, could be impeached.

In one brilliant, breathless oration, Hamilton, with the exception of only term limits and the rules and qualifications for voters, laid out what would become the basic framework of the U.S. government.

Off and on for the next few days, he rose to defend portions of his plan, and then, sure that no one would take his advice, Hamilton went home. Before he left, he went for a "long afternoon's walk" with James Madison, who came away more deeply impressed by Hamilton than his colleagues were.

No immediate action was taken on his recommendations. As William Samuel Johnson of Connecticut put it, Hamilton was "praised by everybody but supported by none."

Ten days later, Lansing and Yates, spurning the convention, opposed to its proceedings, and prepared to fight whatever "national" system the delegates propounded, also returned to New York.

But Hamilton kept abreast of developments, returning to Philadelphia from time to time. He learned that James Wilson of Pennsylvania had broken the deadlock over representation in the lower house by proposing that it be based on the white male population of each state, plus three-fifths of the black population. Southern delegates could see that what would become known as the three-fifths clause assured that the slaveholding states would control the House of Representatives. For purposes of representation, a holder of three hundred slaves such as George Washington would count as 181 voters to Benjamin Franklin's single vote. They eagerly embraced Wilson's proposal.

In return, the Southern delegates swung their support behind the New England states in ending state customs duties and making federal duties the principal means of financing the federal government.

The provision that each state would have an equal vote in the Senate cleared the way for drawing up twenty-three resolutions that made up the rough draft of the Constitution. Presented to the convention, it triggered a four-week-long debate.

The most acrimonious argument produced a resolution that tabled for twenty years any further discussion by Congress of outlawing the African slave trade. Combined with the three-fifths clause, this moratorium revealed that, just below the surface, deep divisions already prevailed between the North and South over slavery.

In revising the draft Constitution, the matter of emoluments to officials at home and abroad surfaced. Many delegates who had attended the Confederation Congresses remembered the uproar over Silas Deane's acceptance of the diamond-studded snuffbox as a parting gift from the French king. As a result, the Articles of Confederation had forbidden "any person holding any office of profit or trust under the United States" from accepting "any present, emolument, office, or title of any kind whatever, from any king, prince, or foreign state."

Now, at the last moment of the Constitutional Convention, emoluments came up again. Benjamin Franklin revealed that as he had prepared to sail home in 1785, the French foreign minister had presented him with a miniature watercolor-on-ivory portrait of King Louis, encircled by two concentric rings holding 408 diamonds. Franklin's grandson, William Temple Franklin, the secretary to the American mission in Paris, estimated that they were valued at 1,000 Louis d'Or (about $270,000 today). Temple apparently accompanied Franklin and his fellow emissaries to Versailles to receive their parting gifts. The king had specifically instructed foreign minister Vergennes to give Franklin a gift "more valuable than those generally given to Ministers Plenipotentiary": *"Je desire que Monsieur Franklin soit bien traite."*

To his younger revolutionary colleagues, Franklin's acceptance of such an elaborate gift from a foreign monarch symbolized everything they considered wrong with the old imperial system. Franklin explained that he had found himself in an awkward position. Not accepting the royal gift would give the appearance of shunning French diplomatic traditions and possibly harm relations between the two allies; acceptance would be seen as making the United States indebted to the French. Before leaving Paris, Franklin had informed Jefferson, his successor, of the gift. He could easily surmise that Jefferson would receive a similar gift when it was his turn to come home. Now Franklin put the conundrum to the Constitutional Convention.

In the rough draft of the new constitution, Article 1, paragraph 4, only banned accepting titles of honor, not gifts. But now Elbridge Gerry of Massachusetts insisted on raising the issue anew:

> Persons having foreign attachments will be sent among us & insinuated into our councils in order to be made instruments for their purposes. Every one knows the vast sums laid out in Europe for secret services.

Gerry argued that, when the Articles of Confederation had been drafted, Congress's concern about emoluments had revolved around the practice of English monarchs buying control of votes in Parliament and the House of Lords by doling out benefices at court that carried lucrative incomes. The prohibition in the Articles of Confederation had been on the holding of multiple offices.

Charles Cotesworth Pinckney of South Carolina now demanded that the wording about the emoluments from the Articles of Confederation be added to the revised constitution to read, "No Person holding any Office of Profit or Trust under them, shall, without the Consent of the Congress, accept of any present, Emolument, Office, or Title, of any kind whatever, from any King, Prince, or foreign State."

Franklin offered to make the jewels a gift to the nation, but Congress refused the offer. In his will, he would leave it to his daughter, Sarah.

After four months, the last debate of the Constitutional Convention took place, on September 10. A five-man committee, including Hamilton and Madison, worked around the clock for two days preparing the final draft for a vote on September 17, when each of the twelve delegations would vote separately and then line up by state to sign the document. Sixteen delegates had already gone home; of those who remained, three—Gerry of Massachusetts, and Randolph and Mason of Virginia— refused to sign.

When he learned that the draft document was ready for final revisions and signing, Hamilton hurried to Philadelphia without informing his fellow New York delegates Lansing and Yates. Defying Governor Clinton and the New York Assembly, he became the only signer from New York State. Without Hamilton's bold act, New York would not have become a signatory to the Constitution of the United States.

Had these delegates allowed their speculative interests to influence their actions in the Constitutional Convention, making each of them "a direct economic beneficiary from the adoption of the Constitution," as Charles Beard alleged? How much of a personal windfall did the delegates who attended the convention reap? An exhaustive study by historian Forrest McDonald shows that, contrary to Beard's theory that the delegates self-interestedly were scrapping the Articles of Confederation to form a centralized government more favorable to their interests, they themselves earned, at best, only a modest return.

In December 1791, when Nicholas Gilman would exchange his old certificates for the new U.S. bonds, he would find his stake in the new republic had grown by $503 ($14,587 today) in four years—about $10 a month. David Brearley's had doubled, from $5 ($145 today) to $10 ($290).

Robert Morris's securities had appreciated by $2,650 ($77,000 today), reaching $7,150, ($207,000), still far short of the $11,000 ($319,000) face value of his Continental securities before the convention.

McDonald offered perhaps the best analysis of Beard's venerable economic judgment on the Founders and their role in crafting the Constitution. When he examined the financial holdings of every delegate to the Constitutional Convention, taking into account every class, faction, geographical sector, and shade of political opinion within each group, he concluded that a simple class analysis simply did not conform to the facts.

Robert Morris, rendering contemporary judgment on the self-interestedness of his colleagues, wrote to a friend, "While some have boasted it as a work from Heaven, others have given it a less righteous origin. I have many reasons to believe that it is the work of plain, honest men."[4]

Despite his failing health, Benjamin Franklin had attended nearly every session of the convention. It was Franklin's presence as well as Washington's that had added gravitas to the convention. Looking back over the four months' proceedings, in a final address read to the convention, Franklin wrote,

> I confess that there are several parts of this Constitution which I do not at present approve, but I am not sure I shall never approve them. . . . I doubt too whether any other Convention we can obtain may be able to make a better Constitution. . . .
>
> Whenever you assemble a number of men to have the advantage of their joint wisdom, you inevitably assemble with those men all their prejudices, their passions, their errors of opinion, their local interests, and their selfish views. From such an assembly can a perfect production be expected?

Franklin expressed wonder that his colleagues had created a new system of government "approaching so near to perfection as it does."[5]

The new Constitution would take effect only after nine states ratified it in a contentious process that would take fully nine months.

While the Constitutional Convention debated in Philadelphia, the last Confederation Congress was meeting in New York City. Its most significant achievement was the ratification of an ordinance to organize all the territories north of the Ohio River that had been ceded by the eastern states.

Based largely on Jefferson's 1784 plan, the Northwest Ordinance provided for subdivision into fourteen new states. Whenever there were five thousand free adult males in a territory, they could establish a bicameral legislature. When the territory's population comprised sixty thousand free inhabitants, it could be admitted to the Union on an equal footing with the original thirteen states.

Ultimately, these new states would possess freedom of worship, right to trial by jury, and public support of education. Most importantly, slavery or involuntary servitude of any kind, except as punishment for a crime, was to be prohibited in any of the Northwest Territories.

An important omission from the ordinance was a ban on corporate land speculations like the Franklins' Vandalia scheme, a loophole that was the direct result of the presence at the New York proceedings of a man who could be called the first American lobbyist, the Reverend Manasseh Cutler. Born in Connecticut, the Yale-educated congressman was a merchant-lawyer who had served as a schoolteacher in Massachusetts before becoming the pastor of a Congregational church and a chaplain in the Revolutionary army. In 1786, the year before the Constitutional Convention, Cutler began speculating in western lands. A founder of a new Ohio Company, he arranged a contract with Congress that allowed Revolutionary War veterans to buy land at the mouth of the Muskingum River with certificates of indebtedness they had been given during the war in lieu of pay.

Surreptitiously, Cutler helped to draw up the Northwest Ordinance, presented to Congress by delegate Nathan Dane of Massachusetts. To smooth its passage, Cutler bribed key congressmen with shares in the Ohio Company. By changing the office of provisional governor of the Northwest Territories from elective to appointive, Cutler was able to offer the post to the president of the last Confederation Congress, General Arthur St. Clair. The last Confederation Congress approved the Northwest Ordinance in early October, two weeks *after* the signing of the new constitution in Philadelphia.

After only brief resistance, the old Congress submitted copies of the new constitution to each state's legislature for submission at a special ratifying convention.

Delaware claimed the honor of being the first, ratifying unanimously. Pennsylvania voted second, the pro-Constitution Federalists drawn from Philadelphia and the commercial towns, overcoming the anti-Federalists' objections to prevail by a 46–23 vote.

New Jersey's strongly Federalist convention approved unanimously; Georgia also ratified by unanimous vote. Connecticut approved overwhelmingly one week later. In divided Massachusetts, a Federalist agreement to attach nine amendments as a bill of rights won over the support of Samuel Adams to yield a 187–168 victory. Rhode Island's legislature refused to call a convention but allowed a referendum: only 237 of the 2,945 eligible voters favored ratification. It would be another four years before Rhode Island became the last state to ratify.

After Maryland ratified 63–11 in April 1788, South Carolina, whose legislature had approved a convention by a single vote, ratified the Constitution by a two-to-one margin, making it the eighth state to ratify and leaving only one more state needed for ratification.

New Hampshire's contentious convention adjourned after only one week, not meeting again for four months, when the Federalists overcame a strong anti-Federalist majority to win ratification of the Constitution, with the requirement of a bill of rights of twelve amendments, by a 57–47 vote. In Virginia, eloquent Patrick Henry led the fight against the Constitution; logical Madison led its proponents to a narrow 89–79 victory with the promise of a bill of rights.

In Poughkeepsie, New York, the most hotly contested convention opened with Governor Clinton's anti-Federalists holding a strong majority. Hamilton, working at first with Madison and John Jay, produced weekly essays—later named the Federalist Papers—that laid out the arguments for a strong federal government. At the convention in Poughkeepsie, Hamilton stalled for time, counting on favorable news from New Hampshire and Virginia to work its effect on the New York Assembly.

When he proposed conditional ratification, his motion was defeated. But then Hamilton resorted to a stratagem—a premature victory parade in New York City that demonstrated strong support among artisans and laborers, usually part of Clinton's base. Calling the vote for ratification, Hamilton prevailed by a narrow 30–27 margin.

With the announcement that the Constitution had been ratified in the requisite nine states, the old Congress dragged its feet one last time. It took three months to adopt an ordinance to locate the interim capital of the new government in New York while a permanent capital was constructed.

Setting the date for appointment of electors and balloting as February 4, 1789, the dying Confederation Congress decreed that the new Congress would convene for the first time on March 4 in New York's City Hall.

It would take four years before the process of ratifying the new constitution was complete. Rhode Island would hold out until 1791, after James Madison wrote, and the First Congress adopted, the Bill of Rights with ten amendments to the Constitution.

But just who had the right to vote? While Gouverneur Morris's eloquent preamble held out the promise that "we the people" would participate in "a more perfect union," according to the first United States census, taken in 1790, out of 3.9 million counted as Americans, only 160,000 white males over the age of twenty-one—only 4 percent of the population—possessed enough property to qualify to vote.

The poor and the debtor were disenfranchised, along with women and Native Americans. Among the excluded were 757,000 enslaved African Americans, nearly five times the eligible white male, property-owning electorate.

At the same time, the new Congress enacted legislation to allow immigrants to become citizens after only two years of residency. Naturalization was a new and powerful idea that would quickly add to the U.S. census rolls.

CHAPTER TWENTY-EIGHT

"THE DINNER TABLE BARGAIN"

On his way to his inauguration, Washington paid a visit to Robert Morris in Philadelphia, inviting him to be the first secretary of the Treasury. To his surprise, Morris demurred: "I can recommend a far cleverer fellow than I am for your minister of finance, your former aide-de-camp, Colonel Hamilton."

Apparently, Washington had not considered Hamilton, in his early thirties and lacking in administrative experience, for the post. Stunned, Washington told Morris he had no idea Hamilton "had any knowledge of finance." Morris did not hesitate: "He knows everything," he told Washington. "To a mind like his, nothing comes amiss."[1]

Inaugurated in April 1789, in New York City, Washington soon announced his selections for his cabinet. Henry Knox, his former chief of artillery who had failed as a land speculator, was appointed secretary of war.

Creating the first federal department, he renamed the Committee on Foreign Affairs the Department of State and asked Madison to write to Jefferson in Paris to feel him out about becoming secretary of state. Leaving the door open for Jefferson to remain in his post if he wished, Washington waited to hear back before publicly naming a replacement ambassador to France.

After five years in Paris, Jefferson had planned to come home only long enough to arrange his daughter's marriage and to straighten out his tangled financial affairs. When he landed in Norfolk in November 1789, however, he was stunned to read in the newspapers that Washington had gone ahead and appointed him secretary of state. He promptly wrote to the president that he preferred to return to Paris.

In a private meeting, Madison pressed Jefferson to accept the job: the South and West were depending on him to represent their interests. His enthusiastic public reception only increased the pressure. A gala welcome by both houses of the Virginia Assembly and a tour of the new capitol at Richmond, which he had designed, filled him with civic pride. Doubtlessly factoring into his decision was that his diplomat's salary of $9,000 (about $258,000 today) would be cut to $3,500 (roughly $100,000) if he returned to his post in France.

It was income Jefferson could scarcely afford to lose. He owed English and Scottish merchants a staggering £5,722 (roughly $6.25 million today). Taking his seventeen-year-old daughter, Martha, home with him, Jefferson arranged for her to marry a cousin and purchased for the couple a thousand-acre plantation near Monticello with twelve families of slaves to work it. To do this, he took out a new loan from Dutch bankers, adding it to his mountain of debt.

He was exasperated to learn that his English agents had fetched very low prices for his 1786 crop and that two-thirds of the proceeds had gone to pay high Virginia property taxes and clothing for the slaves. And he fumed that the old Congress had never reimbursed him for the $9,000, a year's salary, he estimated he had advanced for his diplomat's Paris "kit": carriage, horses, staff, and furnishings.

Before he left Paris, Jefferson had been summoned to Versailles, where, like Benjamin Franklin, Silas Deane, and Arthur Lee, he was presented with a diamond-encrusted royal gift, in Jefferson's case a gold snuffbox valued at 300 Louis d'Or (about $81,000 today). He had no doubt read the emoluments clause in the new Constitution sent to him by Madison and at first believed he would be forced to decline any proffered gift. But then, he reasoned, it was the established custom in Europe that, upon completion of a diplomatic mission, officials exchanged gifts. Jefferson believed that gifts were a form of corruption, but he also believed that in certain cases he was obligated to accept them.

When he learned that French officials would not accept his gifts if he did not accept theirs, he was in a quandary. Jefferson felt obligated to give the officials gifts, which were a big part of their needed income. "They must not lose their perquisites; it is a part of their livelihood," he wrote. He reasoned that, as a mark of respect, he must therefore accept the snuffbox. And he was not at all sure that Congress would reimburse him for these presents.[2]

Ultimately, he decided to accept the diamond-studded royal gift and to have the jewels removed and sold secretly. He would use part of the proceeds to pay for presents for the French officials but then keep any remainder for himself. It would be two years before the sale of all the diamonds was complete.

He netted £300 ($35,000 today) after purchasing the presents. He decided not to apply it to retiring any of his debts.

When he had visited the Adamses in London, Jefferson had been personally confronted by his English creditors. He contended that, before the Revolution, he had sold off lands and assigned the bonds he had received from the buyers to his creditors' Virginia agent. But the creditors' Virginia agent had refused to accept the bonds during the war because the buyers had paid Jefferson in depreciated Virginia currency.

As Virginia's governor, Jefferson had told himself that he must honor the currency of the government he represented. But the English merchants' agent still insisted on payment in gold or silver. In London, Jefferson had been forced to renegotiate directly with his creditors. He promised to pay them off with seven bonds, one to be cashed each year. For the moment, he parted with only a modest £40 (about $6,000 today) in specie.

Arriving home at Monticello in November 1789, Jefferson put off accepting Washington's appointment for two months while he arranged to sell off his war-devastated Elk Hill plantation, along with its enslaved population. Calculating that the damages inflicted by British troops to his properties equaled the full amount of his debts to English creditors made him even more reluctant to pay them off.

Finally, he accepted his appointment as secretary of state in March 1790, nearly a year after Washington's inauguration.

En route to New York, Jefferson stopped off in Philadelphia to visit his old friend Benjamin Franklin, who was dying. Only days later, on April 17, 1790, surrounded by his daughter, son-in-law, and grandchildren, Franklin died at the age of eighty-four. Robert Morris's brother-in-law, the first Anglican bishop in the United States, officiated at Franklin's funeral in Christ Church. The bells overhead, purchased with money Franklin had raised in a lottery, tolled as Bishop William White intoned, "Man that is born of woman has a short time to live." In a corner of the churchyard, Benjamin Franklin was buried beside Deborah, his "plain country Jane."

In his will, published in the Philadelphia newspapers, Franklin publicly disinherited his Loyalist son, William, for "the part he acted against me in the late war."[3] He left the bulk of his estate to his daughter, Sarah.

Soon afterward, Franklin's son-in-law, Richard Bache, chipped enough diamonds from the outer ring of Louis XVI's portrait to finance an extended tour of Europe, including a reunion in London with Sarah's exiled, and divested, brother.

As their first year in office unfolded, the demands on Washington and his administration increased exponentially. The president gave his new secretary of the Treasury 120 days to draw up a plan to pay off the debts of the old Congress, including foreign loans and the war debts of the states. In Hamilton's "First Report on the Public Credit," he proposed to retire all Revolutionary War debts—an estimated $80 million (about $1.5 billion today).

Hamilton proposed replacing all wartime debts with a new kind of currency, a national debt, or a "national blessing," as he called it. Government paper, more than any commercial paper, would be as good as gold "in the principal transactions of business passing as specie."

Hamilton ignored the possibility of favoring only the original hold-ers, the Revolutionary soldiers or their widows or orphans. Current holders of debt certificates would become the new federal bondholders, receiving the full face value of their old securities.

When word of his plan to assume all debts leaked out, the assumption that the government would adopt the recommendation of its own secre-tary of the Treasury triggered a wave of inside trading. In the House, in the Senate, all over New York City, and as far south as Charleston, the hills were alive with speculation.

A corrupt clerk in the Treasury office sold Hamilton's assistant, Wil-liam Duer, a ledger listing the names, locations, and amounts of back pay in the Continental Lines of Virginia and North Carolina. Duer, joining forces with Philadelphia merchant William Bingham, raised large amounts of cash and sent agents south to the backcountry to buy up the cash-strapped soldiers' pay certificates, sometimes offering as little as ten cents on the dollar of the face value of the certificates.

Hamilton's first effort to replace the American economy of debt with a cash economy stalled in the spring of 1790. Few in Congress under-stood that creating a national debt that paid off all existing state and federal debts would give the United States a high credit rating, keep taxes low, encourage foreign loans, and thereby stimulate foreign investment.

In the short term, the news of Hamilton's bold plan produced a Dutch bank loan that bailed out the Confederation's debt and provided the money needed for the federal government's expenses for one year. Overnight, Hamilton had repaired American credit abroad.

But Hamilton still could not win when the House voted on federal assumption of state war debts. Madison, who had as long as the Consti-tutional Convention, favored assumption, was outraged by the specula-tive binge that had targeted so many veterans. He led Southerners in defeating assumption by a narrow 31–29 vote.

Hamilton's plan to have the national government assume the old debts was more than agrarian politicians from the states that had already paid off their war debts could bear. Virginians, even if they had paid for their share of the costs of the war in depreciated currency, especially hated the idea of paying off the war debts of Northern states, which not only hadn't paid their bills as they fought but would reap a bonanza from speculating in the discounted debt certificates.

Washington was careful to stay neutral on the subject of assumption. While he said nothing, many felt they knew his mind. He favored giving special consideration to soldiers who had been forced to sell their pay warrants at a discount. He was hardly able to maintain the appearance of disinterestedness once Hamilton began to strike bargains to maneuver assumption through Congress. When Madison introduced a bill in the House to distinguish between the original bondholders and speculators, it was voted down by the Northern states.

At that moment, the choice of a site for the new national capital came up. Most Southerners, irked by the trouble and expense of traveling all the way to New York City twice a year, insisted on a swampy site along the Potomac, mutually inconvenient to both North and South. Alarmed at the concentration of money and power in the North, especially in the commercial center of New York, the Southerners were willing to move temporarily to Philadelphia, the old capital, while a new capital was built on the Potomac.

One day, Hamilton and Jefferson bumped into each other outside Washington's office. Jefferson had only recently arrived to take up his new post. Hamilton asked him to use his influence with fellow Southerners to get his assumption bill through Congress. While it was part of Jefferson's job to handle domestic as well as foreign diplomacy, he did not want to appear directly involved in Hamilton's scheme but decided on the spot to invite Hamilton and Madison to dinner at his house the next day to discuss the impasse. Inviting congressmen from Pennsylvania and Maryland as well, Jefferson before the dinner meeting worked out a compromise that could lead to congressional passage of assumption in exchange for moving the new capital to the Potomac.

On June 20, 1790, over bottles of Jefferson's best imported French wine, Pennsylvania congressmen agreed to support moving the capital to the South if Philadelphia became the interim capital until 1800 while construction of the permanent capital took place. The Potomac region stood to benefit from the construction of a city most observers expected to become an important new commercial hub, if not *the* commercial capital, of the new nation.

In July 1790, when the debt-funding, debt-assuming, and capital-location bills came before Congress, all three sailed to quick passage. In exchange for siting the capital on the Potomac, two Maryland and two Virginia members changed their votes in favor of assumption. At the time, the "dinner table bargain," as it became known, was believed to have saved the Union.

The new capital site happened to be a short ride from Mount Vernon. The new capital would be linked with the interior of the country by Washington's improved Potomac waterway. The Potomac Company's stockholders included President Washington, who quietly signed the bill into law.

The new capital would be in the ten-mile-square District of Columbia, and the capital city would be called Washington City, the government buildings to be erected on formerly worthless but now valuable swampland yielded in equal parts by Maryland and Virginia. President Washington, buying eight building lots, became one of its first landowners.

Building on his success in the struggle over assumption of the nation's debt, Hamilton proposed the creation of a national bank. On February 8, 1791, the House of Representatives passed a bill establishing the first Bank of the United States. In both the House and the Senate, Hamilton argued that a national bank is "a political machine of the greatest importance to a state" that would enable payment of taxes to provide revenue the new government desperately needed.

Hamilton contended that Article 1, Section 8, of the Constitution permitted Congress to make laws that were necessary and proper for the government, thereby empowering lawmakers to create a national bank.

The bank bill passed the House easily, by a vote of 39–20, and Washington signed it into law on February 25, 1791.

In the short term, Hamilton had prevailed, but in a difference of opinion that would lead to the Civil War and persist into the twenty-first century, Jefferson and Madison disagreed, countering that powers not expressly granted to Congress in the Constitution belonged to the states.

CHAPTER TWENTY-NINE

"Clintonia Borealis"

Suffering from chronic migraines, Thomas Jefferson could find little peace in his rented house on the main wagon route into Philadelphia. Despite the fact the capital was slated to be moved south, in an attempt to make himself more comfortable he made extensive and expensive modifications to the home he did not, in fact, own.

By the end of the First Congress in the spring of 1791, Jefferson needed a vacation. The promise of a welcome respite came when Madison proposed a trip. Knowing the Washingtons would be touring the South, Madison suggested that he and Jefferson make a tour as far north as they could go and still return in a month.

Jefferson especially wanted to visit Vermont. He considered himself the champion of the frontier farmer; he believed the future belonged to the independent farmer, not the urban dweller. He had even come to believe his own state of Virginia was too crowded with wealthy plantation owners. Vermont, which had abolished slavery at its founding, was attracting small farmers, the ideal realization of Jeffersonian democracy, from overcrowded neighboring states. Jefferson had written the new state's application for admission to the Union and had delayed Kentucky's admission to the Union until Vermont could be admitted first as the fourteenth state.

Jefferson had ample reasons for wanting to leave town for a while. Tensions within Washington's cabinet had been escalating for some time. Jefferson was already at sword's points with Hamilton, who advocated pro-British trade policies. Their infighting was about to become public. Jefferson had become alarmed to see his old friend John Adams siding with Hamilton.

Writing under the pen name Davila in a series of columns in the pro-Hamilton *Gazette of the United States*, Adams had been for the last year stressing the dangers of unchecked democracy.

Jefferson was therefore elated to receive a copy of Thomas Paine's latest anti-British blast, *The Rights of Man*, just published in London. Paine, the author of America's bestselling political tracts, had designed a cast-iron bridge that successfully spanned the Schuylkill River in Philadelphia and had traveled to England seeking investors. In a pamphlet, Paine disparaged British parliamentarian Edmund Burke's attack on the French Revolution. Charged with seditious libel, Paine eluded arrest only by fleeing to Paris, where he was honored by the appointment as the only American in France's Chamber of Deputies.

Jefferson wrote a note recommending Paine's pamphlet to readers and sent it off to a printer. He intended his comments to remain private; he was, after all, in Washington's cabinet with Adams and Hamilton. Jefferson was chagrined when the printer published his signed letter as the introduction to Paine's tract. Scores of newspapers reprinted the letter. Overnight, Jefferson became regarded as the spokesman for Americans disenchanted with Washington's pro-British policies. "I am sincerely mortified," he wrote to the president, "to be thus brought forward on the public stage against my love of silence . . . and my abhorrence of disputes."[1]

Jefferson spread the rumor that, as vice president of the American Philosophical Society, he was going with Madison on a scientific trip to trace the ravages of the Hessian fly, which had been devastating grain crops in New York and New England. In addition, he said that in his dual capacity as secretary of the interior he intended to inspect nascent manufacturing projects. In truth, their trip masked a political agenda. He would have a full month for intense discussions with Madison. Along with a note to his son-in-law, Thomas Mann Randolph, Jefferson sent a copy of the *Gazette of the United States* describing its editorial policy as "pure Toryism, disseminating [Hamilton's] doctrine of monarchy, aristocracy, and the exclusion of people":

> We have been trying to get another weekly or half-weekly excluding advertisements set up, so that it could go free through the states in the mails and furnish [our] vehicle of intelligence. We hoped at one time to have persuaded Freneau [Philip Freneau, journalist, poet, and Madison's Princeton roommate] but we have failed.[2]

Here, in a private letter, Jefferson was admitting what he had been denying in public: that he was involved in an opposition faction within Washington's government and was about to launch his own partisan newspaper in which to criticize Hamilton and the president's agenda.

Jefferson's son-in-law was to forward the pro-Hamilton paper each week via government mail to stops along their itinerary so that Jefferson would have the latest political news to discuss in private with Madison during long days on the road. As Jefferson rode out of Philadelphia, Adams was savaging him in the *Gazette of the United States* for endorsing Paine's avowedly radical views.

At first, Jefferson had offered to pay all their expenses, but Madison had insisted that they divide them. As usual, Jefferson was strapped for cash. Before setting out, he had to await the arrival of four hogsheads of Monticello tobacco to sell in Philadelphia for his travel money. But when the shipment finally arrived, it was worthless, already smoke-damaged in a fire. As it turned out, Jefferson would run out of money on the road and end up borrowing from Madison.

Jefferson invariably kept a record of his expenses, even when there was no one to reimburse him. For this journey, he chose a pocket-size *Virginia Almanack*, keeping daily jottings on the backs of its pages, which were printed on only one side. As Jefferson's expense records show, his slave, James Hemings, with money he had saved from tips and presents, often advanced the cost of fresh food purchased along the road.

Rolling out of Philadelphia in his distinctive high, black, Monticello-made carriage, Jefferson overtook Madison in New York City and checked into a boardinghouse in Maiden Lane along with Freneau and John Beckley, clerk of the House of Representatives. Rumors of their meeting fanned reports by Hamilton supporters of political intrigue, but Jefferson and Madison remained silent.

One of Hamilton's friends was George Beckwith, unofficial envoy of Britain to the United States. He reported to Lord Granville, the British foreign secretary,

> I am sorry to inform your Grace that the Secretary of State's party and politics gains ground here. [They] will have influence enough to cause acts and resolve which may be unfriendly to Great Britain to be passed early in the next session of Congress. The Secretary of State, together with Mr. Madison, have gone to the Eastern States, there to proselyte as far as they are able a commercial war with Britain.[3]

Hamilton's youngest son, John, ultimately his biographer, had no doubt that Jefferson was politicking. He flatly asserted that the Virginians were meeting secretly in New York City with the newly elected senator Aaron Burr before going on to Albany to huddle with the anti-Federalist governor Clinton.

If Jefferson and Madison were merely on vacation, they had no reason to conceal or to comment on visits to New York politicians. But if, as John Quincy Adams later wrote, they were engaged in "double-dealing," they had good reason for silence.

It is likely that Jefferson's party called on Burr at his new Richmond Hill mansion. Instead of using his own recognizable carriage, according to his expense records, Jefferson hired a coach for the day.

Even the possibility of such an alliance worried Hamilton's supporters. "They had better be quiet," his friend and former college roommate Robert Troup wrote to Hamilton, "for if they succeed, they will tumble the fabric of the government in ruins to the ground."[4]

In fact, Jefferson and Madison did meet with Freneau to ask him to launch a thrice-weekly newspaper in the nation's capital. In this first clandestine step toward the formation of a political party, Jefferson laid out plans to dip into the State Department's budget and its diplomatic pouch to pay Freneau and produce a partisan critique of Hamilton's policies. Jefferson's *National Gazette* would attack Hamilton's *Gazette of the United States*, each cabinet secretary battering the other's positions under noms de plume while each was fully aware that Washington abhorred discord.

As Madison and Jefferson headed north on the Post Road, Jefferson sent Hemings ahead with the carriage and a little travel money, making a note in his almanac: "James for expenses to Poughkeepsie 6 [dollars]."[5]

After three days on the Hudson River sloop, Jefferson and Madison were ready for the comforts of Henderson's Inn: Jefferson began to rate taverns in his expense record. They hurried on toward Albany, where, according to John Hamilton, they secretly visited Governor Clinton and other anti-Federalists "under the pretext of a botanical excursion." Young Hamilton remained convinced they were studying "Clintonia borealis." They also visited Major General Philip Schuyler, Hamilton's father-in-law, who led them on a tour of overgrown "scenes of blood," as Jefferson described them in a letter to Washington.[6]

Madison, keeping a tiny, palm-size diary, recorded encountering a free black farmer, Prince Taylor, whose house sat all alone at Lake George's northern tip: "He possesses a good farm of about 250 acres which he cultivates with 6 white hirelings." A Revolutionary War veteran, Taylor had paid about $2.50 an acre "and by his industry and good management turns [it] to good account. He is intelligent; reads, writes and understands account and is dexterous in his affairs."[7]

Now nearly a week behind schedule, the travelers had intended to sail the length of Lake Champlain but were forced to turn back by a storm. Backtracking to Saratoga, they crossed the Hudson and rode over a bone-rattling dirt road to Bennington in southwestern Vermont, passing "closely settled" farms, where they first saw sugar maples from which "some sugar is made and much may be."

That spring, Jefferson had been pondering an agricultural question with political overtones. The British government reimposed the rule of 1756 barring American ships from carrying British goods from British possessions in Canada and the Caribbean. Jefferson was determined to break American reliance on its largest import, sugar, a severe drain on hard cash. Before going on vacation, he wrote to President Washington about "the sugar-maple tree."[8]

In Bennington, Vermont's first senator, Moses Robinson, learned they had arrived in town and insisted they stay with him. Jefferson had intended to travel through Vermont incognito but had not reckoned with Anthony Haswell, a fiercely republican fan of Jefferson's who edited the *Vermont Gazette*. Haswell broke the story of the two highest federal officials ever to come to the new state and circulated it to newspapers the length of the country by exchange copies.

Over dinner, Senator Robinson introduced his guests to the local gentry, many of whom had represented Vermont as agents to the Continental Congress during its decades-long quest to enter the Union. At dinner that night, Jefferson proselytized development of a maple syrup industry. He suggested that each farmer maintain a grove of seventy-five maple trees and pledged to help the new state develop a market for maple syrup as a substitute for cane sugar. Indeed, he did arrange for the Dutch to send, in 1792, cast-iron kettles to help farmers boil down their sap.

Before the meal was over, Jefferson learned that the British, in violation of the Treaty of Paris, had built a blockhouse on North Hero Island in Lake Champlain, five miles south of the Canadian line and opposite an American fort at Champlain, New York. The British had stationed the sloop-of-war *Maria* there and were forcing American vessels to heave to, even in storms, to be searched for goods smuggled in violation of the 1756 Navigation Act. As a result, two Vermont vessels had capsized, with one crewman drowning. Vermonters, Jefferson reported, were nervous; Vermont had built a stockade nearby, manning it with two hundred militia. State officials clearly expected trouble.

Jefferson was well aware that the British were refusing to remove their troops and abandon the northern Great Lakes forts on the grounds that Americans, like himself, were violating the peace treaty by refusing to pay their pre-Revolution debts in specie and had confiscated the property of Loyalists.

A clock was ticking now. The two travelers cut short their New England tour to return to Philadelphia and Congress and what was sure to be a major diplomatic crisis.

Jefferson returned to a crisis of a different sort: a "monstrous bill of freight." For packing in Paris and shipping eighty-six crates of books and household goods, he owed another £258 (about $28,000 today). The freight charge aboard the *Henrietta* came to another £544.53 ($60,000).

In all, Jefferson's move from the French capital to the temporary American capital added, in today's money, some $88,000 to his Monticello of debt.

Above all else, President Washington dreaded the prospect of disunion. Despite his repeated personal efforts, his cabinet had divided sharply between Jefferson's Democratic-Republicans and Hamilton's Federalists. The clash became public after news of the execution of Louis XVI in January 1793 and France's declaration of war against Great Britain and the Netherlands. In a heated cabinet meeting, Hamilton insisted that the bloody regime change in Paris from monarchy to republic invalidated the 1778 Franco-American Treaty of Alliance.

Hamilton contended that the treaty, signed by the monarchy, no longer existed. Jefferson countered that treaties were made between nations, noting that the form of government of the United States had also changed—from a confederation to a constitutional republic—without abrogating its treaty obligations.

The cabinet deadlocked over whether the treaty obliged the United States to help France defend its West Indian possessions against the British. Jefferson argued against going to war for any reason. Hamilton and Jefferson clashed over the propriety of formally receiving the new French ambassador, Edmond-Charles Genet. He had been appointed by

Robespierre, the principal architect of the Reign of Terror, which had taken the lives of many French aristocrats who had fought by the side of the Americans.

Determined to steer the United States clear of the twin shoals of European war and diplomacy, Washington insisted on the new doctrine of strict neutrality, even if it meant renouncing the treaty's military obligations. Ultimately bowing to the advice of his secretary of state, Washington upheld Jefferson's opinion on the treaty and instructed that Genet be received, but "not with too much warmth and cordiality."[9]

Despite Washington's official coolness, Genet received a conquering hero's welcome, including a standing ovation in Congress Hall. Misgauging America's enthusiasm, Genet ignored its neutrality. Outfitting privateers and recruiting Americans for a sea-and-land expedition against Spanish-held Florida, he ordered the French consul at Charleston to sell as prizes any merchant ships taken from the British.

When Jefferson upheld Genet's contention that French prizes were French property that could be sold by a French consul, Washington angrily overruled him and ordered all French privateers to leave American ports. He ignored Jefferson's assertion that neutrality was effectively a pro-British stance because it disregarded America's treaty obligations to France.

When Hamilton twice attacked Jefferson's interpretation in print, Jefferson wrote to Madison, "For god's sake my dear Sir, take up your pen, select the most striking heresies and cut him to pieces."[10]

The Genet affair came to a head when a French frigate towed a captured British merchantman, the *Little Sarah*, into Philadelphia. Jefferson ordered Genet to detain the vessel, renamed the *Petite Démocrate*, until Washington returned from his Mount Vernon vacation. Genet refused.

In an impromptu cabinet meeting, Hamilton and Secretary of War Henry Knox clamored to set up artillery along the Delaware River to impede the vessel's departure. Jefferson, aware that a French fleet was approaching Philadelphia, feared this would trigger open warfare with France. Defiant, Genet ordered *Petite Démocrate*, to drop downriver beyond the reach of Knox's guns.

When Washington returned, he accused Jefferson of "submitting" to Genet.

It was Jefferson's last fight as secretary of state. When Washington pleaded with him to stay on, Jefferson assured him that his Democratic-Republican clubs would support Washington through the rest of his first term but that he, Jefferson, was tired of a post that forced him "to move exactly in the same circle which I know to bear me peculiar hatred; that is to say, the wealthy aristocrats, the merchants closely connected to England, the new created paper fortunes."[11] Jefferson knew that Hamilton was also resigning and returning to New York City to galvanize support for the Federalist Party. At that moment, American party politics burst from its chrysalis.

Persistent attacks on Hamilton's fiscal policies appeared in Freneau's *National Gazette*, provoking rejoinders by Hamilton in a six-month series of anonymous articles in the *Gazette of the United States* asserting that Jefferson had been opposed to the Constitution's adoption, that he opposed the programs of Washington's administration, and that he was responsible for political intriguing against the government.

Newly established Democratic-Republican societies, from which the Democratic-Republican Party would take its name, joined anti-Federalist newspapers in attacking Washington's policy of neutrality. Washington had originally favored maintaining friendly ties with France, but after the mass guillotining of the Reign of Terror commenced, Washington veered toward the pro-British Federalists, leaning more heavily on Hamilton for advice on foreign affairs.

Jefferson and Hamilton wrote to Washington to prevail on him to serve a second term. Even when he attempted to heal their differences by writing to them, Washington could see from their replies that their quarrel was unabated. At the same time, despite Washington's invitation for a private meeting at Mount Vernon to ameliorate the rift, Jefferson let it be known that he intended to resign after the close of Washington's first term and submitted his resignation.

In the run-up to the December 1792 election, public opinion split over the war between England and France. Most Federalists supported the

British, regarding England as a bulwark against French anarchy and atheism. Most Democratic-Republicans sympathized with the French, from not only principle but long-standing antagonism toward the British.

Washington was reelected president with 132 electoral votes; Adams received 77 votes, making him, again, the vice president. But the anti-Federalists' toll showed just how deep the party split had become, with 50 electoral votes going to George Clinton of New York for vice president.

Washington's second term began with trouble at home and on the high seas. Discontent over the enforcement of a new excise tax—always the most unpopular form of taxation—on whiskey led to a revolt among farmers in western Pennsylvania.

Fearing another Shays's Rebellion, Washington issued a proclamation ordering the insurgents to return to their homes. He called out 12,900 militia from four states and, when negotiations proved fruitless, ordered the rebellion suppressed.

With his protégé Henry "Light-Horse Harry" Lee of Virginia in command, Washington and Secretary of the Treasury Hamilton rode the two hundred miles together from Philadelphia to Bedford, Pennsylvania, before Washington turned back. None of the "Whiskey Boys" came out to do battle, but Hamilton ordered their two leaders arrested for treason. Washington eventually pardoned them.

The crisis at sea came after British warships began seizing American vessels carrying cargoes from the French-held islands in the Caribbean to France. The Neutrality Act passed by Congress forbade American citizens from enlisting in the service of a foreign power and prohibited outfitting foreign privateers in American ports. But Americans remained aggrieved at Britain for refusing, despite the Treaty of Paris, to evacuate the northern military posts, retarding western settlement and keeping the lucrative fur trade in British hands. The British justified their continued maintenance of frontier garrisons on the grounds that American courts were raising obstacles to their recovery of pre-Revolution debts.

American settlers crowding into the Ohio Country blamed the British for instigating Indians, based and armed at trading posts, for massacres of pioneers. In one raid, one of Washington's own business partners, William Crawford, was captured, tortured, scalped, and burned at the stake.

The Neutrality Act failed to ease tensions between Britain and the United States, which worsened when the British issued orders-in-council that interfered with neutral shipping. Britain seized some 250 American ships and impressed or imprisoned their crews.

As the two nations verged on war, American dependence on customs duties derived from British exports to the United States—the chief source of the government's revenues—led Washington to send Chief Justice John Jay to London as a special envoy to negotiate with the British. But Jay carried instructions that he was to make no commitment that would violate U.S. treaties with France.

In what at first blush appeared to be an American diplomatic triumph, Jay succeeded in securing major concessions. Britain agreed to immediately withdraw its troops, admit American ships to West Indian ports, and resume trade in the Caribbean after the American renunciation of the carrying trade in such staples as cotton, sugar, and molasses.

The treaty also created a joint commission to settle the payments of $2.6 million in pre-Revolutionary debts owed to British merchants. (Those negotiations would drag on for another six years before Jefferson and other debtors finally began to pay up.)

Moreover, the treaty provided compensation for illegal maritime seizures and placed British trade with the United States on a most-favored-nation status but did not provide for impressment of seamen, for slaves taken by the British, or for Loyalists' claims for compensation for their confiscated property.

When the treaty's terms became known in America, Jefferson's Democratic-Republicans organized popular opposition. Riots broke out, and Jay was burned in effigy. The treaty's provision for settlement of debts chagrined Southern planters such as Jefferson, as many of the debts were by Virginians, who also railed at the treaty's silence on slaves stolen by the British in wartime Northern shipping. Commercial interests also attacked the treaty.

Washington considered the Jay Treaty unsatisfactory even as Hamilton entered the fray by supporting it in a series of articles. After a long debate, and after suspending the portion pertaining to the lucrative West Indian trade, the Senate ratified the treaty by a narrow vote.

Democratic-Republicans in the House, demanding all papers relating to the treaty, attempted to block its enactment by refusing funds for enforcement. After a six-week standoff, Washington refused to comply "because of the necessity of maintaining the boundaries fixed by the Constitution," thus establishing the doctrine of executive privilege. Finally, the appropriation passed by a single Federalist vote.[12]

Refusing blandishments from Federalists to seek a third term, Washington reorganized his cabinet to include only Federalists. Long conscious of the importance of free navigation of the Mississippi River, he dispatched Thomas Pinckney, a signer of the Declaration of Independence and now the American minister to Great Britain, to Madrid. The resulting treaty recognized the Mississippi as the nation's western boundary and gave Americans free navigation of the river and the right to deposit their goods in New Orleans for shipment to Europe. For so long George Washington's dream, the Treaty of San Lorenzo opened up the American interior to trade with the Caribbean and with Europe.

But, as Washington wrote to Henry Lee, "no man was ever more tired of public life." To John Adams, he wrote of his "disinclination to be longer buffeted in the public prints by a set of infamous scribblers." With his retirement less than a year away, he set about writing the first draft of his farewell address.

He asked Hamilton to revise his comments. As they passed drafts back and forth, the message grew. The final draft was all Washington's thought, all Hamilton's writing.[13]

In the presidential election of 1796, Jefferson's Democratic-Republicans, running against the Jay Treaty, were defeated, but by a razor-thin margin. John Adams received 71 electoral votes; Jefferson, with 68, became vice president.

On Saturday, March 4, 1797, Adams's inauguration took place in Philadelphia, in Congress Hall, next door to Independence Hall, where

Adams had nominated Washington for commander in chief of the Continental Army twenty-two years earlier.

Washington wore a plain black suit as he walked alone into the hall; Adams, in a lavish new suit, rode in a resplendent new carriage of state. After the brief ceremony, Washington congratulated Adams, who later recounted their last moment together in a letter to Abigail:

> He seemed to enjoy a triumph over me. Methought I heard him say, "Ay, I am fairly out and you fairly in! See which of us will be happier!"[14]

CHAPTER THIRTY

"The Best Room in This House"

As the Napoleonic Wars engulfed Europe, the threat of American entanglement loomed. Since the United States had no navy, both England and France ignored American neutrality.

Nowhere was the crisis more calamitous than in the Caribbean. In the wake of the Jay Treaty, French privateers captured more than three hundred American merchant vessels, pushing Congress to grant President Adams emergency war powers and to create the permanent U.S. Navy. It would be made up of six frigates, the largest ships ever built in America. To finance mobilization, Congress for the first time imposed a direct federal tax on land, houses, and slaves.

Furthermore, Adams summoned sixty-six-year-old George Washington out of retirement, appointing him to command an enlarged army. Washington agreed to accept the position on the condition that he would remain at Mount Vernon and turn over most duties to Alexander Hamilton, who, as inspector general, assumed the rank of major general.

The undeclared Quasi-War, as it became known, began with the French capture of an American schooner in November 1798. Two months later, in the first victory of the new cruising navy, a French frigate surrendered to the American frigate *Constellation*.

As the fighting progressed, American frigates defeated two more French frigates, captured eighty-two privateering ships, and recovered more than seventy merchant vessels. As reports of each victory reached shore, American pride and bellicosity reached new heights.

Except for the solitary visit to Philadelphia to discuss a return to military life, Washington stayed close to Mount Vernon. His eight salaried years as president had helped him stabilize his finances, and now he had time to bring about the restructuring of his various businesses. He had built a state-of-the-art, sixteen-sided threshing barn, similar to the latest model in France, which enabled horses on a treadmill to thresh grain in all weather, giving a boost to his fine-grain flour business. He built a highly profitable whiskey distillery and, riding over from Mount Vernon to a capital city under construction, personally supervised the workers building a pair of three-story townhouses on lots he had bought just north of the Capitol.

Yet he continued to have little success collecting rents for his western lands, even though, as a result of his lifelong efforts to open up the West beyond the Appalachians, more than one million Americans had crossed into the interior valleys and floated down rivers he once had explored to open up scores of new towns.

Washington spent much of his final two years working to persuade talented men who eschewed public life to run for federal office. One of them was Henry "Light-Horse Harry" Lee, who would become governor; another was John Marshall, who had endured the bitter winter at Valley Forge with Washington when many Virginia officers resigned the service. Marshall had studied law and resisted Washington's blandishments to give up his lucrative practice and run for Congress, but he finally acquiesced. No one, including the fiercely independent future chief justice, could refuse George Washington.

When he sat down to draw up his will, dated July 9, 1799, Washington was probably worth $17 million in today's dollars, making him one of the hundred wealthiest Americans, but most of his assets were tied up in 51,000 acres of land and one hundred enslaved people, property his heirs could not easily liquidate.

On elegant 8½ x 6¼-inch paper with the goddess of agriculture as its watermark, Washington meticulously wrote out twenty-eight pages.

He gave cash bequests to friends and all his retainers, including an annuity and immediate freedom to his enslaved manservant Billy Lee, crippled after so many years of dragging Washington's heavy surveyor's chains through the wilderness and shielding him as his bodyguard throughout the Revolutionary War.

All Washington's lands outside Mount Vernon he ordered sold, the proceeds to be distributed equally among twenty-three relatives. He did not want to make anyone too rich to want to work. Everything he did not specifically bequeath, including his home farm of 7,600 acres and one thousand head of livestock, he left to Martha during her lifetime. Then Mount Vernon was to pass to his nephew Bushrod, a future Supreme Court justice.

He left all his slaves to Martha with annuities to provide for them for life and instructions to free them at her death; Martha had already agreed she would free her one hundred dower slaves. Washington had talked of selling off his western lands—"to liberate a certain species of property which I possess, very repugnantly to my own feelings"—to free his slaves to become tenants on his home farms.[1]

George Washington's end came suddenly on December 13, 1799. He had made his usual morning ten-mile ride around his farms in subfreezing weather. When he came back, his greatcoat was soaked through, and snow was hanging from his white hair. He came to the dinner table without changing his damp clothing.

After a sleepless night of coughing, he summoned an overseer to bleed him while Martha summoned his doctor. Three doctors came and argued over his treatment as they drew pint after pint of blood, purging him with calomel and applying leeches to his neck to draw blood into a blister.

Washington finally refused further treatment. He asked to "be permitted to die without further interruptions." He said he looked at dying as "the debt which we all must pay."[2]

Robert Morris learned of Washington's death in his cell in the Prune Street Prison—Philadelphia's debtors' prison—where he had resided for nearly a year. As the British blockade of American ships had tightened to prevent Americans from aiding the French, Morris had abandoned his successful import-export trading practices and turned to speculating in land. With two young partners—one the comptroller of Pennsylvania, the other a New York banker with supposed Dutch banking connections—Morris committed to buying more than three million acres of wilderness from Pennsylvania to Georgia. Endorsing one another's notes to multiply their credit, the trio piled up huge obligations.

Ignoring warning signs, Morris began to build an opulent mansion that took up an entire city block, hiring Pierre L'Enfant, architect of the new capital city. Then, after France declared war on Britain, the Bank of England halted payments in gold and silver for debts backed by notes, shaking international markets. Among the bankruptcies was a small London bank where Morris lost £125,000 (about $15 million today).

A congressional committee auditing the books of the wartime Secret Committee on Trade declared that Morris owed the federal government $93,000 ($2.5 million today). Disputing the bill and insisting it was based on wartime depreciation, he nevertheless paid it with a note. Its security: land he had already sold.

In a desperate attempt to cover his losses, Morris and his partners formed a new company to sell stock secured by their six-million-acre investment in lands. Morris sent a dozen agents, including his son William and future son-in-law, the brother of John Marshall, to Europe to sell shares, but European investors were uninterested.

The lands Morris and his partners were trying to peddle had value and one day would reap handsome profits, but Morris needed to turn a quick profit to satisfy increasingly nervous creditors.

He had given promissory notes to the commissioners who were building the new capital for land he was now required to develop. But a partner who had arranged a loan from the Dutch to fund the construction pocketed the money, leaving Morris with no funds to improve his lots.

When Morris failed to pay his share in hard money, fellow investor George Washington appealed personally to him to pay up—it was his "public duty"—to avoid suspension of construction of public buildings.

After Congress finally agreed to underwrite the construction of public buildings, Morris peddled several of his lots to George Washington at a substantial profit.[3]

His confidence restored, Morris went on another land-buying binge. He bought up seventy-six thousand acres in Ohio and Virginia, paying for them by signing over a debt due to him—by an investor who had already gone bankrupt.

"This was the same sort of bill kiting Morris had used to such good effect in supporting the government during the Revolution," wrote Morris biographer Charles Rappleye, "but then he'd still had his personal fortune and the goodwill of Britain's European rivals to support his notes. But this time his credit was slender and his resources exhausted."[4]

In December 1796, James Wilson, signer of the Declaration of Independence and the Constitution, was stripped of his bench on the Supreme Court and sent to the Prune Street Jail, becoming the first major Philadelphia land speculator imprisoned for debt.

Thoroughly alarmed as creditors daily dunned him, Morris deposited his family in a rented house in the city and fled to their rural summer retreat beyond the county sheriff's jurisdiction. But creditors pursued him, camping and waiting for him to come out. When a constable appeared with a posse armed with pickaxes on Christmas Day 1797, Morris and several visitors drove them off by training guns on them.

But by February 1798, Morris could no longer stave off his creditors. He summoned the sheriff to arrest him and walked the two blocks from his rented house to the Prune Street Prison—one block from the statehouse where, two decades earlier, he had signed the Declaration of Independence and where, as the financier of the American Revolution, he had nearly held presidential power.

Morris's wife, Mary, was able to raise enough money to rent what he called "the best room in this house" and to pay the jailer for his meals. He was allowed to have visitors. Only months before he died, while in Philadelphia for a meeting with President Adams, Washington visited Morris and stayed to dine with the man who had fed his army.[5]

Robert Morris's onetime partner Gouverneur Morris, acting as his land agent, was able to arrange an annual annuity of $1,500 ($30,000 to-day) for Mary, enough for her to rent a small house on an unpaved street on the edge of the city. There, Abigail Adams, in her first year as First Lady, called on Mary Morris and invited her to tea, but she was too em-barrassed to accept the invitation.

When, nationwide, land values failed to recover and a tidal wave of bankruptcies swept the country, in the spring of 1800, Congress passed the nation's first bankruptcy relief law. Morris was one of ninety for-merly wealthy Americans who faced a panel of commissioners and laid out in detail his once-great holdings, debts, and remaining assets. Morris insisted he had made his speculations in good faith and that, one day, he would be able to repay his debts when his creditors repaid him. "I have every reason to believe that at this day I should have been the wealthiest citizen of the United States."[6]

On August 26, 1801, after the federal district court accepted Morris's written "Account of Property" and discharged the claims against him, after three years and six months in prison, Robert Morris, America's first billionaire and the architect of its successful struggle for independence, walked out of debtors' prison and wrote to his son, "I now find myself a free citizen of the United States without one cent I can call my own."[7]

Acknowledgments

For many years, my friend and neighbor Jan Rozendaal, a successful businessman, has asked me, "How did the money work" in the American Revolution and during the early years of the United States? I've put him off as I've written about the lives of individual Founding Fathers.

When I decided to tackle this book, I intended to explore the individual financial affairs of the Founders. But my friend and agent, Don Fehr, persuaded me that readers might be far more interested in a narrative that allowed each player to step to the footlights and explain his contribution as events unfolded.

From my biographical research, I already had some idea of the finances of several key players: Benjamin Franklin's "penny saved is a penny earned" way to wealth; George Washington's vast landholdings; and Alexander Hamilton's grand financial planning, despite which he amassed so little money that his friends had to pass the hat to pay for his funeral. But how had these individuals managed to finance and survive a revolution and then launch a new nation when their money "wasn't worth a Continental"?

Many people helped me to find answers even before I formed the question. Whitfield J. Bell, librarian of the American Philosophical Society, read my feature articles on historical topics in the *Philadelphia Bulletin* and encouraged me to apply for a grant to study the life of Franklin's little-known son, William. Biographer Catherine Drinker Bowen, a director of the Society, took the time to meet with me several times and personally recommended me for the grant.

Exploring the life of the son led me to the father's speculations in frontier lands and to his expense accounts as, first, a British postal official, then American postmaster general.

When Mrs. Bowen died, I was asked to eulogize her at the first international conference on the Loyalists, where I met the late Robert A. East, distinguished professor on the City University of New York graduate faculty, an expert on merchants in the Revolution, and his son-in-law, James E. Mooney, who introduced me to the troves of financial papers at the Historical Society of Pennsylvania and the New-York Historical Society.

The Franklins' attempts to corner vast acreage in today's Midwest led me next to young Thomas Jefferson's fruitless legal career in the Shenandoah Valley. I plowed through one hundred–plus reels of microfilm lent me by the Library of Congress before finding the unpublished doctoral dissertation of Steven Harold Hochman, a thorough financial biography. I could see how Jefferson amassed debts despite his marriage to the wealthy heiress of a land-rich importer of enslaved people.

The manuscript archives of the New York Public Library yielded daily expenses of Jefferson and James Madison as they took a junket to the new state of Vermont. There, the late J. Robert Maguire generously allowed me access to his private collection to see Madison's account of the same trip. In a subsequent visit to the J. Pierpont Library, curator Robert Parks alerted me to letters Jefferson wrote on the membrane of birch bark when he ran out of foolscap on Lake George.

When I turned to George Washington, I visited Mount Vernon, where librarian Barbara McMillan showed me years of weekly plantation reports. Denis Pogue, director of restoration, led me on a tour of Washington's home farms and explained the stages of expansion of the legendary mansion.

As I retraced Washington's early military career, experts in local history led me to sites that are rarely mentioned in archives. Local historians do tireless and creditable spadework. Members of the Braddock Trail Historical Society took me to the forested glen where young Colonel Washington attacked a French diplomatic party, triggering the Seven Years War. During a speaking engagement at Edinboro University, I piled into a pickup truck with Donald Sheehy III, editor of the correspondence of Robert Frost, for a ride to the site at French Creek in northwestern Pennsylvania where young Washington warned French officers to leave the Ohio Valley or face expulsion by the British.

It was Washington's aide and choice as the first secretary of the Treasury who has in recent years become perhaps the best loved figure of the revolutionary era. Many brilliant scholars have paved the way for the resurrection of a once-discredited figure. On the bicentennial of Hamilton's death in a duel, many of them were summoned to participate in a symposium at the New-York Historical Society attended by some 750 high school history teachers. Richard Sylla, distinguished economic historian at New York University, encouraged me as I presented my terse biographic findings and then invited me to speak at the Stern School of Business of New York University.

To help fund my research, administrators at Champlain College have provided a number of grants. I thank, especially, retired President Roger W. Perry and former provost Laurie Quinn. I am also grateful to the staff of Miller Information Commons, especially interlibrary loan librarian Brenda Racht and reference librarian Tammy Miller.

At E. P. Dutton, I am indebted to my extraordinarily patient and skilled editor, Brent Howard, for teaching this longtime teacher to tell the reader what I have found—and not just show it. His able assistant, Grace Layer, has helped me to gather illustrations from curators at, among other places, the American Philosophical Society (Mary Grace Wahl), from the Webb-Deane-Stevens Museum (Richard Malley), and the Massachusetts Historical Society (Hannah Elder). I especially want to thank my superlative copy editor, Maureen Klier, for questioning, trimming, buffing, and polishing my prose.

But most of all I want to thank my two closest editors and friends. My wife, Nancy, for thirty-five years now has listened, challenged, encouraged, and generously shared her deep knowledge of the culture and history of the times I find so interesting and so important. Our daughter, Lucy, a wise and gifted senior editor at Oxford University Press, unselfishly and often helps me to think about my craft and my calling.

Notes

PROLOGUE

1. GW to David Humphreys, quoted in Randall, *George Washington*, 437.
2. GW to Henry Knox, March 1, 1789, *PGW, Confederation Series*, 1:345–46.
3. GW to George Augustine Washington, March 31, 1789, *PGW*, Presidential Series, 1:472–73.
4. Maier, *American Scripture*, 149.
5. Van Doren, *Benjamin Franklin*, 554.
6. Beard, *Economic Interpretation of the Constitution of the United States*, 10.
7. Beard, *Economic Interpretation of the Constitution of the United States*, 17.

CHAPTER ONE. "A PENNY SAVED"

1. *ABF*, 164.
2. BF to William Strahan, February 12, *PBF*, 3:13.
3. *PG*, May 3, 1733.
4. Chapin, *Benjamin Franklin's Autobiography*, 177.
5. Lambert, "'Pedlar in Divinity,'" 821, 836.
6. *PBF*, 3:184.
7. *PG*, March 8, 1748.

CHAPTER TWO. "MY CONSTANT GAIN EVERY DAY"

1. Conkling, *Memoirs of the Mother and Wife of Washington*, 43–44.
2. Lengel, *First Entrepreneur*, 21.
3. Lengel, *First Entrepreneur*, 22–23.

CHAPTER THREE. "JOIN, OR DIE"

1. Lewis, *For King and Country*, 42.
2. *DGW*, 1:40.
3. *ABF*, 210.
4. *ABF*, 211.

CHAPTER FOUR. "WHO WOULD HAVE THOUGHT IT?"

1. GW to Robert Orme, March 2, 1755, *PGW*, Colonial Series, 1:244.
2. *ABF*, 130.
3. *ABF*, 131.
4. GW to John Carlyle, May 14, 1755, *PGW*, Colonial Series, 1:274.
5. GW to John Augustus Washington, May 28, 1755, *PGW*, Colonial Series, 1:289–92.
6. Lewis, *For King and Country*, 357.
7. DH, 16–18.
8. *ABF*, 134.
9. "Instructions," August 14, 1755, *PGW*, Colonial Series, 2:4–6; Lengel, *First Entrepreneur*, 2.

CHAPTER FIVE. "TRIBUNE OF THE PEOPLE"

1. *PBF*, 6:219.
2. BF to Peter Collinson, October 25, 1755, *PBF*, 6:229.
3. John Harris to BF, October 31, 1755, *PBF*, 6:232–33.
4. Thomas Penn to Richard Peters, March 30, 1748, *PBF*, 3:186.
5. "Reply to the Governor," August 19, 1755, *PBF*, 6:151.
6. BF, "Observations Concerning the Increase of Mankind, Peopling of Countries, etc.," *ABF*, 115:n4.

7. BF to Peter Collinson, June 15, 1756, *PBF*, 6:456–57.
8. Richard Peters to Thomas Penn, June 26, 1756, Penn Papers, 8:123–25.
9. William Allen to Ferdinand Paris, October 25, 1755, in Walker, *Burd Papers*, 24–25.
10. William Allen to Thomas Penn, October 26, 1755, in Walker, *Burd Papers*, 25–26.

CHAPTER SIX. "BETWEEN TWO FIRES"

1. BF to George Whitefield, July 2, 1756, *PBF*, 6:468–69.
2. Freeman, *George Washington*, 1:335.
3. DH, 21–22.

CHAPTER SEVEN. "THE CHILD INDEPENDENCE IS BORN"

1. Gipson, *American Loyalist*, 112–13.
2. *Proceedings of the Rhode Island Historical Society*, as cited in Andreas, *Smuggler Nation*, 21.
3. Barrow, *Trade and Empire*, 161–62.
4. *Correspondence of William Pitt When Secretary of State*, London: Macmillan, 1906, 2:351–55.
5. Pencak, "John Adams."
6. Catherine Drinker Bowen, *John Adams and the American Revolution*, 214.
7. Bowen, *John Adams and the American Revolution*, 215.
8. Bowen, *John Adams and the American Revolution*, 217.

CHAPTER EIGHT. "AN ILL-JUDGED MEASURE"

1. Egremont to Shelburne, May 5, 1763, *Public Records Office, Colonial Office Papers, Series 5*, 323, 16.
2. *Papers of Sir William Johnson*, 26 vols., Albany: New York State Library, 1:528–30.
3. Barrow, *Trade and Empire*, 176.
4. Barrow, *Trade and Empire*, 175.
5. GW, "Articles of Association," June 3, 1763, *PGW*, Colonial Series, 7:219–25.
6. GW to William Crawford, September 17, 1767, *PGW*, Colonial Series, 8:279.

CHAPTER NINE. "WHAT MORE CAN THEY DESIRE?"

1. Barrow, *Trade and Empire*, 185.
2. JA quoted in Puls, *Samuel Adams*, 107.
3. Maury, *Memoirs of a Huguenot Family*, 421.
4. SA, May 15, 1764, in "Instructions of the Town of Boston to Its Representatives, in the General Court," MS, Boston Public Library.
5. GW to Robert Cary and Co., September 20, 1765, *PGW*, Colonial Series, 7:402.
6. Quoted in Collier, *Roger Sherman's Connecticut*, 52.
7. *PBF*, 13:124–59.

CHAPTER TEN. "HALF OF ENGLAND IS NOW LAND-MAD"

1. BF to DRF, June 22, 1767, *PBF*, 14:192–95.
2. George Croghan to Sir William Johnson, March 30, 1766, *Papers of Sir William Johnson*, 5:128–30.
3. Sir William Johnson to WF, June 20, 1766, quoted in Alvord and Carter, *New Regime*, 318–19.
4. BF to WF, September 12, 1766, *PBF*, 13:415.
5. GW to William Crawford, September 21, 1767, *PGW*, Colonial Series, 8:29.
6. Freeman, *George Washington*, 2:46.
7. Stuart, *Life of Jonathan Trumbull, Senior*, 94.

CHAPTER ELEVEN. "BONE OF OUR BONE"

1. BF to WF, March 13, 1768, *PBF*, 15, 75–76.
2. Quoted in Barrow, *Trade and Empire*, 276.
3. GW to George Mason, April 5, 1769, *PGW*, 8:178.
4. Thomas Gage to Lord Barrington, November 12, 1770, quoted in Fischer, *Paul Revere's Ride*, 38.
5. Gage to Hillsborough, October 31, 1768, quoted in Fischer, *Paul Revere's Ride*, 40.
6. Middlekauff, *Glorious Cause*, 209–213.
7. Quoted in Barrow, *Trade and Empire*, 246.
8. Gilje, *Rioting in America*, 40.
9. JA, *Diary*, April 24, 1773.
10. *PBF*, 20:515–16.
11. Quoted in Fleming, *Liberty!*, 79.
12. JA, *Diary*, December 17, 1773.

CHAPTER TWELVE. "THE PRIME CONDUCTOR"

1. Transcript of Wedderburn speech, *PBF*, 21:43–49.
2. Quoted in Aldridge, *Benjamin Franklin*, 247.
3. GW to James Wood, February 20, 1774, Founders Archives, National Archives.
4. GW to Bryan Fairfax, July 4, 1774, *PGW*, Colonial Series, 10:109–10.
5. GW to Bryan Fairfax, August 24, 1774, *PGW*, Colonial Series, 10:154–55.
6. GW to Bryan Fairfax, July 4, 1774, *PGW*, Colonial Series, 10:109–110.

CHAPTER THIRTEEN. "IMPROVING OUR FORTUNES"

1. AFC, 1:107.
2. *LDC*, 1:193n.
3. James Duane, "Notes for a Speech to Congress," October 3, 1774, *LDC*, 1:189–91.
4. Samuel Ward, "Notes for a Speech to Congress," *LDC*, 1:184–89.
5. *JCC*, 1:75–80.
6. Beeman, *Our Lives*, 161.
7. Beeman, *Our Lives*, 277.
8. *New York Journal*, January [?], 1776, in Randall, *Little Revenge*, 283.
9. Randolph, *History of Virginia*, 205.
10. Beeman, *Our Lives, Our Fortunes and Our Sacred Honor*, 290.
11. GW to Robert Mackenzie, October 9, 1774, *LDC*, 1:167.
12. GW to John Augustine Washington, March 25, 1775, *PGW*, Colonial Series, 10:308.
13. GW to George William Fairfax, March 25, 1775, *PGW*, Colonial Series, 10:308.

CHAPTER FOURTEEN. " 'TIS TIME TO PART"

1. Quoted in Unger, *John Hancock*, 50.
2. BF to David Hartley, May 8, 1775, *LDC*, 1:335–36.
3. Thomas Hutchinson, *Diary* 2:287. *Diary and Letters of Thomas Hutchinson*, 2 vols., New York: AMC, 1973), 2:287.

CHAPTER FIFTEEN. "UNPARDONABLE REBELLION"

1. JA, *Diary*, August 29, 1774, in *LDC*, 1:5.
2. SD to Elizabeth Deane, September 10, 1774, *LDC*, 1:62.
3. JA, *Diary*, August 29, 1774, in *LDC*, 1:1–5.
4. GW to MW, June 18, 1775, *LDC*, 1:509–510.

5. JA to James Warren, June 20, 1775, *LDC*, 1:518.
6. RM to William Bingham, October 20, 1776, in Versteeg, *Robert Morris*, 16.
7. Rappleye, *Robert Morris*, 33.
8. RM to SD, June 5, 1776, quoted in Rappleye, *Robert Morris*, 58.
9. JA to Horatio Gates, *LDC*, 3:586–87.
10. Henry Mowat, extract of Henry Mowat logbook from HMS *Canceaux*, 1775, LCC.
11. McGrath, *Give Me a Fast Ship*, 21.
12. John Page to TJ, November 11, 1775, *PTJ*, 1:258.

Chapter Sixteen. "Independence like a Torrent"

1. York, "Clandestine Aid," 27.
2. TJ to John Randolph, August 25, 1775, *PTJ*, 1:241.
3. TJ to John Randolph, November 29, 1775, *PTJ*, 1:268.
4. JA to AA, May 20, 1776, AFC, 4:195.
5. McCullough, *John Adams*, 109.
6. JA to AA, July 3, 1776, Massachusetts Historical Society, masshist.org.digital archive.
7. AA to JA, November 5, 1775, AFC.
8. Founders Online, National Archives, https://founders.archives.gov.

Chapter Seventeen. "A Free and Independent People"

1. Randolph, *History of Virginia*, 5.
2. Samuel Ward to Henry Ward, June 22, 1775, *LDC*, 1:535.
3. Stanger, "The First Whistleblowers," 70.
4. *Autobiography of TJ*, 44.
5. AFC, 2:30.
6. AFC, 2:46.

Chapter Eighteen. "Very Useful Here & and Much Esteemed"

1. Ferling, *Independence*, 149.
2. Rappleye, *Robert Morris*, 47.
3. RM to William Bingham, April 25, 1777, *LDC*, 6:651.
4. Chastellux, *Travels in North-America*, 1:200.
5. Abernethy, *Western Lands and the American Revolution*, 184.
6. Quoted in Fleming, *Liberty*, 201.

Chapter Nineteen. "For a Little Revenge"

1. Quoted in Fleming, *Liberty*, 202.
2. GW to John Hancock, September 25, 1776, Founders Online, National Archives, founders.archives.gov.
3. Randall, "Burgoyne's Big Fail," 48.
4. Randall, "Burgoyne's Big Fail," 50.
5. Deane Papers, 5:249.
6. Quoted in Fleming, *Liberty*, 267–68.
7. Ibid., 268.
8. Quoted in Aldridge, *Benjamin Franklin*, 247.

Chapter Twenty. "Discordant Parts"

1. GW to Lee, October 17, 1777, *WW*, 9:387–89.
2. GW to Lee, January 2, 1778, *WW*, 10:176.

3. Gouverneur Morris to JJ, quoted in Rappleye, *Robert Morris*, 157.
4. Ibid.
5. GW to Benjamin Harrison, December 30, 1780, *WW*, 13:462.
6. RM to BF, March 31, 1780, Deane Papers, 9:213–18.

CHAPTER TWENTY-ONE. "THE PESTS OF SOCIETY"

1. GW to Joseph Reed, December 12, 1778, Reed, *Life and Correspondence*, 2:41–42.
2. GW to Andrew Lewis, October 1, 1778, Founders Online, National Archives, https://founders.archives.gov.
3. Sellers, *Charles Willson Peale*, 208.

CHAPTER TWENTY-TWO. "FOR WANT OF PAY"

1. AH to RM, April 30, 1781, in *PRM*, 1:32.
2. AH to GW, April 8, 1783, Founders Online, National Archives, https://founders.archives.gov.
3. RM to JJ, November 27, 1783, *PRM*, 8:785.
4. RM to BF, July 13, 1781, quoted in Versteeg, *Robert Morris*, 67–68.
5. JA to AA, AFC, 3:9.
6. Boldt, *Founding City*, 44.
7. Quoted in JJ, *Diary*, 3:77.
8. *PRM*, 7:249n3.
9. Ibid.
10. JM, "Notes of Debate," January 7, 1783, *JCC*, 25:847.
11. GW to Theodoric Bland, April 4, 1783, *WW*, 26:285.
12. "Circular to the States," June 8, 1783, *WW*, 26:283–96.
13. Quoted in Rappleye, *Robert Morris*, 381.

CHAPTER TWENTY-THREE. "THE MOST SORDID INTEREST"

1. TJ to JM, February 20, 1784, *PTJ*, 6:549.
2. AH to James Duane, August 5, 1783, *PAH*, 3:430.
3. RL to AH, August 30, 1783, *PAH*, 3:434–35.
4. AH to John B. Church, March 10, 1784, *PAH*, 3:520–23.
5. Lafayette to GW, *PGW*, Confederation Series, 2:175.
6. GW to William Crawford, September 1789, WW, 27:346.

CHAPTER TWENTY-FOUR. "HEAVEN WAS SILENT"

1. Abernethy, *Western Lands and the American Revolution*, 365.
2. TJ to JM, April 25, 1784, *PTJ*, 7:118.
3. TJ to Jean Nicolas Démeunier, June 22, 1786, *PTJ*, 10:58.

CHAPTER TWENTY-FIVE. "I SHALL NOT REST"

1. Hochman, "Thomas Jefferson," 178.
2. GW to Chastellux, October 12, 1783, *WW*, 27:188–90.
3. TJ to JM, February 20, 1784, *PGW*, Confederation Series, 2:86.
4. GW to Thomas Johnson, October 15, 1784, *PGW*, Confederation Series, 2:86.
5. GW to Jacob Read, November 3, 1784, *PGW*, Confederation Series, 2:118–23.
6. GW to R. H. Lee, December 14, 1784, *PGW*, Confederation Series, 2:181–83.
7. *Virginia Gazette,* December 4, 1784.
8. GW to JM, November 28, 1784, *PGW*, 2:155–57.

9. GW to GWF, February 27, 1785, *PGW*, 2:386–90; GW to RM, February 1, 1785, *PGW*, 2:309–315.

10. GW to RM, February 1, 1785, *PGW*, Confederation Series, 2:309–315; R. H. Lee to William Short, June 13, 1785, quoted in Rick W. Sturdevant, "Quest for Eden: George Washington's Frontier Land Interests," PhD diss., University of California at Santa Barbara, 221.

11. Quoted in Randall, *George Washington*, 428.

12. R. H. Lee to William Short, June 13, 1785, quoted in Sturdevant, "Quest for Eden," 221.

13. "Address of the Annapolis Convention," September 14, 1786, *PAH*, 3:686–89.

CHAPTER TWENTY-SIX. "THE IMPENDING STORM"

1. Beeman, *Plain, Honest Men*, 17.

2. Henry Lee to GW, in Beeman, *Plain, Honest Men*, 17.

3. Henry Lee to GW, in Beeman, *Plain, Honest Men*, 17.

4. JM to James Madison Sr., November 1, 1786, *PJM*, 9:154.

5. R. H. Lee to GW, November 11, 1786, Founders Online, National Archives, https://founders.archives.gov.

6. TJ to AA, February 22, 1787, *PTJ*, 11:174.

7. GW to JM, November 5, 1786, Founders Online.

CHAPTER TWENTY-SEVEN. "PLAIN, HONEST MEN"

1. Quoted in Stewart, *Summer of 1787*, 112.

2. McDonald, *We the People*, 40–52, 91.

3. Quoted in William Jay, *Life of John Jay*, 1:70.

4. Quoted in Beeman, *Plain, Honest Men*, 17.

5. Farrand, Max, ed. *Records of the Federal Congress of 1787*. New Haven, Yale University Press, 1911, 2:641.

CHAPTER TWENTY-EIGHT. "THE DINNER TABLE BARGAIN"

1. Custis, George Washington Parke, *Recollections and Private Memoirs of Washington*. New York: Derby and Jackson, 1860, 349.

2. Quoted in Forrest McDonald, *AH*, 128.

3. BF, "Last Will and Testament," *Writings of Benjamin Franklin*, 10:493–510.

CHAPTER TWENTY-NINE. "CLINTONIA BOREALIS"

1. Quoted in Randall and Nahra, *Forgotten Americans*, 107.

2. TJ to Thomas Mann Randolph, Randall and Nahra, *Forgotten Americans*, 109.

3. Randall and Nahra, *Forgotten Americans*, 109.

4. Ibid.

5. Randall and Nahra, *Forgotten Americans*, 110.

6. Randall and Nahra, *Forgotten Americans*, 113.

7. Randall and Nahra, *Forgotten Americans*, 114.

8. Randall and Nahra, *Forgotten Americans*, 116.

9. GW to TJ, Freeman, GW, *First in Peace*, 7:73–75.

10. TJ to JM, quoted in Seth Lipsky, *Citizens' Constitution*. New York: BasicBooks, 2009, 148.

11. TJ, Memoir, *Correspondence and Miscellanies*, TJ Randolph, ed. Charlottesville, Va.: F. Carr, 1829, 492.

12. GW to Congress, March 30, 1795, in Bemis, Stanley Flagg, *Pinckney's Treaty: America's Advantage from Europe's Distress, 1783–1800*, 19.

13. GW to Henry Lee, quoted in Richard Norton Smith, *Patriarch*, 229.

14. JA to AA, March 5, 1797, *Adams Family Correspondence*. ed. by L. H. Butterfield et al. Cambridge, Mass.: Harvard University Press, 12: 244.

CHAPTER THIRTY. "THE BEST ROOM IN THIS HOUSE"

1. GW to Tobias Lear, May 6, 1794, *PGW*, Presidential Series, 16:2.

2. Lear, Letters and Recollections of GW. New York: Doubleday, 1906, 129–41.

3. Quoted in Rappleye, *Robert Morris*, 504.

4. Ibid.

5. Rappleye, *Robert Morris*, 509.

6. RM to John Nicholson, May 11, 1798, Huntingdon Library.

7. Rappalye, *Robert Morris*, 512.

BIBLIOGRAPHY

Abernethy, Thomas Perkins. *Western Lands and the American Revolution*. Charlottesville, Va.: University of Virginia Press, 1937.

Aldridge, Alfred Owen. *Benjamin Franklin: Philosopher and Man*. Philadelphia: Lippincott, 1936.

Alvord, Clarence Walworth, and Clarence Edwin Carter. *The New Regime, 1765–1767*. Springfield: Illinois State Historical Library, 1916.

Anderson, D. K., and G. T. Anderson. "The Death of Silas Deane." *New England Quarterly* 62 (1984): 98–105.

Andreas, Peter. *Smuggler Nation: How Illicit Trade Made America*. New York: Oxford University Press, 2013.

Appleby, Joyce O. *The Relentless Revolution: A History of Capitalism*. New York: W. W. Norton, 2011.

Baker, Mark Allen. "Silas Deane." In *Spies of Revolutionary Connecticut*. Charleston, S.C.: History Press, 2014.

Barrow, Thomas C. *Trade and Empire: The British Customs Service in Colonial America, 1660–1775*. Cambridge, Mass.: Harvard University Press, 1967.

Beard, Charles A. *An Economic Interpretation of the Constitution of the United States*. New York: Macmillan, 1913.

Beeman, Richard. "The British Secret Service and the French-American Alliance." *American Historical Review* 29 (October 1932–July 1924): 491.

———. *Our Lives, Our Fortunes and Our Sacred Honor: The Forging of American Independence, 1774–1776*. New York: Basic Books, 2013.

———. *Plain, Honest Men: The Making of the American Constitution*. New York: Random House, 2009.

Bemis, Stanley Flagg. *Diplomacy of the American Revolution*. Bloomington: University of Indiana Press, 1935.

——— Bemis, Stanley Flagg. *Pinckney's Treaty, America's Advantage from Europe's Distress, 1783–1800*. New Haven, Yale University Press, 1965.

Berkin, Carol. *A Sovereign People: The Crises of the 1790s and the Birth of American Nationalism*. New York: Basic Books, 2017.

Bezanson, Anne, et al. *Prices and Inflation During the American Revolution*. Philadelphia: University of Pennsylvania Press, 1951.

Billias, George Athen. *Elbridge Gerry: Founding Father and Republican Statesman.* New York: McGraw Hill, 1976.

Boldt, David R., ed., with Willard Sterne Randall. *The Founding City.* Philadelphia: Chilton Books, 1976.

Bowen, Catherine Drinker. *John Adams and the American Revolution.* New York: Grosset and Dunlap, 1949.

———. *Miracle at Philadelphia: The Story of the Constitutional Convention, May to September 1787.* Boston: Little, Brown, 1966.

Bowen, H. V. *Revenue and Reform: The Indian Problem in British Politics, 1757–1773.* Cambridge: Cambridge University Press, 1991.

Bowman, Frank O., III. *High Crimes and Misdemeanors: A History of Impeachment for the Age of Trump.* Cambridge: Cambridge University Press, 2019.

Boyd, Julian P. "Death of a Kindly Teacher of Treason." *William and Mary Quarterly,* 3rd ser., 16 (2–4): 165–87, 310–42, 515–50.

———, ed. *Papers of Thomas Jefferson.* Princeton, N.J.: Princeton University Press, 1950—.

Brands, H. W. *The First American: The Life and Times of Benjamin Franklin.* New York: Doubleday, 2000.

Breen, T. H. *Tobacco Culture: The Mentality of the Great Tidewater Planters on the Eve of the Revolution.* Princeton, N.J.: Princeton University Press, 1985.

Buel, Richard. *In Irons: Britain's Naval Supremacy and the American Revolution.* New Haven, Conn.: Yale University Press, 1998.

Bunker, Nick. *Young Benjamin Franklin: The Birth of Ingenuity.* New York: Alfred A. Knopf, 2018.

Burnett, Edward C. *The Continental Congress.* New York: W. W. Norton, 1943.

Burstein, Stanley M. "The Classics and the American Republic." *The History Teacher* 30, no. 1 (November 1966): 29–44.

Butz, Stephen D. *Shays' Settlement in Vermont: A Story of Revolt and Archaeology.* Charleston, S.C.: History Press, 2017.

Calloway, Colin G. *The Indian World of George Washington.* New York: Oxford University Press, 2018.

Carp, E. Wayne. *"To Starve the Army at Pleasure": Continental Army Administration and American Political Culture.* Chapel Hill: University of North Carolina Press, 1984.

Chapin, Joyce E., ed., *Benjamin Franklin's Autobiography.* New York: W. W. Norton, 2012.

Chastellux, Marquis de. *Travels in North-America in the Years 1780–81–82.* New York: White, Gallaher, & White, 1827.

Chernow, Barbara Ann. *Robert Morris: Land Speculator, 1790–1801.* New York: Columbia University, 1974.

Coe, Alexis. *You Never Forget Your First: A Biography of George Washington.* New York: Viking, 2020.

Coleman, Peter J. *Debtors and Creditors in America: Insolvency, Imprisonment for Debt, and Bankruptcy, 1607–1900.* Madison: University of Wisconsin Press, 1974.

Collier, Christopher, and David Lovejoy. *Roger Sherman's Connecticut: Yankee Politics and the America Revolution.* Middletown, Conn.: G. B. Wilson, 1973.

Conkling, Margaret C. *Memoirs of the Mother and Wife of Washington.* Auburn, N.Y.: Derby-Miller, 1850.

Deane, Silas. The Deane Papers, 1774–90. 5 vols. New York: New-York Historical Society, 1887.

Davidson, James West, and Mark Hamilton Lytle. *After the Fact: The Art of Historical Detection.* 5th ed., New York: McGraw-Hill, 2004.

Doerflinger, Thomas M. *A Vigorous Spirit of Enterprise: Merchants and Economic Development in Revolutionary America*. Chapel Hill: University of North Carolina Press, 1986.

Downing, Ned W. *The Revolutionary Beginning of the American Stock Market*. New York: Museum of American Finance, 2010.

Dull, Jonathan. *Diplomatic History of the American Revolution*. New Haven, Conn.: Yale University Press, 1985.

East, Robert A. *Business Enterprises in the American Revolutionary Era*. New York: Columbia University Press, 1938.

Ellis, Joseph J. *His Excellency, George Washington*. New York: Random House, 2004.

———. *The Quartet*. New York: Penguin, 2015.

Ernst, Joseph Albert. *Money and Politics in America, 1755–1775: A Study in the Currency Act of 1764 and the Political Economy of Revolution*. Chapel Hill: University of North Carolina Press, 1973.

Feer, Robert A. "Shays's Rebellion and the Constitution: A Study in Causation." *New England Quarterly* 42, no. 3 (September 1969): 338–410.

Fenster, Julie M. *Jefferson's America: The President, the Purchase, and the Explorers Who Transformed America*. New York: Broadway Books, 2016.

Ferguson, H. James. *The Power of the Purse: A History of American Public Finance, 1776–1790*. Chapel Hill: University of North Carolina Press, 1961.

Ferling, John. *Independence: The Struggle to Set America Free*. New York: Bloomsbury Press, 2011.

———. *John Adams: A Life*. Knoxville: University of Tennessee Press, 1992.

Ferris, Robert, and James Charlton. *The Signers of the Constitution*. Flagstaff, Ariz: Interpretive Publications, 1986.

Fischer, David Hackett. *Paul Revere's Ride*. New York: Oxford University Press, 1994.

Fleming, Thomas. *Liberty! The American Revolution*. New York: Viking, 1977.

———. *The Perils of Peace: America's Struggle for Survival After Yorktown*. New York: HarperCollins, 2007.

Flower, Milton E. *John Dickinson, Conservative Revolutionary*. Charlottesville, Va.: University of Virginia Press, 1983.

Franklin, Benjamin. *The Autobiography of Benjamin Franklin*. Ed. by Leonard W. Larrabee et al. New Haven, Conn.: Yale University Press, 1964.

Freeman, Douglas Southall. *George Washington: A Biography*. 7 vols. New York: Scribners, 1948–1957.

Friedenberg, Daniel M. *Life, Liberty and the Pursuit of Land: The Plunder of Early America*. Buffalo, N.Y.: Prometheus Books, 1992.

Gilje, Paul A. *Rioting in America*. Indianapolis, Ind.: Indianapolis University Press, 1996.

Gipson, Lawrence Henry. *American Loyalist: Jared Ingersoll*. New Haven, Conn.: Yale University Press, 1971.

Goldstein, Kalman. "Silas Deane's Preparation for Rascality." *Historian* 43 (1980–81): 75–97.

Gordon, John Steele. *Hamilton's Blessing: The Extraordinary Life and Times of Our National Debt*. New York: Walker, 2010.

Green, James N. "Benjamin Franklin as Publisher and Bookseller." In *Reappraising Benjamin Franklin: A Bicentennial Perspective*, edited by J. A. Leo Lemay. Newark: University of Delaware Press, 1976.

Gross, Robert, ed. *In Debt to Shays: The Bicentennial of an Agrarian Revolution*. Charlottesville: University of Virginia Press, 1993.

Hamilton, Alexander. *Papers*. Ed. by Harold C. Syrett and Jacob E. Cooke, 26 vols. New York: Columbia University Press, 1961–87.

Hammond, Bray. *Banks and Politics in America: From the Revolution to the Civil War.* Princeton, N.J.: Princeton University Press, 1957.

Hancock, David. *Citizens of the World: London Merchants and the Integration of the British Atlantic Community, 1735–1785.* London, Cambridge University Press, 1995.

Henderson, H. James. *Party Politics in the Continental Congress.* New York: McGraw-Hill, 1974.

Hochman, Steven Harold. "Thomas Jefferson: A Personal Financial Biography." Unpublished doctoral dissertation, Charlottesville: University of Virginia, 1987.

Humphreys, David. *Life of General Washington.* Athens: University of Georgia Press, 1991.

Hutchinson, Thomas. Diary and Letters. 2 vols. Boston: Houghton Mifflin, 1884. Press, 1991.

Irwin, Douglas A., and Richard Sylla, eds. *Founding Choices: American Economic Policy in the 1790s.* Chicago: National Bureau of Economic Research, 2011.

Isaacson, Walter. *Benjamin Franklin: An American Life.* New York: Simon & Schuster, 2003.

James, Coy Hilton. *Silas Deane, Patriot or Traitor?* East Lansing: Michigan State University Press, 1975.

Jay, William. *Life of John Jay.* 2 vols. New York: Harper and Harper, 1833.

Jefferson, Thomas. *Papers.* Julian Boyd et al., eds. Princeton, N. J.: Princeton University Press, 1950–.

Jensen, Merrill. *The Articles of Confederation.* Madison: University of Wisconsin Press, 1948.

———. *The Founding of a Nation: A History of the American Revolution, 1763–1776.* New York: Oxford University Press, 1968.

Johnson, Paul. *A History of the American People.* New York: HarperCollins, 1998.

Journals of the Continental Congress. 1774–89. Library of Congress, Washington, D.C.

Ketcham, Ralph. *James Madison.* Charlottesville: University of Virginia Press, 1990.

Kiernan, Denise, and Joseph D'Agnese. *Signing Their Lives Away: The Fame and Misfortune of the Men Who Signed the U.S. Constitution.* New York: Penguin Random House, 2009.

Konkle, Burton Alva. *Thomas Willing and the First American Financial System.* Philadelphia: University of Pennsylvania Press, 1957.

Lamb, Brian, Susan Swain, and C-SPAN. *The Presidents: Noted Historians Rank America's Best—and Worst—Chief Executives.* New York: PublicAffairs, 2019.

Lambert, Frank. "'Pedlar in Divinity': George Whitefield and the Great Awakening, 1737–1745." *Journal of American History* 77, no. 3 (December 1990): 821–36.

Larson, Edward J., and Michael P. Winship. *The Constitutional Convention: A Narrative History from the Notes of James Madison.* New York: Modern Library, 2006.

Lengel, Edward G. *First Entrepreneur: How George Washington Built His—and the Nation's—Prosperity.* New York: Da Capo, 2016.

Lewis, Thomas A. *For King and Country: George Washington, the Early Years.* New York: John Wiley, 1993.

Liss, Peggy. *Atlantic Empires: The Network of Trade and Revolution, 1713–1826.* Baltimore: Johns Hopkins University Press, 1983.

Maier, Pauline. *American Scripture: Making the Declaration of Independence.* New York: Random House, 1997.

———. *The Old Revolutionaries: Political Lives in the Age of Samuel Adams.* New York: Knopf, 1980.

Maury, Ann. *Memoirs of a Huguenot Family.* New York: G. P. Putnam's Sons, 1872.

McAnear, Beverly. "Personal Accounts of the Albany Congress of 1754." *Mississippi Valley Historical Review* 39, no. 4 (March 1953): 727–46.

McCraw, Thomas. *The Founders and Finance.* Cambridge, Mass.: Harvard University Press, 2006.

McCullough, John. *John Adams.* New York: Simon & Schuster, 2001.

McCusker, John J., and Russell R. Menard. *The Economy of British America, 1607–1789.* Chapel Hill: University of North Carolina Press, 1985.

McDonald, Forrest. *We the People: The Economic Origins of the Constitution.* Chicago: University of Chicago Press, 1958.

McGrath, Tim. *Give Me a Fast Ship: The Continental Navy in the American Revolution.* New York: Random House, 2015.

Middlekauff, Robert. *The Glorious Cause: The American Revolution.* New York: Oxford University Press, 2007.

Mitchell, Brian R. *British Historical Statistics.* New York: Cambridge University Press, 1988.

Morgan, Edmund S., and Helen M. *The Stamp Act Crisis: Prologue to Revolution.* Chapel Hill: University of North Carolina Press, 1953.

Morton, Bryan, and Donald Spinelli. *Beaumarchais and the American Revolution.* Lanham, Md.: Regnery, 2002.

Murphy, Orville T. *Charles Gravier, Comte de Vergennes: French Diplomacy in the Age of Revolution, 1719–1787.* Albany: State University of New York Press, 1982.

Nash, Gary. *The Unknown American Revolution: The Unruly Birth of Democracy and the Struggle to Create America.* New York: Penguin, 2005.

New-York Historical Society. *Collections of the New-York Historical Society for the Year 1886.* New York: Printed for the Society, 1887.

Noble, John. "A Few Notes on the Shays Rebellion." Notes from the *Proceedings of the American Antiquarian Society.* Worcester, Mass.: Charles Hamilton, 1903.

Nuxoll, Elizabeth. *Congress and the Munitions Merchants: The Secret Committee of Trade During the American Revolution, 1775–1777.* New York: Garland, 1985.

Padover, Saul K. *The Living United States Constitution.* New York: Meridian, 1995.

Patten, Robert. *Patriot Pirates: The Privateer War for Freedom and Fortune in the American Revolution.* New York: Pantheon, 2008.

Paulo, Joel Richard. *Unlikely Allies: How a Merchant, a Playwright, and a Spy Saved the American Revolution.* New York: Riverhead Books, 2009.

Pencak, William. "John Adams." *American National Biography.* 24 vols. New York: Oxford University Press, 1999.

Penn, William. *Papers.* Historical Society of Pennsylvania, Philadelphia, Pa.

Petersen, Randy. *The Printer and the Preacher: Ben Franklin, George Whitefield, and the Surprising Friendship That Invented America.* New York: Thomas Nelson, 2015.

Phillips, Philip Lee. "Washington as Surveyor and Mapmaker." *Daughters of the American Revolution Magazine* 55, no. 3 (1921): 115–32.

Platt, J. D. R. *Jeremiah Wadsworth, Federalist Entrepreneur.* New York: Columbia University Press, 1955.

Potts, Louis W. *Arthur Lee: A Virtuous Revolutionary.* Baton Rouge: University of Louisiana Press, 1981.

Puls, Mark D. *Samuel Adams: Father of the American Revolution.* New York: Palgrave Macmillan, 2006.

Rakove, Jack. *The Beginnings of National Politics: An Interpretive History of the Continental Congress.* New York: Knopf, 1979.

Randall, Willard Sterne. *Alexander Hamilton: A Life.* New York: HarperCollins, 2003.

———. *Benedict Arnold: Patriot and Traitor.* New York: William Morrow, 1990.

———. "Burgoyne's Big Fail." *MHQ: The Quarterly Magazine of Military History* 32, no. 3 (Spring 2020): 48.

———. *Ethan Allen: His Life and Times.* New York: W. W. Norton, 2011.

———. *George Washington: A Life.* New York: Henry Holt, 1998.

————. *A Little Revenge: Benjamin Franklin and His Son*. Boston: Little, Brown, 1984.

————. *Thomas Jefferson: A Life*. New York: Henry Holt, 1993.

————. *Unshackling America: How the War of 1812 Truly Ended the American Revolution*. New York: St. Martin's, 2017.

Randall, Willard Sterne, and Nancy Nahra. *American Lives*. 2 vols. New York: HarperCollins, 1997.

————. *Forgotten Americans: Footnote Figures Who Changed American History*. Reading, Mass.: Addison Wesley Longman, 1998.

Randolph, Edmund. *History of Virginia*. Richmond: Virginia Historical Society, 1970.

Rappleye, Charles. *Robert Morris: Financier of the American Revolution*. New York: Simon & Schuster, 2010.

————. *Sons of Providence: The Brown Brothers, the Slave Trade, and the American Revolution*. New York: Simon & Schuster, 2006.

Reed, Joseph. *Life and Correspondence*. Ed. by William B. Reed. 2 vols. Philadelphia: Lindsay and Blakiston, 1847.

Richards, Leonard L. *Shays's Rebellion: The American Revolution's Final Battle*. Philadelphia: University of Pennsylvania Press, 2002.

Roberts, Cokie. *Founding Mothers: The Women Who Raised Our Nation*. New York: William Morrow, 2004.

Rossiter, Clinton. *1787: The Grand Convention*. New York: W. W. Norton, 1987.

Schaeper, Thomas J. *Edward Bancroft: Scientist, Author, Spy*. New Haven, Conn.: Yale University Press, 2009.

Sellers, Charles Coleman. *Charles Willson Peale*. New York, Scribner's, 1979.

Shannon, Timothy J. *Indians and Colonists at the Crossroads of Empire: The Albany Congress of 1754*. Ithaca, N.Y.: Cornell University Press, 2000.

Signer, Michael. *Becoming Madison: The Extraordinary Origins of the Least Likely Founding Father*. New York: PublicAffairs, 2015.

Smith, Paul H., ed. *Letters to Delegates of the Continental Congress, 1774–1789*. 26 vols. Washington, D.C.: Library of Congress, 1976.

Smith, Richard Norton. *Patriarch: George Washington and the New American Nation*. Boston: Houghton Mifflin, 1993.

Stanger, Allison. "The First Whistleblowers." *MHQ: The Quarterly Magazine of Military History* 32, no. 3 (Spring 2020): 68–74.

Stevens, Benjamin F. *B. F. Stevens's Facsimiles of Manuscripts in European Archives Relating to America 1773–1783, with Descriptions, Editorial Notes, Collations, References and Translations*. London: Malby and Sons, 1889–1895, no. 1371.

Stewart, David O. *The Summer of 1787*. New York: Simon & Schuster, 2007.

Stinchcombe, William. "A Note on Silas Deane's Death." *William and Mary Quarterly*, 3rd ser., 32 (1975): 619–24.

Stuart, I. W. *Life of Jonathan Trumbull, Senior*. Boston: Crocker and Brewster, 1859.

Sylla, Richard, and David J. Cowen. *Alexander Hamilton on Finance, Credit, and Debt*. New York: Columbia University Press, 2018.

Szathmary, David. *Shays' Rebellion: The Making of an Agrarian Insurrection*. Amherst: University of Massachusetts Press, 1980.

Unger, Harlow Giles. *John Hancock: Merchant King and American Patriot*. Edison, N.J.: Castle Books, 2000.

Van Alstyne, Richard W. "Great Britain, the War of American Independence, and the 'Gathering Storm' in Europe, 1775–1778." *Huntington Library Quarterly* 27, no. 4 (August 1964): 328.

Van Doren, Carl. *Benjamin Franklin.* New York: Viking, 1938.

———. *Secret History of the American Revolution.* New York: Viking, 1941.

Van Doren, Carl, and Julian Boyd. *Indian Treaties Printed by Benjamin Franklin.* Philadelphia: Historical Society of Pennsylvania, 1938.

Van Schreeven, William J. et al. *Revolutionary Virginia: The Road to Independence.* 7 vols. Charlottesville: University Press of Virginia, 1973–1983.

Van Vlack, Milton C. *Silas Deane: Revolutionary War Diplomat and Politician.* Jefferson, N.C.: McFarland, 2013.

Versteeg, Clarence. *Robert Morris: Revolutionary Financier.* Philadelphia: University of Pennsylvania Press, 1954.

Washington, George. *Diary.* Ed. by Donald Jackson et al., 5 vols. Charlottesville, Va.: University of Virginia Press, 1976–79.

———. *Papers.* Charlottesville, Va.: University of Virginia Press, 1968–.

Wiencek, Henry. *An Imperfect God: George Washington, His Slaves, and the Creation of America.* New York: Farrar, Straus and Giroux, 2003.

Wood, Gordon S. *Creation of the American Republic, 1776–1787.* New York: W. W. Norton, 1972.

Wright, Esmond. *Franklin of Philadelphia.* Cambridge, Mass.: Belknap Press of Harvard University, 1986.

Wright, Robert E. *One Nation Under Death: Hamilton, Jefferson, and the History of What We Owe.* New York: McGraw-Hill, 2008.

Wright, Robert E., and David J. Cowen. *Financial Founding Fathers: The Men Who Made America Rich.* Chicago: University of Chicago Press, 2006.

York, Neil L. "Clandestine Aid and the American Revolutionary War Effort: A Reexamination." *Military Affairs* 43, no. 1 (February 1979): 26–30.

INDEX

ABOUT THE AUTHOR

During his seventeen years as a journalist, Willard Sterne Randall was a feature writer for the *Philadelphia Bulletin,* a magazine writer for the *Philadelphia Inquirer,* and an investigative journalist for *Philadelphia* magazine. His reportage won the National Magazine Award for Public Service from the Columbia Graduate School of Journalism, the Standard Gravure Award, the Hillman Foundation Prize, the Gerald Loeb Award, and the John Hancock Award for Excellence in Financial Writing. Since pursuing advanced studies in history at Princeton University—where he received the Davis Prize in British History—he has authored biographies of Benjamin and William Franklin, Benedict Arnold, Thomas Jefferson, George Washington, Alexander Hamilton, and Ethan Allen. His Benedict Arnold biography received four national best book awards, was a *New York Times* Notable Book, and was a finalist for the *Los Angeles Times* Book Prize. *Publishers Weekly* deemed his biography of Jefferson one of the ten best biographies of 1993. He received the American Revolution Round Table's Award of Merit, its highest honor, and the Thomas Fleming Award for Outstanding Military History Writing from *MHQ: The Quarterly Journal of Military History.* He has taught American history at John Cabot University in Rome, at the University of Vermont, and at Champlain College, where he is a Distinguished Scholar in History and an emeritus professor. He lives in Burlington, Vermont, with his wife, the poet Nancy Nahra, with whom he has coauthored three books.

Printed in the United States
by Baker & Taylor Publisher Services